Internationalism
in the Age of Nationalism

PENNSYLVANIA STUDIES IN HUMAN RIGHTS

Bert B. Lockwood, Jr., Series Editor

A complete list of books in the series is available from the publisher.

INTERNATIONALISM IN THE AGE OF NATIONALISM

Glenda Sluga

PENN

UNIVERSITY OF PENNSYLVANIA PRESS

PHILADELPHIA

Published by
University of Pennsylvania Press
Philadelphia, Pennsylvania 19104-4112
www.upenn.edu/pennpress

Printed in the United States of America
on acid-free paper

10 9 8 7 6 5 4 3 2 1

Library of Congress Cataloging-in-Publication Data
Sluga, Glenda.
  Internationalism in the age of nationalism / Glenda Sluga. — 1st ed.
      p. cm. — (Pennsylvania studies in human rights)
  Includes bibliographical references and index.
  ISBN 978-0-8122-4484-7 (hardcover : alk. paper)
  1. Internationalism—History—20th century. 2. Internationalism—Psychological
aspects. 3. Nationalism—History—20th century. 4. Nationalism—Psychological
aspects. I. Title.
  JZ1318.S5965 2013
  320.54'8—dc23
                                                    2012041246

It is, indeed, a strange and for all appearances absurd scheme
to want to write a history based on an idea of how the course of
the world must go if it is to approach a certain rational goal; it
seems that such an attitude can only result in a *romance*.

—Immanuel Kant, "Ninth Thesis," *Idea for a Universal History
with a Cosmopolitan Intent*, 1784

Contents

Introduction

In the steamy summer of 1948, a group of thirty-six teachers representing twenty-one countries—nearly half the number of internationally recognized sovereign states in the world at that time—met at Adelphi College on New York's Long Island, a few miles from the United Nation's own makeshift headquarters in an old munitions factory at Lake Success.[1] They were guests of a UNESCO seminar on "world understanding," tasked with discussing education programs that would promote interest in and knowledge of the workings of the UN and its specialized agencies. They also took it upon themselves to determine the proper progress of internationalism.

Refusing to be defeated by the heat and humidity, or by the challenges of translation, the teachers talked, ate, and made the most of photo opportunities. They listened to lectures by UN personnel, toured Lake Success, met with Eleanor Roosevelt on the grounds of her home at Hyde Park, and Dwight Eisenhower, then president of Columbia University. In the cool of night, they entertained each other with "National Evenings," celebrated independence days, exhibited national movies, listened to music, and performed folk dances. At the end of six weeks of seminars and socializing as an "international group," they concluded that "adult" internationalism welcomed "the nation-state structure of mankind."[2]

The seminar on "world understanding" was precisely the kind of internationally minded cultural event that Hans Morgenthau, the American political scientist and proclaimed founder of post–World War II realist theory, disdained as irrelevant to a hard-headed pursuit of peace. A German-Jewish émigré from the Weimar Republic, Morgenthau was based at the University of Chicago in 1948 and had just published his seminal study *Politics Among Nations*, with its lively dismissal of the futile idealism of UNESCO's educational programs. History had taught Morgenthau that "world understanding" could never guarantee peace because of the unreliability of human nature and the complex interests of states.[3] It is all the more surprising then to find that in *Politics Among Nations* Morgenthau postulated "the creation of an international community as foundation for a world state" and as "the first step toward the peaceful settlement of the international conflicts which might lead to war."[4] Into the 1950s, as the UN and UNESCO succumbed to the politics of the Cold War, in a succession of new editions of *Politics Among Nations*, Morgenthau anticipated "the obsolescence of the sovereign national state" and the transformation of "the existing international society of sovereign nations into a supranational community of individuals."[5] Although Morgenthau thought little of UNESCO's cultural content, he presumed that its institutional existence had contributed to the "spreading web of international activities and agencies, in which and through which the interests and life of all the nations would be gradually integrated."

Internationalism has long been regarded as a story of ideologues and radicals—whether nineteenth-century pacifists driven by utopian dreams of a parliament of man or working-class revolutionaries urging the workers of the world to unite. This book recovers a distinctively twentieth-century internationalism that was imagined through the same dominant lens of realism as nationalism, often with a similar defensiveness about its realist and idealist imperatives, and that culminated in the League of Nations and United Nations as unprecedented experiments in what was sometimes termed "international government." From the turn of the twentieth century, internationalism captured imaginations as "new" because its characteristics were the product of the social and political modernity of the times, including new international institutions, new international forms of sociability, and the importance of, as the UNESCO teachers would pronounce, "human beings with the right outlook."[6] Writers, intellectuals, and political activists, men and women, from across the liberal political spectrum, remarked on the sociological or objective character of an "era of internationalism," and its *réalité*. The stimulant for this popular and intellectual interest in a new internationalism was not only the transnational spread of ideas and power of "public opinion" that accompanied mass literacy, but also the constant threat of war and the evidence of atrocities in the name of nationalism. In the circumstances, internationalism seemed to many the most likely path to a "permanent peace" and to the fulfillment of the democratic ambitions of men, women, and anticolonialists who had limited political representation in nation-states and empires.

Throughout the twentieth century, the significance and meaning attributed to internationalism emerged out of the same questions of modernity and democracy, and political idealism that shaped the twentieth century into a corresponding age of nationalism. Like the dominant national trend, internationalism appeared as a story of political and social evolution in the interests of liberty and peace. As twinned liberal ideologies internationalism and nationalism inspired a wide range of imagined communities, but at their core were the same unresolved questions about the nature of individuals and groups, and the extent to which human beings could fashion a destiny of their choice. This meant that internationalism, particularly as it was institutionalized in the league and UN, was also imagined through the same language of race and civilizational difference that gave twentieth-century nationalism its unflattering timbre. Some of the more inspiring words on which twentieth-century talk about the relationship of the national to the international hung—particularly international society, interdependence, and transnationalism—have made the transition into the twenty-first century. Others—including internationality, international minds, world citizenship, and world government—were forgotten or rendered foreign, from one decade to the next.

Through the linguistic transformations and shifting emphases of internationalism ran the thread of an Enlightenment promise of evolving political, economic, social, and cultural progress, from the empires of the ancien régime to the nations of liberty and fraternity, and toward the universalism of a broader horizon of humanity. In the twentieth century, perhaps humanity's darkest century, the paradoxes of this promise and its potential came to the fore as a new internationalism.

Narratives of nationalism have become so engrained in our understanding of history, that we have forgotten the long, intimate, conceptual past shared by the national and international as entangled ways of thinking about modernity, progress, and politics.[7] Their symbiotic origins take us back at least to the 1780s, when the English philosopher Jeremy Bentham coined the term "international" as an appellation for law that extended beyond the state, governing the "mutual transactions of sovereigns."[8] It could be argued that the availability of the term "international" may have even encouraged familiarity with the nation as a synonym for the state. We can easily imagine, as exemplary of this new interest in the international, Immanuel Kant's 1784 essay "Idea for a Universal History with a Cosmopolitan Intent" and its discussion of how best to regulate relations between nations in the interests of permanent peace.

Kant famously concluded that human "unsocial sociability" would eventually drive humans to a federation of peoples or "universal *cosmopolitan* state."[9] In the century that followed, the Enlightenment language of stages, with its confident assertion of progress and universalism and the inevitable evolution of communities from family to nation to humanity, established a crucial ideological connection between the national and the international as successive phases of social and political life.

It is not difficult to find a universal cosmopolitan intent and an engagement with internationalism layered through all manner of nineteenth-century political texts, including those most famous for promoting nationalism as well as socialism. From the 1830s, Giuseppe Mazzini, exiled in England amid a community of English-speaking supporters of his Italian national cause, publicized a progressive vision of ever-widening concentric circles of association, in which nations existed as one stage of political and social evolution that would eventually link humanity.[10] The same Garibaldi who is recognized as the hero of the Italian Risorgimento, or national revival, was in 1867 the president of the newly formed International League of Peace and Liberty convening in Geneva and circulating its own journal under the masthead *États-Unis d'Europe*, or "United States of Europe."[11]

The abstract noun "internationalism" was an innovation (in both English and French) of this mid-nineteenth century, intended to capture the fulcrum of a new class-based political imaginary that we associate with the First International, and the workers' anthem "The Internationale."[12] Although it was still relatively easy to confuse and fold together ideologically divergent visions of international and national communities, the proletarian internationalism of the latter half of the nineteenth century was specifically opposed to nationalism, supporting instead transnational, non-state-bound class interests as the stepping-stone to radical economic egalitarianism. Even so, political versions of this class-conscious internationalism reiterated the familiar Enlightenment script of the evolution of human communities from the local to the universal, with a place for the nation. Writing in 1876, the German socialist August Bebel adapted an evolutionary vision of change to his own international ends: "The family forms a tribe, and several tribes form a state and the nation and finally the close interaction of nations will result in internationality."[13]

A similar script exuding faith in the evolution of internationality shaped the nationalisms of the later nineteenth century across national and linguistic borders. Here we might recall Woodrow Wilson, American president and attributed architect of both the League of Nations and the principle of nationality. Wilson's teacher was Herbert Baxter Adams, the progenitor of a national American historiography, who conceived of the nation as a stage in the evolution of human society in the general direction of a world-state. Adams, in turn, took his own understanding of the international destiny of nations from his mentor at Germany's Heidelberg University, the Swiss political scientist and international jurist Johannes Bluntschli.[14] By the end of the nineteenth century, Wilson shared Adams' and Bluntschli's historically specific conception of the evolution of humanity from ancient and medieval times to the late nineteenth-century epoch of international congresses and internationality.[15] It was an understanding that, from Wilson's perspective, presumed that some nations and "races" were more likely to take the lead in this process. He was hardly alone in his opinion that the federalism of the United States stood as a model of the momentum of political unification into ever-larger communities, including a "United States of Europe."[16]

By this time, profound social, political, and cultural changes had radically altered the landscape of the international and the national as inevitable forms of political community. More than half a century after the English poet Tennyson's famous 1835 invocation of the "Parliament of Man"—the oft-quoted albeit ahistorical prelude to twentieth-century international organizations— the political significance of internationalism was self-consciously distanced from its poetic or revolutionary nineteenth century intonations.[17] In the latter decades of the nineteenth century, interest in the promise and predictability of internationalism was invested in the "sociological" evidence of a seemingly endless concatenation of international associations and congresses, international administrative organizations, law and peace initiatives.

Symptomatic of this international turn was the growing talk of a new, "real" internationalism with social as well as political dimensions. As nationalists grabbed the center stage of political life, and communist internationalists preached the inevitability of class revolution, the liberal cast of a twentieth-century internationalism—built, like nationalism, out of institutions and sociability—came clearly into view. Indeed, at the end of World War I, the principle of nationality and the League of Nations were the shared basis for a new international world order. The etymological link between proletarian politics and the term internationalism still endured in demands for radical economic change and democratization. But a liberal, nation-embracing, and anticommunist version of internationalism was palpably on the rise. Leaders of powerful Western states, middle-class women and feminists, anticolonialists, social scientists, and moral reformers, now organized around the "international question" as well as the "nation question." A composite picture of their imagined internationalism would reveal a liberal international world order compatible with national patriotism and "collective security" (a term coined only in the 1930s), and profoundly connected to the history of democracy as well as peace and moral improvement.

In the 1940s, surveys of British and American public opinion confirmed that politicians, pamphleteers, scholars, and the public alike had come to identify being internationally minded as the most realistic alternative to the perils of nationalism and invested their hopes in the creation of the United Nations Organization. During the UN's early existence, cosmopolitanism came to favor in its literal translation as "world citizenship," as did the prospect of a world federation on the American model. The spectrum of these hopes and assumptions were captured in the UNESCO seminar discussions of the ideal international civil servant employed in "world government." There the teachers representing geographically dispersed states mulled over the idea that all members of the UN Secretariat ought to have "world citizenship"; countered that "world citizens" in fact did not have the freedom of the world "since there was from the point of view of passports, residence, etc., no 'world' but merely nation-states and their dependencies;" and then agreed that the ideal international civil servant should have "a national outlook."[18]

Although the Cold War swung the balance toward nationalism—as the political objective supported by all sides—in the 1970s, the significance of internationalism in this oscillating relationship was restored, its meaning again radically renovated.[19] From a *longue durée* perspective, the motifs that historians now describe as characteristic of the seventies as a "global" period were the same as those that featured at the beginning of the twentieth century, namely the exponential proliferation of international institutions and a new international society. What had changed were the kinds of nonstate and state actors that had begun to populate the international sphere. They included on the one hand, mass-based organizations such as Amnesty International and, on the other hand, a "Third World UN," representative of new postcolonial states and demands for global social and economic reform. Throw the visual impact of television into the mix and this was the setting for a truly expansive mass, and even international, public sphere. Since then, the concept of "civil society," borrowed from its Eastern European context, has become the tag for the power of nongovernment initiatives and actors that in the seventies drew legitimacy and authority away from the state at a global level. When the end of the Cold War ushered in a "fourth age of nationalism," another new concept, postinternationalism, was simultaneously born.[20]

During these historical ebbs and flows, the political and institutional spaces that opened up around the idea of "the international" crossed with the multiple strands of democratic, liberal, socialist, feminist, nationalist, imperialist, capitalist, federalist, and anticolonialist aspirations. To a significant extent, visions of international community were carried into the twentieth century on the back of eighteenth-century celebrations of global trade and commerce. By the end of World War I, however, there was more disillusionment with the regional and social inequities of free trade and its promise of peace through markets. Capitalism, and the economic precepts of "social justice," were the conditions of this new internationalism and defined its difference from nineteenth century proletarian internationalism. As the sovereignty of states as nations became an almost sacrosanct law of political life, the social justice perspective kept alive a longer standing tradition of international humanitarianism and intervention.[21] Through all these transformations, the liberal character of the new internationalism propelled social and political change, it spurred old and new questions about how to change and improve the world, and, depending on who you were and where in the world you lived, encouraged all manner of answers always in combination with thinking about the nation and the state.

At the end of the twentieth century, on the tail of the end of the Cold War, anthropologists and cultural theorists pondered the relationship between nationalism and internationalism as "neither antagonistic nor even analytically separable principles, but . . . rather, mutually entailed aspects of a wider process of categorical thought and action."[22] Around the same time, cultural and imperial historians began to launch quite separate self-conscious investigations of the transnational dimensions of the past, and the history of internationalism.[23] They probed the intersecting stories of imperialism, decolonization, and development. Nudged by the sixtieth anniversary of the UN and UNESCO, some even turned their enthusiastic attention to the significance of emblematic twentieth-century international institutions.[24] As a result, we know more and more each day about the workings of the League of Nations, the International Labour Organization, the Institute for International Intellectual Cooperation, the World Health Organization, and the United Nations itself. Yet we still know relatively little about the range of ideas and ambitions associated with these organizations or abandoned at their creation, especially beyond the metropolitan cultures of Western Europe and North America. The closer we look, the more apparent are the holes in our knowledge about the breadth and complexity of internationalism as an idea or its influence across the twentieth century, and the lives of the people it involved.

This study offers an introduction to the history of internationalism at specific moments of the twentieth century when international visions of community occupied the liberal political mainstream. It aims to correct a distortion of historical vision that has featured nationalism in the foreground, while keeping internationalism beyond view. As a result the emphasis in this narrative is on internationalism, even as my intention is to restore internationalism to the history of nations and nationalism. It is not written as a survey, or a complete compilation of every configuration of internationalism. Nor does it proclaim the objective sociological status of internationalism in the twentieth century. Instead, this history of internationalism in the age of nationalism draws its momentum from the historically specific ideas and institutions that were named "international" by citizens, and women and men who lacked basic rights. Putting the international back into the big picture of the twentieth century, I would argue, gives more space to the perspectives of men and women who regarded international institutions, and the league and UN, as contexts in which they could improve their status as national citizens as well as build an international community.

The teachers who finished up writing the report on their UNESCO seminars in 1948 concluded that persons wanting to write on the UN should go there and "trace the theoretical structure in tangible objects and persons." This book started out as just that kind of study of the early years of the United Nations seen through its people. My research into their stories led me to this cultural history of the rise and demise of twentieth-century internationalism with its focus on the intersections of the social, political, and intellectual. Those same stories opened my eyes to a century of politics that we have tended to historicize and remember as organized solely around the principle of nationality and the realism of the nation-state.

Although the most easily available evidence of internationalism draws us into a European world, in assembling this argument I have made use of the archives of "universal history," and the scholarship of historians who have begun to explore the archives of mobility to capture the references to an international present or future that surfaced not only along a transatlantic passage nor simply in the interests of colonialism.[25] Together these archives indicate that in different parts of the world internationality was refashioned in the cause of an anticolonial internationalism increasingly, although not solely, in support of nation building.[26] By focusing too on the place of women in this international history, my aim is to show they were there, even though we may have lost sight of them, and that where they are absent there may be a gender story to tell.[27] As important, I have taken as my approach the same methodologies that have been used to study nationalism, with particular attention to the "imagined" and "invented" dimensions of internationalism, as well as the mutually reinforcing relationship between the talk of internationalism and its realism, and the importance of the international for understanding the history of the nation. I have tried to look through to the cultural underpinnings of visions of international community, the invisible moral order that internationalism implied, and its political implications in what I think of as the "five ages" of the "new internationalism": the turn of the twentieth century, the end of World War I, the apogee of internationalism at the end of World War II, its reprise in the "global" seventies, and the "postinternational" nineties.[28]

Some years ago, the historian Akira Iriye argued the importance of internationalizing history. Iriye began to trace the outlines of a twentieth century "cultural internationalism" as "the exchange of ideas, cultures, and persons" and as distinct from "the world order defined by military power and considerations of national interests."[29] I endeavor to continue what Iriye began, but I weave the strands of the modern history of internationalism as an idea back into narratives of the twentieth century as an age of nationalism and national interests. My reading of that past and the relationship between internationalism and nationalism is indebted to the international optimism that inspired the work of Iriye and other social scientists at the approach of a new millennium. But my argument has been shaped as much by the global politics of the twenty-first century in the wake of the events of 9/11, and the relative absence of the talk of internationalism in our own time. And that leads me to my opening historical gambit—this absence throws into stark relief the persistence of internationalism as a peculiarly twentieth-century phenomenon. Without the impact and influence of internationalism, the twentieth century would have looked radically different.

Chapter 1

The International Turn

In the early twentieth century, if someone had asked Europeans or Americans to predict where the world was headed, chances were they would have pointed toward internationalism of a new twentieth-century kind. As John Hobson, the British economist, explained, it had become impossible "to trace down those issues which are presented to us as great social issues, political or economic, and to find any solution which is satisfactory that does not present the elements of internationality."[1] For the future American secretary of state Robert Lansing, the nineteenth century belonged to nationality; the driving force of the twentieth century was internationality.[2]

Those of us fed on a more conventional historical diet might consider these assessments, made only a few years before the outbreak of the world's first "total war," misguided. The turn of the twentieth century was after all the apogee of nationalism, an era marked by the invention of new nationalities and nations.[3] Nationalism is as commonly named the culprit of the outbreak and violent force of World War I as credited with the legitimation of the principle of nationality in the peace process that brought the war to an end. The apogee of nationalism was simultaneously the apogee of empire, accompanied by the rivalrous militarization of the world's empires and acts of state-coordinated violence in the name of national pride, economic necessity, or territorial expansion.[4] Given these circumstances, the claims made by Lansing and Hobson begin to make sense only once we parse the historical specificity of their political language and its intended meanings, and assess the extent to which their views of an international turn were shared.

As we will see, the turn-of-the-twentieth-century fascination with the novelty of internationality and the passing of the national reflected the self-consciousness with which an increasingly literate and mobile mainly middle-class public heaped their own ambitions for change onto the material changes in their everyday lives, and how they imagined those lives. Those same material changes were simultaneously opening up national and international public spheres, furnishing new public spaces of national and international congress that allowed for transnational connections and the "contamination of ideas."[5] Nationalism and internationalism were still likely to be perceived as antithetical or even agonistic: the revolutionary political internationalism of the working class opposed to the liberal nationalist aspirations of Europe's middle classes. But the concept of a "new internationalism," born of the "objective facts" of modernity, and out of the same historical processes as nations offered an increasingly attractive political conception of modernity and progress. The first historian of this phenomenon, Christian Lange—a Norwegian parliamentarian and founding member of one of the most significant experiments in the political scoping of internationalism in this period, the Inter-Parliamentary Union—went so far as to enthuse that the ideological innovation of the new internationalism was in essence its embrace of the nation.[6]

This chapter draws the strands of the history of nationalism back into the story of internationalism in the decades that Europeans like to refer to as the Belle Époque. It maps the contours of an international turn marked by the confident pre-World War I narratives of internationality and "objective internationalism" and the influential wartime associations that caucused the prospects for international government as a League of Nations. As important, it reconnects this early twentieth-century history of internationalism to the debates about race, empire, and nationalism that were intrinsic to contemporary liberal conceptions of progress and modernity. In all these ways, the history of turn-of-the-twentieth-century new internationalism provides us with the ideological and social backstory to the advent of the league and the UN.

Objective Internationalism at the Turn of the Twentieth Century

If we can trace the truth of the past by attention to principles that were constantly talked about, then the early twentieth century took a self-consciously international turn.[7] As contemporaries understood it, the mechanisms of that turn were the new "objective facts" of steam, electricity, and trade. Roads and railways, canals and ocean carriers, and telephone, telegraph, cable, wireless, news, and mail services had all transformed economies and provided the opportunities for cooperation and sociability across the political borders of empires and nations. Even more importantly, they provided the infrastructure and motivation for the international institutions and associations devoted to all manner of internationalized political, economic, religious, and humanitarian issues proliferating across the world.[8]

The novelty of international organizations, their impact on everyday life, and their significance for the future are all the more apparent as the subject matter of contemporary commentaries and investigation. For those who were counting, it was possible to number ten new international organizations for each year of the 1890s and contrast them with the mid-nineteenth century, when there were only five.[9] The International Telegraphic Union (1865), the Universal Postal Union (1874), the International Union for Weights and Measures (1875), the International Union of Custom Tariffs (1890), and the International Office for Public Hygiene (1907) all featured on the accumulating and increasingly well-rehearsed listings of the objective facts of internationalism.[10] There were the international organizations with distinctive constituencies, such as the still familiar International Olympic Committee (1894), the International Co-operative Alliance (1895), the Universal Esperanto Association (1908). Some international organizations, such as the International Committee for Relief to the Wounded (1863, renamed the International Committee of the Red Cross in 1876), traced their origins back to the nineteenth-century humanitarian societies set up in the wake of the Congress of Vienna. The Young Men's Christian Association (1844) gathered momentum in the latter decades of the nineteenth century, espousing "Christian principles of social and international conduct" and "the development of a right public conscience such as shall strengthen all those forces which are working for the promotion of peace and better understanding between classes, nations, and races."[11] Middle-class European women had not always found it easy to access the international societies of the earlier nineteenth century such as the YMCA or the abolitionist movement (the 1840 World Anti-Slavery Conference held in London had actively excluded women). When the opportunities arose, women were quick to organize their own international associations and coordinating bodies, such as the International Council of Women (1888) and the International Woman Suffrage Alliance (1904). By 1910, an international conference and the Brussels-based Office Central des Associations Internationales coordinated the multiple interests of this burgeoning international society, as it was commonly identified.

Many of these international organizations were based in Europe (most popularly Berne, Brussels, Paris, and London); however, they were as remarked on in North and South America, and in the urbanized outposts of empires. Their activities extended into the non-European parts of the world, particularly Japan.[12] Some were the instruments of state cooperation, others were the manifestations of individual and social initiatives. As the sheer number of international organizations, their variety, and their functions as settings for transnational sociability, cooperation, and the spread of ideas captured the imaginations of their membership, they became the basis of claims that "objective internationalism" had arrived. Regardless of parochialism or vintage, these organizations were construed as evidence of the difference between twentieth-century internationalism and previous nineteenth-century versions.[13] From a historical perspective, the articulation of this difference is less evidence of a really-existing internationalism, than of a new self-consciousness of the internationality of everyday life.

A typical product of this self-consciousness was the doctoral thesis on "Internationalism and the international administrative organization," published in 1910 by a young French political science student in Lyon named Jean Claveirole.[14] Claveirole was particularly endeared to the Berne-based Universal Postal Union, an international organization that had liberated postal delivery from incompatible national and local administrative practices and tariffs. The significance of this organization lay not just in the facility with which mail could now be sent but also the new ways of seeing oneself in the world it invited. Claveirole's observations of the new age augured by the international administration of postal services entice the twenty-first-century reader into a past as foreign as it is familiar: "When I throw a stamped card for 10 centimes into a letter box, to some part of another continent, and it arrives in a few days; when I address a letter to a stranger and I add an 'international response' coupon, exchangeable in every country against a post stamp for the same value; can't I say, even more justly than Socrates, that I am a citizen of the world?"[15]

For Claveirole, the act of posting a letter demonstrated the realism of the new internationalism, as it drew the individual into an international realm of sociability. As significantly, Claveroile claimed, the effect of the existence of international administrative organizations literally repeated the institutional and sociological processes that had led to the creation of nations such as France itself, albeit on a new international scale.

Before World War I, then, internationality was a word that signified both the existence of international organizations and practices and their social and cultural effects. Like the equally ambiguous "nationality" (a term that had worked its way into the majority of European political and legal lexicons only in the latter decades of the nineteenth century), internationality was used to bolster arguments for a particular way of being in the world.[16] For John Hobson, internationality meant that "anything happening in the most remote part of the world makes its immediate impression upon the society of nations."[17] It could also imply an international subjectivity, what Hobson would describe as a new kind of "international man," simultaneously national and international.[18] Claveirole's own fascination with internationality resonated the pervasiveness of nationality.

The Viennese-born Alfred Fried pushed the conceptual relationship between nationality and internationality almost as far as it could go. Born into the simultaneously polyglot and nationalist rhythms of the Habsburg Empire, Fried was an archetypal turn-of-the-century self-identified internationalist—an enthusiast of Esperanto as a universal language and a publisher of journals with pacifist and internationalist leanings. In 1892 (twenty years after the establishment of Germany as a political state), Fried set up the German Peace Society; twenty years later, he created the Verband für internationale Verständigung—the Society for International Understanding. He was not only a founder of and subscriber to international organizations, he made it his business to document their existence. The purpose of Fried's directory, the *Annuaire de la vie internationale*, for example, was to log the manifestations of objective internationalism—and it remains a useful catalogue of turn-of-the-twentieth-century visions of "international life."[19] When in 1908 Fried published his *Das Internationale Leben der Gegenwart*, "International Life Today," he wrote it as a travel guide to the country known as "*das internationale Land*," a territory imagined through the mapping of intergovernmental treaties and the new Public International Unions.[20]

There are good reasons why Fried's map was dotted with public international unions or, as Claveirole preferred, international administrative organizations.[21] In the early twentieth century, the organizations that coordinated and regulated the movement of people, things, and diseases across the borders of member political states were attributed a simultaneously political and social influence on internationalism by virtue of their administrative internationality; since then historians have credited these public international unions with the introduction into international relations of "new themes, new actors" and new "international norms."[22] The Universal Postal Union was exemplary of these organizations, down to its use of the language of "Union." Its shared laws and rules were conceptualized as building administrative links between states and nationally defined practices, and, on that foundation, a future form of international government. It was not only nations as states that were invited into the sphere of international administration. In pursuit of its practical international goal, the United Postal Services included among its founding members a "non-sovereign" entity, Egypt.[23]

Christian Lange's involvement in the first Inter-Parliamentary Union conference held in Norway in 1899, was as indicative of the governmental dimensions of the new internationalism. The Inter-Parliamentary Union collected together parliamentarians, predominantly from Western and Northern Europe, committed to the development of international rules and laws for cooperation between liberal democracies.[24] For Lange, as for many parliamentarians of states designated "national," the mutuality of national and international sociological phenomena determined their intrinsic compatibility. Undoubtedly this compatibility was often consummated as a union of political convenience. The historian Madeleine Herren has shown how, regardless of individual motivations, the creation of international administrative organizations suited the purposes of state government agendas, as a "back door to power."[25] The Swiss government, for example, was extremely aware of the symbolic capital that could be accrued from the fact that its political capital Berne was the headquarters of many of these new public international unions. Swiss politicians made strategic use of the impetus of the new internationalism to compensate for what the Swiss federal government lacked in foreign policy initiatives.[26] Although the United States exhibited more than enough domestic foreign policy clout, in 1908, Theodore Roosevelt was sufficiently seduced by this new kind of "backdoor" power to lure international gatherings away from the European continent onto welcoming American shores.[27]

In the age of the nation-state, there were many strategic or even pragmatic considerations underlying the recovery of the nation's compatibility with internationalism. After all, the objective facts of steam, electricity, and trade, like international institutions that enabled an *international* sociability and allegedly fostered internationality, were the acknowledged framework connecting *national* communities across otherwise disconnected domestic landscapes. This nationalizing process was as relevant at the turn-of-the-twentieth-century in relatively new states such as Italy, Thailand, and Australia, as in the older political communities of Japan, France, and the United States. Such conceptual coincidences sometimes also made it difficult to think of the national and international as consecutive stages in the evolution of political communities. Consider the quandary faced by French-based peace societies gathered in Toulouse in 1902 for their first national congress. The most successful of these, the Association de la Paix par le Droit—with 1,200 members in 1902 and 3,250 in 1912—defined its internationalism in terms of its support for the introduction of international laws enforcing cooperation and arbitration between states, not unlike the ambitions of the Inter-Parliamentary Union.[28] Yet here was the Association organizing a national coalition. Would national meetings of peace societies encourage a partisan and even parochial nationalism rather than the kind of internationality that they also believed to be the prerequisite of peace? These were questions its members asked themselves. The advice offered by their president—the philosopher and staunch French republican Theodore Ruyssen—was that the national and international should be regarded as complementary. Ruyssen explained that by capitalizing on the resources of national organization they would be more effective in their promotion of the *mystique* of internationalism as a secular religion larger than that of the nation, "the religion of humanity."[29]

The narrative of a new internationalism was constructed then out of leaps of imagination, over the ambiguities and paradoxes of sociological and political modernity. This process is particularly striking in the gradual disambiguation of the liberal characteristics of this new internationalism from more politically radical versions of internationalism through the excision of unwelcome ideas, people, and politics. Accounts of the objective facts of a new internationalism rarely gave space to the evidence of wildly successful meetings of the International Working Men's Association or the class-based political agenda that spread across Europe among the dissidents of empire and industrialization, under the aegis of the First International (1864) and then the Second International (1889). Instead, the narrators of the new internationalism's sociological realism tended to relegate class-based internationalism to the nineteenth century. Similarly, they made no mention of the less ideologically admirable facts of inter-nation-state cooperation obvious in the tightening regulation in the United States and British settler societies of cross-border movement by certain race-identified groups, particularly the Chinese and Japanese, or the impact of the world's growing interconnectedness on the burgeoning international traffic in arms, narcotics, and women and children. Nor did they pay attention to the signs of the international revitalization of "old channels of migration" taking place beyond the borders of Europe and which could be counted, for example, in the rising number of annual hajis from the Dutch East Indies to Mecca and Cairo.[30] While Ruyssen resolved on the "mystique" of internationalism, he still tolerated the anarchists who appeared at the fringes of the meetings of the Association de la Paix par le Droit.[31] Eventually, however, ideologies critical of the nation and state alike, particularly communism and anarchism, along with citizens and subjects who regularly moved across national or simply state borders in search of work, lost their place in the mainstream narrative of a new twentieth-century internationalism with its emphasis on progress and modernity in the image of the liberal nation-state.

From a distance, the political and social meaning attributed to the ostensibly objective facts of internationality cannot help but appear subjective, particularly when we consider that many of the political representatives of states involved in intergovernmental organizations—even those devoted to the more mundane challenges of sanitation—were motivated by the cause of national health and security, as well as a "back door to power," or that the new internationalism comprised the same implicit assumptions of class, race, and gender difference that confined visions of national community to their historically specific limits. However, recognizing the subjective ways in which the objective qualities of the new internationalism were constituted—out of the selective interpretation of social change and legitimate social actors—does not make it any less historically significant an idea. Instead, it merely makes it an idea of its times, put to work in the context of the issues of the day.

The next section situates the invented tradition of internationalism in that historical context. It looks in greater detail at the historically-specific social and political dimensions of the narrative of a new internationalism and the extent to which its key components—international organizations, international law, and international government—attracted a wide range of political causes. This is a story that has its conventional beginning in 1899, at an international peace conference held at The Hague, but in this chapter leads us to the League of Nations Associations of World War I along the less conventional route of the Universal Races Congress of 1911.[32] As we will see, across this period, the nation question and the more general preoccupations of empire, race, and civilization imbued the new internationalism with its distinctive twentieth-century character.

Reinventing a Tradition

There were eventually two Hague Peace Conferences before World War I, in 1899 and 1907. Together they came to stand for the extraordinary expansion of public interest and political investment in international law and international institutions as the instruments of a permanent peace. The 1899 conference was called by the Russian tsar to bring a halt to the escalating arms race and military rivalry among the imperial powers. It could be said that Nicholas II was acting in the tradition of a century of diplomatic congresses and continental gatherings traditionally described as the Concert of Europe. Since the end of the Napoleonic Wars, and the convening of the Congress of Vienna (1814–15), the politically conservative governments of European states had regularly sought shared solutions to threats to stability and prosperity, even if for selfish national ends. In the latter half of the nineteenth century, representatives of European states under pressure to improve the living standards and opportunities of their national citizenry had also begun to gather more regularly to consider questions of shared social as well as political interest, from questions of imperial rivalry to sanitation, health, labor, policing, and peace itself.

Against this background, the 1899 Hague peace conference illustrated not only the expanding social dimensions of the nineteenth century practice of international conferencing, but also the accumulating political status of intergovernmental administration and international law. By the turn of the twentieth century, international law was widely considered a crucial facilitator of the political ideals and administrative practices that had putatively made internationalism real. It was assumed to encourage shared, or at least negotiable, precepts of justice, as well offer an effective means of resolving disputes between states, and averting wars. The story has its beginnings in the mid-1860s, when two lawyers—Tobias Michael Carel Asser and Gustave Rolin-Jaequemyns—lit on *l'esprit d'internationalité* as the motto for the world's first international law journal, *Revue de Droit International et de Législation Comparée*. Asser and Rolin-Jacquemyns associated the "spirit of internationality" with a set of common principles of law that could be infused into domestic legislation and foster closer relations between nations, including freedom of association and the abolition of slavery. The story of the progress of international law becomes more complicated, however, when we discover that their enthusiasm was stymied by their English collaborator John Westlake, an expert on British laws dealing with cross-border or transnational issues.

Westlake refused the inclusion of *l'esprit d'internationalité* as part of the journal's explanatory rubric, on the grounds that "the humanization of national policies and development of a liberal spirit" was in practice unsustainable, utopian, and irreconcilable with the realism of state-based international law.[33] As the historian Martti Koskenniemi has described, in the decades that followed, as the discipline of international law accrued adherants and practitioners, its purpose was inextricably entangled in both impulses—the "spirit of internationality" and state-based realism.[34]

The logic of late nineteenth century international law also connected international values with the nation and imperialist accounts of civilization through the precepts of Enlightenment-fostered Orientalism. When the Scottish political and legal philosopher James Lorimer pondered the questions of territory, frontiers, and legislation that he believed were at the heart of military conflicts, he imagined their resolution in the form of an international government with its headquarters as likely in Constantinople as Geneva. This was because he believed that while only some states and men were fit to assume the role of international adjudicators—Germany, France, Russia, Austria, Italy, and Britain— Constantinople could be legitimately occupied as a geographically suitably international site and the sovereignty of the ruling "Turks" ignored because of Turkish "political incapacity."[35] Similarly, the German lawyer Walther Schücking, who was convinced that nationalism was an ideology of the past, and internationalism the future, thought international law would assist "the long-term objective of a World State" through "a gradual Europeanization of the world."[36] At the same time, through the efforts of the expanding community of legal experts who came to know each other under the auspices of the *Revue de Droit International*, and the networks of the corresponding Berne-based Institute of International Law and International Law Association, international law became the sign under which the competing colonial ambitions of the self-styled "civilized states" were resolved in the interests of the colonial powers themselves.[37]

The institutional and disciplinary developments in international law exemplify the tensions that characterized narratives of a new internationalism and its liberal universal aspirations. In other words, the political dimensions of the international communities imagined out of the sociological stuff of modern technology and commerce and universal ideals of justice and peace were as vulnerable to the civilizational and racial language that at the turn of the twentieth century carried European empires across the world and legitimized the newly exclusivist national citizenship and immigration domestic policies of European and settler societies. It is difficult to imagine that we would not find those same tensions at the heart of the 1899 Hague Peace Conference, regardless of its reputation as "The Parliament of Man, the Federation of the World,"[38] or as Schücking, present at The Hague as a German delegate, brazenly described it, an existing "World Confederation."[39]

At first glance there was nothing outstandingly representative about the so-called parliament assembled at the summer palace of the Queen of the Netherlands, in the tranquil park setting of the Haagse Bos in May 1899. The Central and South American Republics, Sultanates of Morocco and Muscat, Orange Free State, Principality of Monaco, Republic of San Marino, and Kingdom of Abissina were not even invited. Instead, there were the predictable representatives, including those from Europe's growing cohort of empires. The only nonmonarchs to sign the concluding agreements of the conference were the Swiss Federal Council and the presidents of the United States, the United Mexican States, and the French Republic. However, the world's remaining sovereign entities—including the Ottoman Empire, Siam, China, Persia, Japan, Luxembourg, Serbia, Bulgaria, and Romania—were all invited to send delegates, a curious but still significant formal guest list. As importantly, the conference generated unprecedented levels of popular interest thanks to the same revolution in technology counted among the objective facts of internationalism.[40]

For many of its participants and a newly constituted reading public fed a daily diet of information by the tabloid presses of England, America, and Europe, the Hague peace conferences announced a new age of emboldened public opinion. Since then, historians tend to agree that the Hague peace conferences cultivated an international sociability and a specifically internationally minded public opinion, at least in part thanks to the efforts of William T. Stead, the English newspaperman. Stead is often thought to have been behind the calling of the conference, and he was certainly committed to using the tools of the tabloid newspaper industry in the interest of generating enthusiasm for world peace.[41] His own conception of the road to world peace happily combined a pacifist interest in the newly invented international language Esperanto, the idea of a United States of Europe, and an International High Court, along with undiscriminating faith in spiritualism, imperialism and the enforcement of international law.[42] At The Hague, Stead supped with the tsar and banked on the interest of readers whose only access to conference proceedings and dramas came through publications such as his own *Review of Reviews* and *Courrier de la Conférence de la Paix*. The same calculation must have been made by the *Manchester Guardian, Nouvelle Revue,* the *Times, Morning Post, Figaro,* and the more parochial European and American papers that sent reporters to the sleepy capital of the lowlands.

It was as important a sign of the times that not all those invested in the internationalism of the Hague conferences were men. Bertha von Suttner, a prominent Austrian feminist and pacifist, participated in the proceedings from the sidelines—her task in 1899, on American invitation, was to work on the German-language press to drum up more public support for the international ambitions of the meeting. She had come to her role at The Hague through her long involvement in international humanitarian organizations, women's associations, and peace societies. After attending the third Universal Peace Congress in Rome in 1891, von Suttner had established an Austrian peace society on the model of the famous pacifist societies in England. She was also responsible for setting up an Austrian interparliamentary group linked to the work of the Inter-Parliamentary Union.[43] She knew the Swedish industrialist Alfred Nobel and encouraged him to create an international peace prize. (She herself won the prize in 1905, and knew many of the recipients in other years, including Alfred Fried.) The energy she brought to her convictions is apparent in the fine web of international connections that she carefully worked for her pacifist ends.

Ensconced at The Hague, von Suttner noted in a diary entry for June 10, 1899, that much of the energy of the conference came from unexpected sources such as the retinue of reporters and lobbyists and overwhelming popular interest: "I have never before in the course of a whole year received so many letters, telegrams, and voluminous writings as now, while I am here at The Hague. They announce schemes, proposals, infallible methods for securing peace. And all of this I am expected to make comprehensible to the delegates!" Von Suttner was especially skeptical of the "aeronautical letter writers" who sought support from the peace conference for their inventions of "airships and flying machines" that would, "by the conquest of the atmosphere," bring an end to customs houses and border fortifications. Her skepticism was aroused less by their dreams of planes, than by her expectation that "all new inventions are invariably employed by the war authorities." And yet, she added, "I am firmly persuaded that every technical improvement, especially all means of easier communication, ultimately leads to universal peace."[44]

Among the correspondents who deluged von Suttner and other prominent participants at The Hague were the working-class and religious groups from all over the European world linked through pacifist organizations. The chief American delegate, Andrew White recorded in his diary (and few did not keep one) that he was inundated by "plans, schemes, nostrums, notions and whimsies of all sorts," thanks to new communication technology and the services of the Universal Postal Union.[45] White only reluctantly concluded that these letters and petitions were evidence of a feeling more earnest and widespread than he had ever dreamed. Writing from the 1907 Hague conference (instigated this time by peace and arbitration societies and a new Cercle International), von Suttner too claimed, albeit with more enthusiasm, that public opinion, "expressed, organized, made palpable and even disagreeable to those who oppose it," was "the master, and even the god, of the conference."[46] From her perspective, the events that went on around both peace conferences, including public lectures and debates, and the socialist, anarchist, and Zionist organizations that shadowed its meetings, were all evidence of a clamor for democratic representation in international affairs.

When it comes to the concrete international detail of the Hague conferences, the substantial gaps between the aspirations attached to it by supporters of disarmament and arbitration and what could actually be agreed upon have inspired mixed historical assessments. Certainly, the conference established the international machinery that would be interpreted in the ensuing decades as crucial to the growing authority of international law. This included sixty-one articles for curbing the arms race, the humanization of the conduct of war, and the formation of a Permanent Court of Arbitration. Historians with an eye to the wars that punctuated the first decade of the twentieth century in the wake of the conferences have focused quite rightly on its relative failures, including the rejection by almost all its delegates of the Russian proposal for compulsory arbitration between states.[47] For contemporaries, however, the conference also had social or cultural implications. Stead wrote to the tsar on the mounting cachet of internationalism for "old men . . . hoping to crown a long career by a great achievement in the cause of international peace," and young men "using the success of the Conference as the starting-point of their ascent to high places."[48] The creation of the Permanent Court of Arbitration even launched the international careers of men who were not at the conference. John Westlake was by then a Cambridge professor of international law and took a close interest in The Hague events, eventually turning up at the new Permanent Court of Arbitration to represent Great Britain (1900–1906). Asser was a Dutch delegate to the 1899 conference and went on to a career as an arbitrator at The Hague court too, acting in the dispute between Russia and the United States over the Bering Strait, for which Robert

Lansing was the American representative before he went on to political life as the U.S. Secretary of State.[49] Stead's observations also attributed cultural capital to the new internationalism in other ways, whether the homage that the conference committees paid to the "One and Great International Society," or contemporary analyses of the appearance on the international political scene of "non-sovereign territory" as a "new voice."[50]

Despite the best or worst of any one participant's intentions, the Hague conference was spun by men like Stead into "a fact in the evolution of human society . . . greater than all its works."[51] For Léon Bourgeois, head of the French delegation, it had accentuated the "bonds of humanity" over the primacy of national frontiers. Carefully crafted conference legal documents delimited the authority to decide those bonds to the "society of civilized nations." Even so, the representatives of societies only ambiguously awarded civilized status acknowledged the conference's universal implications. The Chinese delegate Lou Tseng-Tsiang was fundamentally suspicious of proposals put at the conference for a future "High Assembly" monitoring questions of peace and disarmament, on the assumption that it might not be to China's advantage, because any "High Assembly" would include the European imperial powers alone. Regardless, and unlike some of his European peers, he agreed to support the prospect of international intervention on "humanitarian" grounds.[52]

The conference vision of a future "High Assembly" may have come to nothing, but the humanitarian objectives of The Hague Peace Conference impressed representatives of the new international organizations that harbored strictly religious or moral ambitions and sought a political voice. The American feminist May Wright Sewall, who went to The Hague in her capacity as the president of another new international organization, the International Council of Women, was struck in particular by the extent of Quaker and Christian interest.[53] We know too that the provincial American pastor James Van Kirk's experience of that conference led him to take to the road preaching interdependence and friendship. In 1909, Van Kirk stopped before the Liberty Bell in Philadelphia to read his "Declaration of *Inter*dependence" and make the point that the world was moving from patriotism to humanitarianism and political unity.[54]

The history of ecumenicalism intersects profoundly with the universalist and pacifist intentions that gave such momentum to the idea of internationalism and international law in this period and found some satisfaction at The Hague. Just as religion still defined moral and social life, and religious exclusivity was often a nationalist cause, the prospect of a universal Christianity or internationality connected religiously and morally like-minded individuals, and linked the prospects for peace with "Christian values." Ecumenicalism also tied the new internationalism more closely to its nineteenth-century past, particularly the British and North American peace and abolition societies, and the missionaries who were among the first groups to espouse universalizing transnational causes.[55] Even as narratives of a new internationalism cast off the nineteenth-century versions of internationalism as "dreamlike" and unreal by comparison, religiously motivated peace movements embraced the new century's inclination to a self-conscious internationality. In 1891, Berne became home to an International Peace Bureau coordinating the interests of the nation-based peace societies mushrooming in the "nations between the Ural Mountains and the Rockies" and finding some supporters in Japan, Australia, and Argentina.[56]

"Pacifism" was coined in this period to describe the force of these peace societies and "pacifists." Although pacifists were often accused of national disloyalty and dysfunctional idealism, by 1899 their number included prominent politicians as well as international lawyers, some of whom joined organizations such as Ruyssen's Association de la Paix par le Droit with its practical international program for peace through law. Others considered the new internationalism the vehicle of a universal, Christian religion.

Wilbur Fisk Crafts, a religious moral reformer whose ideas led to the formation of another of those international associations littering the fin de siècle, the International Reform Bureau (1895) based in Washington, D.C., might otherwise not be remembered to history. Yet, in the excavation of a past in which the international was thought of as a force for change at least equal to the national, his life and writing offer evidence of internationalism imagined as binding the world together through the shared imperatives of universal moral values with profoundly Christian roots.[57] For Crafts, internationalism was "fitted to be in the twentieth century of largest interest because of greatest novelty and of largest human importance." Crafts was an adept customer of the "international travel and international commerce" and international trading that he believed were also "developing an increasing group of international men, whose hearts, like the ocean, reach out helpfully to all shores." In his own mind, the mechanics of internationalism had rendered him an "unofficial diplomat at large, seeking not the advantage of one nation but of all, through the promotion of those moral and social reforms which history proclaims are the real questions of life or death to nations."[58]

In the fall of 1906, Crafts's addiction to internationality compelled him to address "the shipmates of several nations in an entertainment on an Atlantic liner" on the evils of narcotics, gambling, alcohol, and prostitution. His audience may not have welcomed his message, but they were only one among the many Crafts approached on his travels to Japan and China on a well-trodden American missionary trail. He met with foreign secretariats and preached his mantra of international philanthropy and social ethics. He also took heart in the fact that in 1908 there were nearly four hundred Esperanto societies in Europe, America and Asia, including Japan, and thirty Esperanto-language journals published every month disseminating knowledge about not only ethics and religion but also general science and medicine.[59] Crafts used these avenues of transnational publication to disseminate his view of the importance of internationalism as a modus and means of moral reform, in French, German, Spanish, Arabic, Urdu, High Wenli, and, of course, Esperanto, which his wife taught through the *New York Christian Herald*. The rhetorical questions Crafts canvassed in these writings were characteristic of the controversies raised by twentieth-century discussions of internationalism: "Is a broad sociality essential to the noblest individuality?" "Is foreign travel, on the whole a benefit?" "Is the watchword 'My country, right or wrong,' justifiable?"[60]

On May 28, 1899, the Honorable William H. Fremantle, Dean of Ripon, preached a sermon for the international peace conference at the English Church in The Hague that suggests the anxiety surrounding just this last question, or as he named the conundrum, "patriotism and cosmopolitanism." Fremantle advised of the "compatibility" of the "general welfare of mankind" and national patriotism, and of "taking up the white man's burden among the weaker races."[61] There was no contradiction on his account among international, national, and imperial interests or identities. In the same way, the first wave of mainly middle-class feminists like May Wright Sewall who had ventured into the terrain of the Hague peace conferences identified themselves as intrinsically international, "without country," precisely because they were denied the political and legal rights of national citizenship. The point of the International Council of Women was to lobby for national rights, and in support of the rights of unrecognized nations repressed by empires.[62] While meeting at the Hague peace conference of 1907, a number of women's and men's organizations organized a new umbrella organization, the Subject Races International Committee, which would shelter the National Council of Ireland, the Egyptian Committee, the Friends of Russian Freedom, and the Georgian Relief Fund—as well as explicitly international associations built out of imperial networks, including the Anti-Slavery and Aborigines

Protection Society, the International Arbitration and Peace Association, and the Positivist Society. This last was a loose following of Auguste Comte's mid-nineteenth-century vision of a future in which the religion of humanity would replace monotheism and technocrats would oversee a world made up of small temporal states. For all their divergent causes, the member groups of the Subject Races International Committee committed themselves to the defense of "the principle of Nationality, to maintain for each nation the management of its own internal affairs, to protect subject races from oppression and exploitation."[63]

The credo of the Subject Races International Committee recognized demands for individual and collective liberties as appropriately international, humanitarian, and pacifist. The satisfaction of those demands, it was presumed, would lead to a more just, internationally conscious, and thus more peaceful world. The committee's first conference, held in London in 1910, gave voice to independence claims for Finland, Georgia, Persia, and Poland, declarations against domination by Russia, calls for home rule for British-occupied Ireland and India, and demands for the end of slavery in Mexico, Brazil, and Peru. In each of these cases, mainly British spokespersons carefully distinguished between the status of "subject races," which, they argued, required imperial protection because of their alleged relative political incapacities, and "subject nationalities" that demanded emancipation.[64]

The Universal Races Congress held in London the following year collected together all these new impulses and the increasingly familiar faces of turn-of-the-century international organizations. The inspiration of Felix Adler, the German-American (and Jewish) founder of an international ethical cultural movement, and the German-Jewish Gustave Spiller, a known author of educational and psychological studies, the Universal Races Congress was to pose "the great question of International Relations" or, in the words of Léon Bourgeois, another Hague veteran and honorary president of the congress, "the securing of harmony between the various races of men . . . [as] an essential condition of any serious attempt to diminish warfare and extend the practice of arbitration."[65] For some of its European participants—and the list was self-consciously long—the 1911 congress was to take the measure of the changed relations between "Occidental and Oriental peoples" brought about by the military and imperial rise of Japan. Examined in hindsight, the congress usefully recapitulates the related imperial, race, and nation questions enmeshed in the "international question," as it was understood at the time. It also introduces us to an even broader cohort of actors whose ideas and experiences flesh out this sketch of a new internationalism in the decades just prior to World War I.

Among the most important of the figures in attendance at the Universal Races Congress was the great African American sociologist W. E. B. Du Bois, who insights and activism follow the story of internationalism through into the latter half of the twentieth century. In 1903, Du Bois had famously pointed to the "color-line"—"the relation of the darker to the lighter races of men in Asia and Africa, in America and the islands of the sea"—as definitive the so-called "international question."[66] In 1911, he made the Atlantic crossing to London to act as secretary of the U.S. section, alongside Adler, on the expectation that the Universal Races Congress was to be "the meeting of the World on a broad plane of human respect and equality," aiming at "human understanding and world peace and progress."[67] After it was over, he described it to the readers of the Chicago-based NAACP newspaper, *The Crisis*, as "a great and inspiring occasion bringing together representatives of numerous ethnic and cultural groups and bringing new and frank conceptions of scientific bases of racial and social relations of people."[68] Certainly the logistics of the conference confirm Du Bois' appraisals. The Universal Races Congress involved fifty countries, more than thirty presidents of parliaments, the majority of the Permanent Court of Arbitration, and delegates to the Second Hague Peace Conference. It brought to London the grand dame of the Hague conferences, Bertha von Suttner, as well as twelve British governors and eight British premiers, over forty colonial bishops, some one hundred thirty professors of international law, leading anthropologists and sociologists, the officers and council of the Inter-Parliamentary Union, and more.[69]

On the long list of the congress's "vice presidents" were men from France, England, and the United States, Arthur Balfour and other prominent British politicians and university vice chancellors, well-known internationalists of a liberal democratic cast, such as Theodore Ruyssen, Alfred Zimmern—a classicist and eventually first professor of international relations in the world—and H. G. Wells, the English writer. Given its London location, English participants were bound to dominate. However, the congress rallied speakers and the support of persons from across the world, Brazil, China, Cuba, Ecuador, Greece, Guatemala, Haiti, Japan, Mexico, Persia, and Turkey among others. Lou Tseng-Tsiang returned as an "honorary vice president" thanks to his Hague role, William T. Stead was on the congress's Executive Council. By this time, there was also a new generation of female ecumenicists, humanitarians, and pacifists, some of whom, like the British theosophist Annie Besant, were given a platform in front of the thousand-strong crowds. Other women took a back seat, including the prominent American feminists Jane Addams, Carrie Chapman Catt, and Emily Greene Balch.

The congress program fielded a strange mix of social scientists for whom race resonated quite differently, including James Baldwin, John Dewey, William I. Thomas, Walter Pillsbury, Ferdinand Tönnies, and Emile Durkheim. Among Du Bois' favorite speakers were John Hobson, who critiqued the exploitative basis of imperial capitalism, and the "jetblack" Haitian General Légitime, who insisted on the capacity of Haitians for advancement. A few speakers argued on psychological and sociological grounds that evolution was progressing beyond the narrowness of nationality and toward a greater humanity.[70] In these scenarios, race was a more inclusive, universalistic category than nationality given, so the argument ran, there were fewer races than nations. The challenge was only to see them as equal. Franz Boas warned more simply, and fundamentally, "against such stability of type as would give rise to a definite hereditary superiority of one race over another."[71]

In the final session of the congress, Edwin Mead, the American director of the World Peace Foundation, celebrated the influence of the first journal devoted to the study of international relations, the *Journal of Race Development* (1910, renamed as the *Journal of International Relations* in 1919 and, a few years later, *Foreign Affairs*).[72] From our perspective, the journal's origins in the academic collaboration of the psychologist and Freudian G. Stanley Hall and historian George Hubbard Blakeslee, its title, and topics make plain the intersections between scientific conceptions of race as a fixed category of human difference, and the cultural as well as political underpinnings of the new internationalism.[73] For Edwin Mead, the journal was evidence that science could affect "interracial goodwill."

The Universal Races Congress reflects distinctively twentieth-century anxieties, from the competing social and political realism of nationalism and internationalism, to the significance of race, civilizational, sex, and class difference in the constitution of international laws, organizations, and government. Even though the most prominent voices and names were those of white Western males, its program and audience is further evidence that they did not have the stage to themselves. That same program also illustrates the extent to which debates about the biological origins of race and theories of human nature shaped the search for common international ground in the early decades of the twentieth century. This was a period when newly credentialed scientific disciplines, among them sociology and psychology, were emerging out of the heterogeneous philosophical forms of moral and scientific inquiry prevalent until the latter nineteenth century. Just like other natural and social scientists, sociology and psychology's recruits contested the political significance of sex and race (sometimes class and national) differences and the relative influence of biological determinism and social environment on those differences. Because of their scientific authority, their claims and their methods (especially intelligence testing) influenced education, citizenship, and immigration policies.[74]

The international resonance of the language and themes of these new sciences rings clearly in John Hobson's speeches and publications in the aftermath of the Universal Races Congress on the new internationalism. Hobson, who had spoken at both the Subject Races International Committee Conference and the Universal Races Congress, now contrasted the social philosophy of the eighteenth century, which had produced a laissez-faire individualism built on "the notion that a sound society required nothing more than a set of these hard-headed, intelligent, self-centred monads, each vigorously asserting his rights, pursuing his separate material interests of his neighbours," with the lessons taught by modern economics, politics, and psychology, which had destroyed the idea "that such a separate 'self' exists at all." The self was amorphous, uncontained by "skinhood" and determined by its social relations "expressed in a number of concentric circles of widening area: self, neighbourhood, city, nation, mankind."[75] Hobson's own description of concentric circles was not that different from the Enlightenment stagism articulated a century earlier. His point, however, was that even though human subjectivity was environmentally determined, the "slow-growing sentiments of common humanity" were just not keeping up with the pace of social changes summed up as objective internationalism. This same psychological disjuncture, Hobson explained, was the reason for "the sudden flare-up of intense hostility towards Germany or Russia or France which from time to time possesses the personality of the ordinary British citizen."

Amidst the facts of hostility and violence, the concept of an "international mind" gained popularity as one of the many kinds of minds that were the subject of scientific and more popular discussion, from war minds to herd minds, women's minds, and national minds.[76] In popular evocations, the international mind became a useful way of conveying an international subjectivity or *mentalité*. Nicholas Murray Butler, the president of Columbia University, for example, made the international mind—by which he meant "the habit of thinking of foreign relations and business in such a way as to inspire friendly and cooperative relations"—an argument for international law.[77] Butler maintained that an evolutionary process had begun that would see war disappear, and the nurturing of an "international mind" would help that evolution along.[78] Unsurprisingly perhaps, he believed that those responsible for that nurturing were men like himself, "an international elite instructing public opinion on ethical principles civilized standards, and respect for law."

Like Léon Bourgeois, Christian Lange, Bertha von Suttner, and many other protagonists in the history of the new internationalism, Butler was an eventual winner of a Nobel Peace Prize (1931). He was as well known, however, for his anti-Semitism and suspicions toward the Japanese. Nevertheless, his concept of an international mind not only made its way into the thinking of the newly formed Carnegie Endowment for International Peace, of which Butler was a trustee, but also echoed through a Carnegie report into the growth of internationalism in Japan, authored by Tsunejiro Miyaoka, a Tokyo-based former diplomat keen to establish the liberal and international credentials of his countrymen.

Miyaoka's career had taken him to Washington as secretary of the Japanese legation, and then a postdiplomatic life as an international lawyer, working in international arbitration at The Hague Permanent Court on the opium trade disputes.[79] He came to his work for the Carnegie inquiry convinced of the naturalness of the Japanese-American relationship mapped onto a regional geography of "the Pacific Slope." By the time he published his findings in 1915, Japan (unlike the still-neutral United States) was already a participant in Europe's war against the Central Powers, drawn in through its alliance with Britain. Miyaoka reported to the Carnegie Endowment that he had found proof of an "international mind" corresponding to Butler's concept, now inflated to "the awakening of the human conscience to this broader horizon,"[80] "the rise of human conscience from a lower to a higher plane, from narrow self-interest or welfare of family."[81] For lack of acknowledged alternative evidence, however, his conclusion pointedly settled on less sensational examples of the movement of people and ideas between the United States and Japan, across what Miyaoka described, in the manner of the Universal Races Congress, as the civilizational boundaries of West and East.

The Carnegie report on the growth of internationalism in Japan is one more example of the extent of fascination with a new liberal internationalism, as well as the selectivity with which it was observed. (Japanese immigration to the United States had long been stymied by American race-based policies, and Butler's anti-Japanese views would have been on Miyaoka's own mind.) Miyaoka's approach to internationalism reinforces too the centrality of the image of "modern man's" mobile and expansive belonging.[82] By 1915, that mobility was already under threat from the conflict engulfing the European continent. Sigmund Freud would soon bemoan the barriers to movement set up by new passport systems and borders. Before then, however, there was cognizance of a "new kind of people," described by H. G. Wells as a "floating population" working for the new international institutions.[83] We might put under that heading diplomats and international lawyers such as Miyaoka himself, and the "international financiers and entrepreneurs" that the American philosopher Horace Kallen identified as proponents of an international mind—Kallen may have been thinking of William T. Stead as much as Andrew Carnegie.[84] Certainly the audiences for international gatherings such as the Hague peace conferences and the Universal Races Congress were marked by the divides of race and class as well as the relative growth of public spheres in societies such as prewar Japan.[85] Ironically, if Miyaoka had conducted his survey at the end of World War I rather than its beginning, he may have been able to plumb richer sources of internationally minded thought and action, both in Japan and in the United States.

International Government and World War I

At the outset of World War I, it would have been difficult to predict internationalism's move to the center of discussions and debates regarding a postwar international order that could ensure permanent peace. The declaration of war drove members of many international associations to declare their national allegiances uppermost. Yet within the spate of a year, the conflict's furious and relentless course had revived the relevance of internationalism as a political project.

During her wartime trips to England, the American feminist, pacifist, and moral reformer Jane Addams noted a discernible difference between the "Victorian man" and the young man being sent to war.[86] Addams concluded that there were now two kinds of masculinity in England, corresponding to two kinds of internationalism: the moral romanticism of the Victorians who dreamed of a far-off "Federation of the World" to be brought about by the wise men of many nations; and the young conscripts "who do not talk much about internationalism, but they live in a world where common experience has in fact become largely internationalised."[87] Whether she intended it or not, Addams (who would share the Nobel Peace Prize with Butler) was in effect repeating the prewar mantra of internationalism and its sociological realism.

Political visions of international community with federalism as their method had also preceded the war. The new internationalism of the turn of the twentieth century circulating in the cities of Western Europe and North America had invited political projections that Edward Krehbiel—a historian and eventually American delegate to the 1919 peace conference in Paris—described as "a sort of confederation, a cooperative union of sovereign states, a true concert of powers."[88] In 1910, Gustave Hervé, a minor figure in French socialism, had taken up his pen in support of the same model of a United States of Europe propagated by Stead, and hoping for "perhaps a United States of the world."[89] In the United States itself, and especially along its East Coast, an extraordinary number of organizations and movements, few of them socialist, and including the World Federation League (set up also in 1910), had advocated a federal internationalism. These organizations focused on synchronizing decisions made at the international or world level with national concerns and imagined a World Court at the legal heart of any future political alliance.[90]

The deep tributaries of international law and liberal models of representative government fed the tides of the specifically federal perspective on government internationalism. Hayne Davis, a New York attorney who joined the Inter-Parliamentary Union and the League for Peace and Arbitration and went on to found the American Association for International Conciliation, directed his overlapping enthusiasm for international law and democratic politics toward support for "a world system resembling the United States, known as the United Nations, and including constitutional limitations upon governmental powers."[91] While the world waited for the evolution of this system, he counseled the wisdom of increasing American armaments. Further north in Massachusetts, the state legislature had accepted the arguments of 1899 Hague Peace Conference stalwarts and petitioned the U.S. Congress to promote a world legislature that would periodically call international assemblies to make recommendations to national governments. The agent behind this initiative was Raymond Bridgman, another newspaperman and author of *World Organisation* (1905). Bridgman believed in a world bill of rights, a world executive or secretariat for evolving world boards and bureaus, and a universal principle of world community that would replace the doctrine of national sovereignty. He backed these causes again in 1915, when the Massachusetts Assembly agreed to adopt a resolution favoring "a world-state unhindered by national sovereignty."[92]

By then, a raft of associations supporting a League of Nations had begun to appear in Britain. The similar societies organized in the United States, and Europe and then around the world emerged from the networks that had promoted international and national causes before the war and that brought together imperialist viewpoints with internationalist ambitions and nationalities causes. The Oxford classicist Gilbert Murray, who was among the organizers of the London Conference on Subject Races, was also a keen member of the League of Nations Society founded in 1915 by his fellow Cambridge classicist Goldsworthy Lowes Dickinson. Murray, born in the British colony of Australia, went on in the interwar period to take a leading role in the creation of the International Organization for Intellectual Cooperation attached to the League of Nations, and, when the league collapsed, he helped establish an organization for education in "World Citizenship." Dickinson was part of a British network of academics who, like Hobson, published in progressive American journals on international ethics and social reform. By late 1918, the League of Nations Society had amalgamated with the League of Free Nations Association to form the League of Nations Union. Dickinson and Murray now mingled with Alfred Zimmern, the Fabians, H. G. Wells, and Leonard Woolf, and a bushel of British politicians, including the former (Liberal) prime minister H. H. Asquith and (Conservative) former prime minister *cum* foreign secretary Arthur Balfour.

Although oriented toward legal forms of internationalism, particularly international law and arbitration, the League of Nations Union also spoke to the cause of political self-determination. For many League of Nations Union members there seemed no contradiction between the idea of self-determination and the viability of the British Empire both because self-determination could imply "home rule" as much as a nation-state, and because the empire was imagined as a political form on which an international government built out of the structures of nation-states might be modeled. The British prime minister Lloyd George described Britain as "the only embryo League of Nations because it is based on the true principles of national freedom and political decentralisation."[93] He would have found no disagreement from Lim Boon Keng, a prominent Straits Chinese intellectual from Malaya. Educated in British medical schools, in later life Keng was "an architect of Confucian revival, and a founder of the revolutionary forerunner of the Kuomintang." During the war, however, he portrayed the British Empire as the "prelude to the federation of the world."[94]

French supporters of a future Société des Nations intentionally emphasized its form as a society, not just "league," insisting on its potential for international sociability.[95] Adherents of the Association francaise pour la Societé des Nations (French Association for the Society of Nations) set up in 1918 were a familiar mix of academic and political figures of the French establishment as well as its more progressive left wing.[96] They imagined their activities as part of a longer tradition of political pacifism, including the Ligue International de la Paix (1896), which promulgated the right of people to self-determination as a tenet of internationalism, or the Hague conference, at which, as Léon Bourgeois would insist repeatedly, France had proposed a Société des Nations.[97] Bourgeois's intellectual compatriots at the French Collège Libre des Sciences Sociales were as concerned to corroborate the realism of a Société des Nations with roots in "the evolution of civilized humanity."[98] Others deliberated a future Societé that oversaw the implementation of international laws from the perspective of "the rights of the stranger."[99] Regardless of their specific interpretations of international government, by 1920, there were around twenty thousand vocal supporters of what the French persisted in naming the Society of Nations.[100] This compares to the four thousand formal members of the British League of Nations Union in 1919, and the membership of the American League to Enforce Peace, which reached more than a quarter of a million during the war.[101] (The British League of Nations Union established its credentials as a mass organization in the late 1920s when it peaked at 650,000 members.)[102]

Women were intensely and often separately involved in this agitation through their overlapping feminist, nationalist, and internationalist interests. In the late nineteenth century, Bertha von Suttner had grabbed the international mettle, assuming political leadership in ways that women were rarely able to in the denationalized fin-de-siècle Habsburg Empire or in earlier humanitarian international organizations. But von Suttner had no part to play in the wartime league associations—she died in June 1914. The new war generation of female pacifists and internationalists gathered around the figure of Jane Addams, an advocate of the social sciences, national patriotism, and internationalism.

Addams was a member of the American Women's Peace Party (which she proudly claimed antedated the League to Enforce Peace by six months) and the Central Organization for a Permanent Peace (OPP), established in The

Hague in 1915 with an all-star cast of culturally and politically influential Europeans and Americans, including the familiar Ruyssen, Lange, Hobson, Woolf, Dickinson, Emily Greene Balch, and Paul Otlet (secretary-general of the Union of International Associations in Brussels). Although the OPP's professed aim was to study individual and national rights, its members regarded it as a "worldwide" society devoted to an agenda evolved from the legalism of the Hague peace conferences: an international order built on sanctions and arbitration, the abolition of secret treaties, popular control of foreign policy, reduction of armaments, freedom of the seas, and guarantees of religious freedom and equality as international issues.[103] Its female section, the International Women's Committee for Permanent Peace, juggled a commitment to nationalities and a tradition of feminist pacifism and political activism that addressed women's legal and political marginalization in national life.[104] In April 1915, Addams with Balch and her OPP colleagues convened a now iconic international congress of women who braved wartime dangers on the open seas and on the European continent in order to gather at The Hague. Their international mission was to not only bring about an end to the war but also democratize international relations, adding to a growing internationalist agenda the political equality of men and women, and the equal involvement of women in international affairs.[105]

The organization that resulted from the 1915 Hague congress, the Women's International League for Peace and Freedom (WILPF), became one of the most active supporters of a League of Nations. Significantly, its membership pursued the demands for democratization and equality through a balance of national and international causes.[106] The WILPF's British chair, Helena Swanwick (a future delegate to the League of Nations), maintained that only an international organization could prevent nations from oppressing each other and offer democratic control of foreign policy. Under her editorship, *Foreign Affairs: A Journal of International Understanding*—the official organ of the pacifist Union of Democratic Control—enjoined "the evolution of a sane and constructive internationalism" that acknowledged both patriotism and love of country, and "the cause of international reconciliation and understanding among men."[107] Swanwick imagined an International Parliament where nonnational interests, such as shared motherhood (it didn't seem to matter that she was childless), would combine across national lines.[108]

As the war raged on, English- and French-language public spheres were bursting with the urgency of plans for a world federation elected by national populations, or in which national populations would elect regional federations, or states would be given votes on population/wealth coefficiencies, or international representation would be organized according to race.[109] The French, British, and American national associations in support of international government of some kind all countenanced the creation of an Allied League to enforce peace by military means.[110] The French philosopher and government adviser Henri Bergson believed in a federation limited to Allied states, insisting that Germany would never change and thus could not be included in such a federation (nor could any inferior races), and that the imposition of a League of Nations would be an artificial institution lacking any organic growth. Bourgeois (who was chairing the French government committee tasked with exploring the concept of a League of Nations, to which Bergson also belonged) wanted a league that included Germany in order to be able to keep that state within the fold.[111] In *Towards International Government*, John Hobson mulled over the maintenance of state autonomy in the formation of an international government, even though looking back on this period he would recall the talk of a new world order fixated on the significance of a supranational sovereignty.[112] Indeed, the discussions that took place in print, in public meeting rooms and in correspondence, held both themes in constant, even precarious tension: the state as the political form that protected nations, and political suprasovereignty as a necessary dimension of a viable and modern international community.

Progressives or moderate left-wing political groups, such as the English Fabian Society, thought in terms of an "International Council" or federation. Leonard Woolf, the author of the influential Fabian-sponsored tract *International Government* (1916), repeated the view that new international forms of political governance were required to meet the new international conditions of life. Those conditions were not unlike prewar iterations of the ways in which internationality—through the vehicles of steam, electricity, and trade—had affected everyday experience so that life was determined more by "capital, labor, professions etc." than geographical lines, or place of residence.[113] Indeed, for Woolf, the basis of "true international Government" was the "extraordinary and novel spectacle of international voluntary associations." His model of a future international government was shaped out of a coalition of "states, municipal authorities, private individuals, and every sort and kind of national group, society and association." In his wartime pamphlet on a League of Nations, Hobson, who was by now allied with the Union of Democratic Control as well as the Fabians, described these same units as the components of "international society."[114]

Discussions about a postwar order built out of images of international society and internationality draw our attention to the blurrier borders in the imagining of internationalism: who it represented, who it would govern, on what authority, and with what powers? Woodrow Wilson's early proposal for "a universal association of nations" invited the "full submission of the cause to the opinion of the world." But he only vaguely implied the international scope of a future league's reach.[115] By comparison, his political peer, Theodore Marburg, the chair of the American League to Enforce Peace's Committee on Foreign Organization, went so far as to explain in correspondence with the French premier Aristide Briand that creating a league involved the "surrender of a measure of sovereignty, for there is set up a will higher than the will of the nation."[116] When a youthful Walter Lippmann (employed in the U.S. government organization established to explore the principles and details of a postwar peace) asked the equally young English economist Harold Laski his opinion on these questions, Laski offered that the world was on the threshold of "new conceptions" in sovereignty thanks to international trade, whereby "every action in the modern world of any power reverberates through the whole fabric" and "sovereignty necessarily involves interference with interests other than those it theoretically intends to cover."[117] The Republican senator Henry Cabot Lodge of Massachusetts, one of the founders of the American League to Enforce Peace and otherwise an antagonist of Wilson's, drew on an image of the utopian rather than objective qualities of internationalism but arrived at a similar political conclusion. Lodge claimed that "a union of civilized nations" that would "put a controlling force behind the maintenance of peace and international order" was as necessary as it was utopian, since "it is through the aspiration for perfection, through the search for Utopias, that the real advances have been made. At all events it is along this path that we must travel."[118]

Ellen Key, a Swedish self-styled feminist with an enormous following in Europe and the United States—a woman described by the English "sexologist" Havelock Ellis "as one of the chief moral forces of our time," and member of the Organization for Permanent Peace—took a slightly different tack.[119] She responded to the problematics of sovereignty and realism by presenting the nation as utopian as internationalism.[120] Key laid out her vision of internationalism early in the war to an American newspaper reading public over a series of installments later published with the indicative subtitle: *A Consideration of Nationalism and Internationalism, and of the Relation of Women to War*.[121] Her essays condense many of the characteristics of wartime internationalism as they developed in discussions of a new international postwar order: internationalism was a "state of mind" and a form of political life that could be brought about only through the application of international law, and through the accommodation of national patriotism; internationalism had to make space for a "sound nationalism," based on "the concordance between people of kindred race and language." In the inevitable widening of political association into internationalism, nations would be maintained since national patriotism had to be incorporated into internationalism for it to work.

Unlike the discussions among male protagonists, whatever their political persuasion, Key's internationalism also had a feminist bent. It reflected her awareness of the gender implications of internationalism when women were not spoken for. She presumed women would be beneficiaries of this national internationalism because they would gain international recognition of their "equal rights in politics, in nationality, in marriage, and, as parents, equal pay for equal work, and equal moral standards, equal training and opportunities, and the endowment of maternity." "Woman" would also assume new international obligations and a new rationale for her own education, training herself as "a world-citizen for her responsible task as mother of humanity."[122] This essentialized woman would cultivate "an international spirit" and, through instruction in civics, "develop a world consciousness and give an introduction to the duties of world citizenship." More generally, international education would cherish the national literatures and masterpieces of other countries, its proponents would set up international commissions to censor textbooks that disseminated national hatreds, and encourage the learning of foreign languages and a world language. Key was in effect outlining a cultural program of international mindedness that echoed through the rationales for the cultural work of the League of Nations and the United Nations and UNESCO, and that mimicked the already conventionalized gender division of nation-building labor.

There were other ways in which the wartime debates about a postwar internationalism imitated the nation question, particularly in the extent of scientific interest in the forms of subjectivity that could establish the legitimacy of political communities. The foundations of international government was a theme that seeped into the work of psychologists, who claimed to contribute to its illumination through the study of human nature, with varying results. The American psychologist Morton Prince was intentionally upbeat about the evidence for internationalism as a phenomenon with psychological roots as deep as those of nationalism. In 1916, he took this message to the federalist pan-Asian "Japanese Concordia Association," where he proclaimed that the study of psychology was enabling man to dream of a "world consciousness in international relations" through its insight into man's individual striving.[123] By contrast, the transatlantic psychologist William McDougall, best known for his work on the "Group Mind," preferred to emphasize "the great and necessary part played in human life by the Group Spirit and by that special form of it which we now call 'Nationalism.'"[124] Specifically addressing the idea of a league, McDougall proposed that the nation was so closely identified with man's psychological needs that antinationalists could be diagnosed as persons who hated the common man.

In what became a seminal text for early nationalism studies, *The Psychology of Nationality and Internationalism* (1919), the Michigan-based psychologist Walter Pillsbury merged both these perspectives.[125] His inquiry into the importance of race in shaping the "national mind" was spurred by the phenomenon of American Greeks returning to Greece to fight during the Balkan Wars of 1913. By the time he got around to writing up his study, American intervention had helped win the war in Europe, a league of nations loomed, and Pillsbury deemed a final chapter on the psychology of "supranationality" requisite. He now argued that supranationality would always exist as a concentric circle of world consciousness, shadowing local and national consciousness. The question that remained was how to crystallize "the broader sympathies now wasted in more or less vague sentimentalism." Pillsbury believed that once supranational institutions were created, international subjectivity would follow as a result of the social adaptation of instincts and habits. It would take about a century, but after that time the legal foundations of a League of Nations would become as immutable as the constitution of the United States.[126]

The range of psychological theories of instincts and of the unconscious as wellsprings of nationalism or internationalism is a useful reminder that these theories reflected contemporary scientific and political controversies, rather than consensus on the "objective" status of either phenomenon. George Mead, the well-known American social psychologist and proponent of the concept of an international mind (he also played a part in the Universal Races Congress), stayed clear of biology and popularized an analogy between the self constituted through social communication and interaction and nations constituted through international sociability. During the war, Mead made social psychology the raison d'être for an international organization that he conceived of as a "League of Nations," which would eliminate war as "the arbiter of international life."[127] The league, he maintained, would also guarantee "U.S. hegemony over Latin Nations, thus relieving the United States of the burden of maintaining 'a vast military establishment' through which to accomplish the same end." For all their different expertise, Mead's socially constituted international mind looked a lot like Nicholas Butler's. Both men thought of the international mind, like international arbitration, as relevant to the civilized world, namely Europe and white settler colonies, only occasionally Japan and the South American republics.

The influence of the new psychology infiltrated wartime deliberations on the dominion of an international government over nations, empires, and races. The American League to Enforce Peace insisted on the United States's "sovereign right to decide alone and for ourselves the vital question of the exclusion of Mongolian and Asiatic labour," and not to submit questions of race to an international forum, on the grounds that the maintenance of "the purity of the race" was among the "deepest of human instincts."[128] The Oxford historian and Foreign Office advisor John Holland Rose went so far as to berate "the reckless unwisdom of the champions of internationalism and their utter disregard of the claims of country." Nationalism, he suggested, was a "spiritual conception, unconquerable, indestructible [even if] there is a baser side to the instinct."[129] By comparison, internationalism was a political outlook like socialism and other "anarchic and anti-national theories" with a far greater hold on the Slav and Latin peoples.

Like many British liberal imperialists, Alfred Zimmern (who otherwise acknowledged the social conditions of his own conversion from Judaism to English patriotism) more easily accommodated the legitimacy of a liberal form of internationalism focused on law, institutions, and some form of international government, as well as the primacy of national "sentiment." Zimmern insisted that human nature dictated a nationalist path to internationalism. Echoing the fashion for group psychology and national instincts, he was convinced "no theory or ideal of Internationalism can be helpful in our thinking or effective in practice unless it is based on a right understanding of the place which national sentiment occupies and must always occupy in the life of mankind."[130] Harold Laski suggested obliquely to Walter Lippmann that the "complex of psychological relations" was equally as important as the complex of economic relations to the determination of the question of sovereignty.[131] Christian Lange thought of internationalism as having roots in European and Christian intellectual traditions and in the biological truths of group psychology and germplasm theory.[132]

As the war's end looked likely, Hobson composed a new theory of "International Man" out of the observation that the nineteenth-century faith in international peace through laissez-faire economic internationalism had been proven wrong. Under the conditions of modern industrialization and empires, free trade had not generated friendly competition and cooperation, it had led to a cutthroat search for overseas markets and the grim exploitation of colonies and colonial subjects and finally to war. By contrast, the objective facts of steam, electricity, and trade had socialized a new kind of international man. The problem, he added, was that suitable economic and political institutions based on intergovernmental cooperation and economic reform had not yet evolved. These were among the expectations Hobson had for the new League of Nations, in which "it is generally held, the sole hope for civilization resides."[133] Ellen Key's intellectual idol, the immensely charismatic Indian philosopher and antinationalist Rabindranath Tagore, was more sophisticated in his reading, rehearsing the "well-known psychological fact that by adjustment of our mental attitude things seem to change their properties."[134] Of course, it might have been the same premise of mental adjustment that, on Jane Addams's understanding, had instilled a nation-based internationalism in the outlook of young soldiers.

At the end of 1917, these assessments and predictions regarding internationalism were revised in the new circumstances of the spread of revolutionary zeal brought alive by the sudden overthrow of the Romanov monarchy in Russia and establishment of a Bolshevik worker's government. As Vladimir Lenin, the revolution's leader, assimilated the relevance of the "self-determination of peoples" into this new episode in class-based internationalism, the attention of the world's politically disaffected and war-weary turned eastward. For the governments of liberal democratic states, the Russian Revolution was a dramatic reminder that there was still a life pulse in the class and communist body of late-nineteenth-century internationalism. Robert Lansing, now Wilson's secretary of state, described nationalism as the defining characteristic of a version of internationalism opposed to what "most people call Internationalism, but which I think ought to be called Universalism or else Classism."[135] The same Lansing who, prior to the war, posited internationality as the driving force of the new century felt obliged on the eve of Paris peace talks to prepare for Wilson a "Memorandum on the Spiritual Weakness of a World Union."[136]

The Bolsheviks' success did not deter everyone from investing in a liberal conception of internationalism, even when its language overlapped closely with that of class-based internationalism. In 1919, "World Brotherhood," a phrase that throughout the twentieth century would be synonymous with proletarian internationalism, or (in Lansing's words) universal classism, remained the catchcry of a Christian congregation that drew into its community the proponents of a League of Nations.[137] This brotherhood was mainstream enough to bring together Gilbert Murray and Lloyd George in support of the specific civilizing role of Christianity, and a vague litany of "great imperishable dogmas." That litany echoed the reformist temperance agenda that had set Wilbur Crafts on his path: "Sobriety, Continence, Honesty, respect for Justice, Truth, and Reason, and the maintenance of a healthy mind in a healthy body."[138]

In the early days of the war, impressionistic surveys of internationalism in the English-speaking world posited the general public opinion that nationalism was "no longer expressive of the age," and "the present sovereignty of states is detrimental," even though a federation of the world, of the kind envisioned in the organization of the 1899 Hague conference, tended to be thought of as "not yet, feasible."[139] By the end of the war, as the discursive fields of both internationality and nationality were busily tilled, the conceptualization of nationalism and internationalism, and the relationship between them, sprouted clarifications.[140] Good nationalism was patriotic but sociological in origin. Bad nationalism was racialist. Good or, as William McDougall put it, "true internationalism" was the complement of nationalism.[141] Bad internationalism was antinationalist and took the specific name of cosmopolitan internationalism.

Tomas Masaryk, the liberal democrat leader of the newly legitimated Czechoslovak nation, an early political beneficiary of the principle of self-determination promised in Woodrow Wilson's Fourteen Points, was more generous in his parsing of these ideas: "There is no difference between national identity and internationalism, if we understand the point appropriately."[142] How was the point to be understood? For Masaryk, internationalism was to be thought of not "in the old way as a sort of cosmopolitanism and liberalism," instead in a new way, "as an organization of nations which are capable of managing their own affairs." This version of internationalism allowed for static concentric circles of ever-larger communities, rather than consecutive stages of evolution from the local to the universal: "Humanity tends in two directions, national and international. At the moment of liberation of nations, humanity approaches its unity as well." Masaryk too distinguished between a good national internationalism and a bad cosmopolitanism internationalism.

The changing fortunes of the term "cosmopolitanism" is another useful marker of what had changed after the war. In the prewar world of the Belle Époque, cosmopolitanism was a concept celebrated by transatlantic student clubs that practiced race-mixing sociability, and whose members, like the Wisconsin-based editor of the *Cosmopolitan Student*, moved in the circles of the Universal Races Congress. Cosmopolitanism made a brief appearance in the political mainstream in the 1940s through the language of "world citizenship" and the cultural ambitions of UNESCO. In the interim decades, cosmopolitanism conventionally served the antithetical purpose of identifying a bad internationalism. During the war, James Baldwin, the American psychologist who had also attended the Universal Races Congress, pathologized France for its "cosmopolitan culture." Baldwin went so far as to describe the effects of "the theory of internationalism" as not only destructive of "true patriotic feeling," but the source of "symptoms of political palsy," and ultimately national weakness.[143] Even Ellen Key, like Tomas Masaryk, was careful to distinguish between cosmopolitanism, on the one hand, and internationalism anchored in national patriotism, on the other. Hobson distanced his international man from a "shallow cosmopolitan."[144] Cosmopolitanism was not only out of favor, but, during the war and after, it returned as code for Jews—as a race without a nation—and for the proletarian class-based internationalism perpetrated by revolutionaries everywhere.

For all these efforts at separating out nationalism and internationalism, by 1919, contemporaries were still likely to see them as inextricably entangled ideas, particularly since, in different contexts, each answered to the simultaneous demands for democratic representation that defined the modern era. Both the principle of nationality and the League of Nations framed wartime discussions of what peace should look like, and became mainstream political solutions to the challenge of permanent peace in liberal democratic societies, the antithesis of competing working-class-based claims to the representation of those same ideas. Inevitably, arguments that attempted to reconcile the interests of nations and internationalism reinforced their mutual realism and their similar historical and sociological origins. The notion that internationalism was the consequence of changed social conditions and forms of sociability, and the historical stage after the nation in the political evolution of humanity, even supported historical perspectives and sociological answers to the question everyone was still left asking, "What is a nation?"

Chapter 2

Imagine Geneva, Between the Wars

The history of internationalism has always involved forgetting. In the European summer of 1919, the British geologist Mrs. Ogilvie Gordon stood before the National Council of Women of Great Britain and Ireland and announced "a new era which the historian of the future will probably term the Era of Internationalism."[1] Gordon was echoing, intentionally or not, the prewar pronouncements of a new internationalism. Her attention, however, like that of her postwar contemporaries, was not on the past. She had in mind an international future recently inaugurated at the Paris Peace Conference, where victor governments, from President Woodrow Wilson's America to Taishō-era Japan, had signed up to both the principle of nationality and the form of international governance that took shape as the League of Nations. Wilson's informal adviser, Colonel House, reassured the president that commitment to a league had not only inaugurated a new world order but also turned the world upside down.[2]

House did not mention that the support of the great powers for a League of Nations was to a significant degree provoked by alarm at the success of the Bolshevik Revolution that already had taken place in Russia and its reinvigoration of Marxist-inspired internationalism. It was no coincidence that the new experiment in institutional internationalism embraced the language of "social justice."[3] But the significance of the "sentiments of justice and humanity" in this new international order had as strong roots in the liberal inclinations and paradoxes of a distinctively twentieth-century internationalism.[4] This explains why for John Hobson, the league's template was too timid, and he soon gave up on his expectations of an international answer to the world's social and economic injustices.[5] Within a few years of the league's creation, the American epidemiologist and feminist Alice Hamilton wrote to her sister complaining about the ways in which the limitations of the new league had betrayed the hopes of women. Hamilton was as annoyed by the unperturbed optimism of her close friend, the psychologist George Herbert Mead, who remained "a fanatical adherent of the League." Mead, Hamilton mocked, was still convinced that "all the woes of Europe will be over when once we have joined it."[6]

The absence of the United States from the League of Nations has long been at the heart of the historical accounting of the international organization's weakness and ultimate failure—after all the league was not able to prevent outbreaks of conflict in the 1920s and 1930s, or World War II.[7] This chapter concentrates, instead, on the scope of postwar ambitions and disillusionment inspired by the league in the interwar period, as one way of correcting a historical tradition that has written international institutions out of the study of the twentieth century. As we will see, the league was crucial to the mechanics of nationalism as well as to the intellectual, political, and social history of twentieth-century democracy and modernity.

In the early months of 1919, the disillusionment that became such a defining part of the league's history seemed unimaginable, just as the inevitability with which the representatives of the great powers discussed the invention of a league was unprecedented. To begin with, the drafting of the League of Nations Covenant reignited earlier debates about the political nature of internationalism and its possibilities, and made their resolution all the more pressing and real. If there was to be a new representative international organization, should it be an alliance or a federation of nation-states? A dissoluble or indissoluble union? An exercise in sociability among nations or actual governance by an international body? *Who* should be included in this new international community?

The spectrum of suggestions sent to the commission tasked with drafting the league's covenant tells an important tale of the different and changing ways in which the new internationalism was imagined in the postwar, its complex relationship to the institutional and intellectual innovations of nationalism, and the influence of the league on the fate of those fatefully twinned ideologies. Recovering those international imaginaries requires taking stock of how our own memory of the league—as a failure, unable to prevent calamity or exploitation or war—has forgotten the longer history of internationalism and its points of deep institutional and intellectual connection to the history of nationalism.

Drafting the League of Nations Covenant, 1919

Like almost everyone involved in the Paris peace talks of 1919 that brought a formal end to World War I and planned out the new international world order, Harold Nicolson, a young aristocrat and diplomat, and Bloomsbury-based figure, kept a diary. He entrusted to it his growing disenchantment with the claustrophobic processes taking place in the corridors of the Hotel Crillon. This was the eighteenth-century palace skirting the Place de la Concorde in the heart of Paris, and long associated with the bitter fruits of older forms of diplomacy—not an auspicious headquarters for the anticipated new era of transparent foreign policy making and public consultation.[8] The states chosen by the great powers as fellow deliberators of the shape and form of the new League of Nations, however, read like the more inclusive guest lists of the turn-of-the-twentieth-century Hague Peace Conferences, which had included China, Japan, Serbia, Greece, Romania, and Belgium. To these sovereignties were also added Brazil, Portugal, and the newly constituted nation-states of Poland and Masaryk's "Czecho-Slovak" Republic. Léon Bourgeois, the French delegate to the 1919 peace talks, reinforced in his person and perspective the link to the international ambitions of the Hague meetings. Bourgeois took to his new role like the Hague veteran that he was, prodding the commission responsible for drafting the league covenant to reflect on national sovereignty as an obsolescent fiction, and the sovereignty of each state as less than absolute.[9]

Germany, present as a defeated power, was not represented on the covenant-drafting commission, but its delegates submitted a formal contribution to the debate regardless. Their submission outlined a plan for a political "world parliament" on the federal model of the existing German Bundesrat.[10] The author was Walther Schücking, another veteran of 1899, and by this time professor of public law. Whether because the submission was from a Germany in postrevolutionary turmoil or because it celebrated German federalism, British delegates dismissed it as a "typical product of German liberalism."[11] That was hardly a charge that could be made against the Swiss submission, which argued for a league in the image of Switzerland's "indissoluble alliance of states." The Swiss delegates imagined the league as a federal organization requiring some sacrifice of state sovereignty and a proportional system of representation that would, in practice, give populous China more influence than France, Germany, Italy, or Japan.[12]

The list of abandoned versions of the new League of Nations is a long one.

Under Bourgeois's guidance, the French delegation conceived of the league as a *société*.[13] It would be empowered to maintain peace and guarantee sovereignty through the creation of an authoritative international body that could compel its members to accept its decisions as well as those of an international court (of course Bourgeois, like the American secretary of state in Paris, Robert Lansing, had experience working at the Permanent Court of Arbitration set up after the 1899 Hague peace conference). Consistent with the wartime views of French, British, and American league associations, each delegation argued that the league should have influence over the military policy of its members, including the size of contingents that could be contributed to an international force and the right to enforce conscription to achieve those numbers. Even the British delegates, many of them with connections to the wartime League of Nations associations, agreed with the idea of an alliance that could require states to submit disputes to judicial arbitration and deploy forces to defend a member state under attack by a nonmember.[14]

Other submissions to the drafting commission tested the international waters of a new era of internationalism by picturing a league with the power to control the international distribution of foodstuffs and raw materials. The American and Italian delegations proposed that the league should be able to receive petitions from minorities, and that a new Permanent Court of International Justice should give the league scope to intervene in questions of minority rights. The theme of economic and social planning on an international scale, like the principles of petitioning and intervention, would persist in debates about the nature and purpose of international government through the twentieth century.

The international government that was finally given form by the League of Nations Covenant was inevitably the product of compromise but, some argued, to a debilitating degree. Ultimate authority was vested in the League Council, a body of four permanent members, namely, the imperial powers Great Britain, France, Italy, and Japan. The United States should have been the council's fifth permanent member, but it infamously never joined the league because of opposition from the U.S. Congress. There were also four nonpermanent members elected for three-year terms by the league's General Assembly, and playing to the permanent members' tune. The council directed assembly business and controlled the Secretariat. Neither the council nor the General Assembly was allowed to make recommendations that contravened a member's domestic jurisdiction. That meant that although the new body had responsibility for disarmament and the prevention of international disputes, it could take no initiative that involved intervention in deemed matters of national sovereignty, whether the enforcement of arbitration, the status of conscription, the kinds or amounts of armaments being stockpiled, or their reduction! As a result, almost the only easily identifiable prewar internationalist element instituted in the league was a new international court. The Permanent Court of International Justice could hear and determine any dispute of an international character, unlike the existing Permanent Court of Arbitration, which dealt with legal disputes between states. In both courts, however, disputes could be taken up only on the request of the parties involved—when Walther Schücking became the first German judge to preside at the court, in 1930–35, its authority was still relatively limited.

In the end, the Paris peace process instituted an international order that gave the new international organization no explicit political or military power in the international realm or over the affairs of states. The league sat alongside, rather than on top of those states, with explicit authority to determine international concerns that did not contravene national state sovereignty. The peace of 1919 had effectively stamped the century with the imprimatur of nationality as the international norm of statehood, and of institutionalized internationalism. Where there was ambiguity before, now there was certainty about that point at least. Rather than a fiction past its use-by date, the sovereignty of the state was newly reinforced through both the principle of nationality, and the League of Nations.

Despite its limitations, the league's political consequences were not easily constrained or foretold. The organization was embedded in too many strands of influence and aspiration. Its General Assembly may have been given few formal powers, but in the tradition of international organizations such as the Universal Postal Service, which admitted "non-sovereign" entities, "any fully self-governing State, Dominion or Colony" could become a member if it had the agreement of two-thirds of the General Assembly. As a result, the league had forty-two founding members and added another twenty-one during the interwar period. At its peak in 1935, these members ranged alphabetically from Afghanistan to Venezuela.[15] Although the General Assembly's delegates were nominated by the members rather than directly elected, the inclusion of a General Assembly implied a kind of democratic representativeness on an international scale. As we will see, the provision of an international bureaucracy in permanent residence to serve the General Assembly and councils and the committees, copied straight over from conventional forms of state administration, simultaneously reinforced the concept of international government and entertained international equivalents for the national loyalties and interests of state bureaucracies.

The league's international potential, like its limitations, was also decided by virtue of the social and economic questions that the peace process had newly internationalized, in some cases in obvious competition with the Bolshevik Revolution. Race, religious, and sex equality did not make it into the covenant, despite the expectations of some lobby groups. However, the creation of an International Labour Organization, or ILO, backed by the International Labour Charter, was written into the Treaty of Versailles.

The ILO represented perhaps the most ambitious political aspirations associated with the postwar peace and international government.[16] Its governing body was famously a "tripartite" structure: twelve delegates nominated by the "chief industrial" members of the league (left to the League Council to determine); six employer delegates; and, even more radically, six worker delegates. The guidelines prepared by the Commission on International Labour Legislation for the International Labour Charter formalized too international social welfare and labor standards on the model of German social insurance and the French eight-hour-day convention. The charter translated the protection of women before and after childbirth and the regulation of night work for women and children into universal labor and health standards.[17] The rhetoric of "sentiments of justice and humanity" and "social justice" written into the constitution of the ILO may have had a distinctly pragmatic edge—evident in the reference in the final peace treaty to the threat posed by the "conditions of labour . . . involving such injustice, hardship, and privation to large numbers of people" to "the peace and harmony of the world." But these were still powerful ideals to enshrine as an international obligation.[18] Less happy was the status of non-Europeans in this particular international adventure. True to the imperial spirit of the peace, the International Labour Charter stipulated that "differences of climate, habits and customs, of economic opportunity and industrial tradition may restrict uniformity in the conditions of labour difficult of immediate attainment."[19]

Similar prejudices regarding the political significance of difference—even where they referred back to environmental and cultural rather than biological causes—played out in the infamous responses of the leaders of the "new world" to the Japanese delegation's efforts to write race equality into the league's covenant.[20] When it came to the vote among the members of the drafting commission, eleven of seventeen hands supported the contention that race equality was an "indisputable principle of justice."[21] Woodrow Wilson then infamously refused the majority, claiming unanimity was required. Under his influence, the peace process effectively rendered racial equality "an internal matter for states and empires, and not an international issue."[22] It was a particular matter for the member states that led the campaign to refuse race equality, namely Australia and the United States, where race segregation and race-based immigration laws were directed most aggressively against the "yellow race" and their alleged threat to labor standards. As with the introduction of minority laws, the motivations for a race equality clause were not exclusively universalist or internationalist. For the Japanese delegation, it was a matter of the status of Japanese immigrants in California, and the international standing of nonwhite Japan among the white imperial powers.

The demands of the delegates of women's international organizations for women's rights to be made an international concern fared as badly as race equality, even though their aim was at least in part to use the international fora to win national rights.[23] In comparison to race equality, Wilson did not have to press the point of unanimity when it came to sex equality. The Commission of Ten, including the maharajah of Bikaner and the Japanese delegates, supported him to the man in their rejection of the universal applicability of women's equal rights to "self-determination." Their rationale for not including women's rights in the league's covenant turned on the unchallenged view that the determination of the status of (women's) difference was a prerogative of *national* self-determination, and definitive of national sovereignty. The point would be insisted upon repeatedly in the working league.[24]

The formal prerogative given to the principle of nationality by the peacemaking process also made it easier for the governments of victor states to insist on the internationalization of other forms of inequality for imperial ends. At a time when, as the Americans warned, "empire" held negative connotations, the league was made the moral linchpin of a system of colonial trusteeship. The so-called mandate system allowed the victorious imperial powers to add to their colonial territory on the vaguely defined assertion that the empires awarded this "sacred trust" would oversee the transformation of their mandates into nation-states.[25] The classification A to C was introduced as a purported measure of the relative stage of the political evolution of nations among Arabs, Africans, and Pacific Islanders, as if they were taking their place in a queue.[26]

As with the fate of women and Americans in the league, however, the power of the league did not always exert itself in predictable ways. Although the mandate concept was in practice made relevant only to the colonies of the vanquished German and Ottoman Empires, in abstract terms it evoked as universalist ideals both international government and "self-determination," which explains why, despite the paternalistic civilizational and racial language in which the mandates system was often cloaked, the concept of mandates seemed to make benevolent sense to some contemporaries we might otherwise expect to not have supported it. While the League of Nations Covenant was being drafted, W. E. B. Du Bois urged a mandate system that would bring to the attention of "the civilized World" evidence of African natives "not receiving just treatment at the hands of any State," or "any State deliberately exclud[ing] its civilized citizens or subjects of Negro descent from its body politic and cultural."In February 1919, Du Bois organized a parallel Paris conference to promote a "Pan-African" perspective for the drafters' consideration.[27] The American government, wary of the possible implications of Du Bois's activism for race relations at home, tried its hardest to thwart the conference and the participation of Americans. But Du Bois was already in Paris and working on his project with Blaise Diagne—the black Senegalese deputy to the French chamber. Their pan-African conference eventually attracted fifty-seven delegates from the United States, the French West Indies, Haiti and France, Liberia, the Spanish colonies, the Portuguese colonies, San Domingo, Britain, the British territories in Africa, the French possessions in Africa, Algeria, Egypt, the Belgian Congo, and Abyssinia.[28] The final communiqué declared that they represented territories "inhabited by 85,000,000 Negroes and persons of African descent," and gave unanimous support to a mandate system that would improve social and economic conditions and enforce rights for those inhabitants.[29]

The resolutions of the pan-African conference were of little concern to the covenant's drafters. They designed a mandate system that gave no authority to the league to ascertain or actively look out for the interests of individuals and groups ostensibly under international purview.[30] The conditions of the mandate territories remained a matter for the appointed colonial masters, rather than the league's Permanent Mandates Commission. The commission was empowered only to receive the annual reports of the mandatory powers, not to initiate or act on those reports or on the petitions it was allowed to receive from mandate subjects.[31] The mandate system also veiled the reneging of wartime promises of colonial withdrawal. Arab regional leaders who had taken the British at their word and risen up against the Ottoman Empire during the war, helping the Allied cause on the promise of a postwar pan-Arab state, found that ex-Ottoman Arab provinces they assumed would be included in that state were instead to be shared out among the French and British. These were the A-class mandates of Mesopotamia, Syria, Lebanon, and Palestine, which would, it was now claimed, "be prepared for early independence" at some unspoken future date.[32] During the drafting process, Rustem Haida, representing the Kingdom of Hejaz, on the southern fringes of the mandated Palestinian territory, had warned that "the word 'mandate' is used, but the definition of that word is not given. It remains vague and undefined. On the interpretation that will be given to that word depends the freedom of liberated populations."[33] In effect, the league covenant committed to a definition of mandates as the "tutelage of backward people," with no acknowledgment of the available evidence of the political aspirations of those same people.[34]

In the era of new internationalism, the initiative for tackling the international "color line," begun in a peculiarly early twentieth century way by the Universal Races Congress, had become entangled in confused and uncertain "expert" pronouncements on the nature of nations and races. On the back of advice from a corps of English, French, and American historians, classicists, and geographers acting as expert advisers to their respective governments, the 1919 peace reinforced the conception of nationality as either or both cultural and racial, and as *the* foundation for a more peaceful international order, including the new league. The limitation of mandates to the colonial territories of the defeated powers also meant that the principle of nationality was irrelevant in the victor states' colonies. This led to curious and at times tragic contortions of logic in the implementation of nationality as a principle by the league. The treaties that dealt with the collapse of the Ottoman and Habsburg Empires, for example, turned to "population transfers" supervised by the league to reposition designated religious communities on either side of the territorial borders of their respective new nations.[35] Where those transfers did not take place and identified nationalities did not have their own states (namely in the new or altered Poland, Czechoslovakia, Yugoslavia, Romania, Austria, Bulgaria, Hungary, Turkey, Finland, Albania, Lithuania, Latvia, and Estonia), the league was authorized to make the protection of national or racial "minorities" an international matter.

The specific group that the drafters had in mind in this case was Jewish religious minorities, conventionally classed as a "race" and lacking a national home.[36] The significant point here is that neither the principle of nationality nor the rights of minorities were necessarily intended to make the renovated international arena more representative, egalitarian, or inclusive. The drafters of the covenant were more concerned with erecting boundaries around the league as a public opinion forum or as the guarantor of rights, which was why requests for the incorporation of religious equality into the league's covenant died the same quick death as vehement demands for racial and sex equality.[37]

Given the conservative bent of the international context in which the principle of nationality and the conceptualization of international government were manufactured—by the representatives of states that were inclined above all to maintain their influence—it is all the more surprising, and historically significant when one comes across the odd corner of the world in which fuller political expression was given to a sovereign form of international authority. In two specific cases, the league was given responsibility for demarcating and administering international territories. This occurred because, despite the faith of peacemakers and their advisers in the scientific bases of national and racial difference, they found it impossible to translate that knowledge into facts on the ground. As a result, the nationally ambiguous city of Danzig (torn between the new Germany and the new Poland) and the port town of Fiume (disputed between Italy and the new Kingdom of Yugoslavia) were both reinvented as international "free cities," medieval-like microstates, with no single cultural or racial identification. Students of imperial history might be inclined to trace this conception of international territory back to the latter-nineteenth-century Shanghai International Settlement, where colonial powers shared sovereignty. But, by comparison, both Danzig and Fiume were relatively unfulfilled international experiments.[38] Neither survived for very long. More enduring was the conceptualization of the league's own headquarters as international territory. For its first sixteen years, the aptly named Hôtel National (renamed the Palais Wilson in 1924 on the president's death), a five-story and 225-room building by Lake Geneva, was home to the league bureaucracy. It could be argued that the territorial internationalism that established the inviolability of the league's buildings and grounds more profoundly imitated the conventions of national sovereignty.

The existence of alternative versions of the League of Nations explains some of the disappointment that accompanied the new international world order, as well as the more optimistic convictions that it would usher a new era of internationalism across the threshold of the interwar period. Without the background of the international turn, or the intellectual, technological, and ideological innovations that we can usefully term "modernity," the league may have stood for the kind of strategic alliance of states that can be found in the imagined confederations of the late eighteenth century and through the nineteenth. Instead, even the different sources of complaint at the league's expression of a minimalist and at times cynical internationalism are a reminder of the extent to which contemporaries associated the new era of internationalism with political progress, only sometimes invested in the institutional detail of world federalism or a world-state, or the nation-state. The revolutionary mood spreading across Europe and the colonial world had accentuated demands for political and economic rights, and "self-determination." The anticipation of a truly international league linked anti-imperial nationalist and women's rights groups in Turkey, Egypt, India, and China, as well as between anticolonialists and the American race liberation organization, the NAACP.[39] Egyptian anticolonial lobbyists petitioned the league drafters on the understanding that a "new era" was dawning in which disputes over issues such as control of the Suez Canal would be subject to forced and fair international arbitration. Representatives of the anticolonial Indian National Congress and the Muslim League expected from the new international organization support for the "rights of the non-White races."[40] The idea of the league also inspired idiosyncratic imagined communities. William Henry Panton Gibbons from Port-au-Prince, Haiti, wrote to the "British Majestory [sic]" "respectfully" denouncing the limitations of the final version of the league's covenant and demanding an independent "negro state" in the territory of Angola and the Congo.[41] Gibbons's own dream was a particular pan-African vision—a Christian United States of West Africa brought to life under the aegis of a mock flag of his own design.

During the drafting of the league covenant, some British delegates and advisors felt reassured that in its final form the new organization would act more in the mode of a nineteenth-century imperial conference, meeting only occasionally and "composed of statesmen responsible to their own peoples, and dependent on unanimous agreement."[42] Instead, the establishment of the league could not help but extend the political and social dimensions of the international turn, from residual imaginaries of world federation to the more practical conception of a "parliament of man," and even to an international space in which everyone might have the right to a voice. Although the status of internationalism or the league's own internationality in the new world order was not everyone's concern, the objective fact of a League of Nations seemed to change everything.

A League Temperament, the 1920s

At the outset of the Paris Peace Conference, Woodrow Wilson equated the creation of the League of Nations with "a new international psychology," "a new real atmosphere."[43] This may have been less an expression of his conviction than a pandering to expectations. Either way, it amounted to a reinforcement of the significance and objective existence of international mindedness. There were always the skeptics, like Harold Temperley, the erstwhile British adviser and historian of the peace conference, who insisted that the League of Nations unlike the British Empire lacked "bonds of common allegiance and common descent."[44] By contrast, the lingering echoes of prewar internationality made their way into the private correspondence of the cynical junior British diplomat Harold Nicolson, who wrote from Paris to his wife, the writer Vita Sackville-West, playfully commending a "league temperament . . . ready to help me when I become too national and anti-dago." Nicolson also reflected more seriously that for the league to be of any value, "it must start from a new conception, and involve among its promoters and leaders a new habit of thought."[45] Even amid the self-interested maneuvering that characterized the peace process, the imperative of peace and the social and intellectual roots of the international turn were kept alive in the idea that a new international organization could and should nurture internationality. This tension between the league's national and international objectives propelled the organization in its halting progress through the decades of the interwar period.

Expressions such as "League temperament" and "the spirit of Geneva" immersed the new organization in the expectations of international behaviors and identifications. However, Geneva, as much as the league, was no international utopia. Outsiders perceived the picturesque Swiss town as provincial, culturally isolated, and politically conservative. In the decades of the interwar period, locals tended to look down on the arriving international officials as radicals, who in turn stereotyped the Genevans as profascist.[46] Some delegates who doubled as ambassadors to France—this included the Japanese and Haitian emissaries—preferred a commuting relationship from homes in the bustling metropolis that was interwar Paris. In a world of imputed national as well as international intimacy, the advances in transport and communications should have made this a simple enough option, except that both imagined national and international communities had their factual limits, which league officials and administrators soon discovered to their constant frustration. While the French national railway was determined to obstruct the progress of institutional internationality not headquartered in Paris, the Berne-based Swiss rail organization refused to improve connections or the speed of transit across the French-Swiss border for fear of encouraging Geneva's rival provincial prosperity.[47]

The details of the league covenant point to a similar ambivalence among its drafters about Geneva as the new international hub. It gave the League Council the option of deciding "at any time" to establish the league's seat "elsewhere."[48] Geneva had in its favor Swiss neutrality during the war (as did the alternative suggestions of Berne and Lausanne) and its singular history as the headquarters of one of the earliest icons of intergovernmental institutions, the International Red Cross. But Switzerland was not a founding member of the league, and choosing Geneva meant rejecting other traditional European peace cities, such as The Hague, and Brussels, and even Constantinople.[49] Of course, once Geneva was selected as the league's home, its international reputation and its internationality—even if not its train and telephone connections—accumulated the legitimacy of "facts on the ground." More than thirty international bodies soon moved their headquarters from elsewhere and brought with them their particular international perspectives.

The Women's International League for Peace and Freedom, which Jane Addams and others had organized during the war, set up home at the edge of Geneva's old town in the Maison International, which they decorated to project a cozy domestic life.[50] The staff at the newly constituted ILO, by contrast, announced the agency's international ambitions with bespoke furniture made of the woods of many nationalities. The official administrators and delegates of the new institutions made do with the adapted premises of the Hôtel National. In 1937, they all moved into the purposely designed and built campus of the Palais des Nations in the extensive grounds of Ariana Park. Although by then the league was in the waning cycle of its interwar career, that complex of imposing buildings would remain the iconic image of Geneva's reputation as the indomitable, rather than accidental and imperfect, spirit of early twentieth-century internationalism.

According to circulating historical and sociological theories of nationality and internationality, the sociability contrived in the league's bureaucracy and its physical spaces would of themselves foster international mindedness, even where it had not existed before. The focus of this expectation tended to be the new class of international civil servants put to work in the league administration, the men and women servicing its Secretariat, committees, and conferences. In 1921, Sara Wambaugh, an American expert on plebiscites who worked temporarily with the League's Minorities Section, enthused to the *New York Times* over the cosmopolitan flavor of the Secretariat, describing it as a "league in miniature."[51] Diplomats on assignment were also considered, by virtue of their job description, agents of this sometimes cosmopolitan-identified internationality, and many of them became as convinced of the international significance of their roles at the league. Viscount Ishii Kikujiro, Japan's ambassador to France and to the League's council and assembly from 1920 to 1927, reminisced that daily contact between delegates made them lose much of their fierce patriotism, gain moderation and conciliatory tendencies, and made of some pacifists.[52]

If Ishii Kikujiro's memoir seems more wishful thinking than accurate remembering, it is as true that in the league's early years even skeptics found themselves affected by the fervor. In contemporary accounts, a league temperament was caught much as one might contract a fever. George Rich, a justice of the Australian High Court, was initially one of those skeptical delegates to the league, sent in 1922 to sit on constitutional, judicial, and political committees and on the Nauru mandate subcommittee. He was soon won over by Geneva's revivalist atmosphere and the process of "shrewd, practical, able and conciliatory men of the world, meeting together to solve in a common-sense way problems that baffled nations."[53]

In the 1920s, Australian and Japanese intellectual and political elites were among the most involved and publicly active enthusiasts of the league.[54] The league's under-secretary general was Inazo Nitobe, a Japanese diplomat and former colonial adviser. Nitobe became a regular spokesperson for Geneva as the new Mecca, the league as the "conscience" of the world. He also conceived of Japanese-American relations as a manifestation of internationalism (and thereby hung a tradition), and "colonisation as a means to civilisation and world peace, with clear moral obligations for the colonisers."[55] By contrast, his superior, the secretary-general of the league, Eric Drummond, an aristocrat who had previously served as private secretary to the British foreign minister, exuded no personal inclination to international leadership or international mindedness. Nitobe's attitude was relatively more characteristic of the putative international mind suited to transnational mobility and sociability, and international institutions and practices. Fluent in English and Japanese, Nitobe had degrees in agriculture and economics from the United States and German universities (Johns Hopkins and Halle). He was also a Protestant by conversion who had married into a Philadelphia Quaker family. He owed his mixture of ecumenical, social Darwinist, and imperial perspectives on internationalism to this transnational background.[56] He had arrived at the league with experience in the Japanese colonial bureaucracy, as a former colonial administrator in Taiwan, and as professor of colonial policy at Tokyo University. In this latter role, his job was training other Japanese colonial bureaucrats in a view of history as the "irrepressible, onward march of 'superior' civilisations."

Nitobe's appointment as under-secretary general has been explained as compensation by the European powers for the failure of the racial equality clause, or as their half-hearted recognition of Japan's status as a charter member of the league with a permanent seat on the League Council.[57] Regardless of how he ended up so high in the league, Nitobe's particular embrace of the organization suggests the consistent influence in this new era of institutional internationalism of a diplomatic, and, in the tradition of old diplomacy, usually aristocratic class.[58] Transnational and even self-consciously cosmopolitan in their education, these diplomats and administrators shared a conception of imperial civilizing missions, imagined from the "race"-distinctive perspectives of distinct imperial traditions. The masculine values of the frontier, the inevitability of progress, the relative capacity of different races and nations to meet the challenges of modernization, and the role of Japan in bringing progress and universal civilization to Asia, these were all values that sat comfortably with the league's mission as it was seen from Geneva by a member of the league elite.

If we go by the international careers of Japanese and Chinese league officials, it is clear that the transnational circuit of higher education meant that a predominant number were trained in North American and European universities, or worked in London or Paris. In these cases, there could also be heard the complaint from within the organization that they "were not truly representative of their country" and their presence masked the league's failed internationality in the respect of representing all the world.[59] Alternatively, the employment of American citizens in the league Secretariat, like the considerable support the league gained from American philanthropists and banking and finance figures, guaranteed the informal representation of the United States, if not its government, in the league's activities and influence, particularly in the realm of economics and finance.[60]

The importance to contemporaries of the league's internationality was of a particular kind, nurtured in the corresponding expectations of some of its members that it would represent, equally and even democratically, the world's constituent nationalities and civilizations. The geographical and cultural statistics on employee distribution anxiously compiled by league administrators show us that the First Division of directors and chiefs counted a maximum at any one time of three Australians, Canadians, Indians, Japanese (including Nitobe), and New Zealanders; two Chinese; one Albanian, one Iranian, one Thai, and one Turk each. This was in contrast to thirty-nine British staff (including Drummond) and thirty-two French (including Joseph Avenol, secretary-general from 1933 to 1940). Swiss employees were predictably overrepresented in the administration.[61]

League administrators were as self-conscious of what they thought of as civilizational representation. In 1922, they recorded a ratio of Europeans to non-Europeans of seven to one, and in 1930 a slightly less galling five to one.[62] But even these figures could be misleading since they reflected back cultural distortions. Sometimes Europe and Latin America were counted as equivalent, or the single category "Americans" included North and South America. At other times, the Middle East was represented by France (reflecting the French mandates and colonies in that region), hiding the fact that there was only one Persian member of section in 1930. That year the category "Far East" was used to improve the figures for Japanese, Indian, and Chinese employees. The Far East region could boast only six posts overall, even though it supplied 12 percent of the total budget and as a "civilization" it comprised millions of people. British-ruled India paid almost as much into the league's budget as the permanent council member Italy, yet few Indians "competent as well as representative of the Indian civilization" made it into the ranks of the Secretariat. The situation was lamented by the bureaucracy but blamed on the British recruitment of potential league candidates into the Indian Civil Service.

The relationship of national patriotism to the league's own internationality was a particularly hard nut for its civil servants. In 1919, Harold Nicolson had cheekily ventured a league patriotism that was as historically likely as an American patriotism. When the league and ILO administrations came into their own, their training manuals and organizational conferences indicated a different emphasis on the relationship between national and international patriotism, drawing on a fundamental distinction between good and bad internationalism. Harold Butler, the ILO's director-general from 1932 to 1938, was of the view that since the international arena was a space populated by the typical representatives of each country, people who were divorced from their national life were not the kind of people the ILO wanted.[63] "They might speak languages wonderfully, and they might know an awful lot about an awful lot of things," but they could not give "the viewpoint or the slant of their own nation on the various problems with which they were called upon to deal."[64] For Clarence Jenks, the ILO's principal legal adviser, "experience proved that members of the cosmopolitan tribe, globetrotters, and persons without a country are not ideal recruits, and that the man or woman without roots in his own or any other country, even though a fair technician, will never make a satisfactory international official." Jenks had risen to his post from humble origins, by way of the position of treasurer of the British Universities League of Nations Society and chairman of the Cambridge University League of Nations Union during the war. He then went on to spend the rest of his life in Geneva. Despite his own migration, Jenks advised that ideal league civil servants needed to exhibit strong national sentiments if they were to comprehend the realities of international life. As he ticked off his list of the essential qualities required of international officials—"integrity, conviction, courage imagination, drive, and technical grasp—in that order," he was also inclined to consider culturally and racially predetermined qualities. Technical grasp, Jenks offered, was to be found in persons of Latin or Germanic origin. Directors of league departments harbored similar prejudices about national and regional proclivities and tended to regard only Scandinavian workers as "particularly competent, unbiased and trustworthy," Polish and "Balkan" recruits as the opposite.[65]

There were then considerable national and imperial inhibitions and motivations breathing life into the spirit of Geneva. The paradoxes of this new league-focused internationality were not lost on some of its participants. Salvador de Madariaga, a professor of Spanish literature when he was not the league's director of disarmament, was a man who called many places in Europe his home. In the late 1920s, he dryly celebrated Geneva as "the sacred town on which the new Olympus is rising," while observing that the league's "preeminent role was in the reification of national psychologies through its collective life."[66] In effect, the league's meeting rooms were adding a new vigor to national self-consciousness: "Nations meet and discuss in Geneva as nations, and thereby acquire a deeper sense of their existence, a greater sense of their importance."[67] Madariaga's analysis of the league contradicted the assumption that international institutions fostered an international sociability or international minds. But it made sense, given the league's structures and limitations. A 1930 minority report by German and Italian members of a committee appointed to review the administration of the league Secretariat, explained (not without a whiff of irony), "So long as there is no Super-State, and therefore no 'international man,' an international spirit can only be assured through the cooperation of men of different nationalities who represent the public opinion of their respective countries."[68] In this way, league officials were complicit in carefully separating out cosmopolitan lifestyles from the internationalism entertained by the league, particularly through their employment practices and their statistical vigilance. Even if this contradiction suited the dominant understanding of the national origins of the new internationalism, the expectation that "the Secretariat commanded its own loyalties, . . . its own corporate reaction, its own psychology" remained as common an expectation among league workers and was announced most loudly in inverse proportion to the decline of the league's international prestige.[69] Madariaga concluded that in an era in which the nation stood for the end of political progress rather than its means, the league was the only "remedy for the evil."[70]

In the 1930s, Egon Ranshofen-Wertheimer, a diplomat and journalist who had worked for the league in its Social Questions division, undertook a study of the International Secretariat in which he asserted that "at a time of rampant nationalism," "the citizens of more than forty nations . . . with no precedents to guide them, collaborated as one team for a common purpose."[71] League officials, he claimed, were remarkably free from national prejudice and felt free to criticize, even to oppose, their own governments. We can conjecture that Ranshofen-Wertheimer's assessment of the league's internationality was influenced by his scholarship on the unpredictable destinies of laws and states, and his unpredictable personal history as a Catholic with Jewish roots, born at the end of the nineteenth century in multinational Habsburg Austria.[72] As xenophobia and fascism took political root around Geneva in the 1930s, enthusiasts of the new internationalism such as Ranshofen-Wertheimer were even more determined to keep their faith in the remedy of international conventions and practices associated with the league and the survival of "supranational allegiance" as an ideal.[73] The league Committee for International Intellectual Cooperation (CIIC)—which boasted the membership of Albert Einstein, Henri Bergson, Sarvepalli Radhakrishnan, and Marie Curie—maintained as determined a focus on the cultural and social role of intellectuals moving themselves and ideas across national borders in aid of the development of a "League of Minds" and a "universal conscience."[74] The CIIC's chair, Gilbert Murray, was an acknowledged British imperialist who disliked the antinational implications of world citizenship and had an unmistakable class-, race-, and gender-bound view of internationalism's reach. However, like the organization Murray established in the latter 1930s, the

London-based Council for Education in World Citizenship, the CIIC aimed to train individuals to an international consciousness of their place in a variegated world, through education in geography, languages, and broad-minded history teaching.[75]

Over those same interwar decades, the spirit of the new internationalism did not take all its vitality from the league, although the league's physical terrain remained an important point of orientation. The social history of internationalism in this period includes the NGO networks that grew up around the league, or in competition with it, and the women and "non-Europeans" who made up their population. The interwar period is counted as the second "golden age" of international organizations, as the nongovernmental variety more than doubled—estimates suggest that by 1939 there were around 730.[76] Some of the adherents of these bodies collaborated with the league; many worked across their own networks. Intergovernmental organizations or public international unions still oversaw international telegraph and telephone infrastructure, shipping regulations, and the increasing demand for airspace. Such organizations also drew in the citizens of nonmember states such as the United States. All were part of "a more complex, technically sophisticated and interdependent international system."[77]

The most famous internationalist of the immediate postwar period, Fridtjof Nansen, was a Norwegian delegate to the league, but when he won the Nobel Peace Prize in 1922 it was in recognition of his autonomous Relief Organization and his idiosyncratic invention, the International Passport for people with no citizenship, recognized by fifty-two governments and bearing his own photo. Although this passport became known as a League Passport and Nansen was a league delegate, his internationalism was pragmatically radical and ultimately effective thanks to his individual international statesmanship. Nansen for his part liked to credit the league, expecting that it would eventually evolve into a parliament for a "United States of Humanity."[78]

While a sizable population of interwar internationalists disillusioned with the league kept a keen eye on the communist internationalism espoused from Moscow, for NGOs dedicated to the rights of indigenous groups, Hawaii was the "New Geneva."[79] Honolulu was home to the Institute for Pacific Relations (IPR), created in 1926 from the good intentions of a YMCA Pacific Conference. The IPR stood for an internationalism built out of regions, for the importance of cultural information and exchange, and for the social experiments in racial equality that the league was not equipped to tackle.[80] Ken-Sheng Chou, from the Hunan province of China, a law professor trained in Edinburgh and Paris, came to the IPR in the interwar period to promote a plan for a regional Pacific Association of Nations with its own administrative council, judicial system, military staff, and armed force (this path led him to become an adviser to the Chinese delegation at the San Francisco conference deliberating a United Nations in 1945).[81] Mary Woolley, who was on the IPR's Executive Committee, was simultaneously a member of the American Peace Society and the World Alliance for Promoting International Friendship Through the Churches. She was also the only female American delegate to the 1932 Geneva Conference for the Reduction and Limitation of Armaments.[82]

Although the U.S. government was formally absent from the league, its citizens took an interest in the interwar vogue for internationality in other ways. In a new age of publicity and literacy, the American public sphere was filled with magazines with titles such as *Our World* or *Our World Weekly* or *Cosmos*. In the early 1920s, some of these gained print runs of up to forty thousand copies. Many of these publications were financed by a league advocate from Illinois named Herbert Houston, whose "Newspaper Syndicate" provided newspapers with editorials that attracted much larger readerships. Together with another leaguer, Raymond Fosdick, Houston founded the League News Bureau.[83] The American Carnegie Endowment produced *L'Esprit International* for a European market and lent its efforts to the establishment of International Mind Alcoves in community libraries, where the great texts of the world would be available to the average reader.[84] The league was also quick to take up new media technology, parlaying its message of internationalism through its own station "Radio Nations," and appointing the Hollywood megastar Charlie Chaplin as foreign ambassador to the world. In other words, in the interwar decades you did not need to be a member of the league or working at the league to hear about internationalism, as mixed as the message of internationalism could be.

Religion remained a definitive strand of that message, and not only among the ecumenical internationalists who were linked to the league through pacifist and church organizations. Florence Kitchelt, a Rochester-based social worker with links to the Connecticut International Association and devotee of the league, was a Unitarian.[85] The founding editor of *World Unity*, an interwar monthly that espoused the virtues of the league, was John Randall, an ordained Baptist minister who had set up the World Unity Foundation in North America. Randall's world unity would take form through a "new consciousness of world community" and the promotion of a "universal religion of brotherhood" as the antidote to political and economic nationalism.[86]

The Baháʼí movement was equally involved in the promotion of internationalism through its *World Order* magazine.[87] The World Brotherhood continued to build a successful following into the mid-twentieth century as Fraternité Mondiale. Meanwhile, the British historian Arnold Toynbee's version of league internationalism as a new world religion synthesizing Christianity, Islam, Hinduism, and Buddhism (although not Judaism) led back to the secular Mecca and mystique of Geneva and the league.[88] Within the league, Norman de Mattos Bentwich, the director of the league's Commission for Jewish Refugees, was a Zionist promulgating a league of religions to further universal peace.[89] Overall, the emphasis among the league's supporters was on a language of civilization commonly linked to Christianity on the implication that pacifism was a specifically Christian virtue, in much the same way that nineteenth-century European imperialism was grounded in the language of Christian proselytization. James Garnett, the secretary of the English League of Nations Union, for example, was drawn by his Christianity to the mystique of a secular internationalism.[90]

It is difficult to think about the League of Nations and the complex of organizations and networks that it encompassed in the interwar years without feeling it takes us, as it took so many of its adherents and employees, back and forth across an ocean of international objectives, methods, and obstacles. As an institution, the League of Nations had to navigate all these expectations, including the shifting currents that were carrying the concept of internationalism away from "a moral space defined through abstract principles of peace and humanity," toward "the moralism of positions taken in the name of democracy or freedom."[91] Bobbing alongside the association of internationalism with a culture of international mindedness and national states of mind, with middle-class rather than proletarian values, were the demands for progress and liberty on an international scale and on behalf of politically marginalized cultures and races as much as classes, women as well as men, those whom the nation had failed, and those who still awaited the nation's arrival.

An International Society, the 1930s

In 1932, a young black American, Ralph Bunche, wrote home that he had decided to stop off in Geneva to observe the league machinery in action and was thrilled "to see the delegations from Liberia, Haiti, and Abissinia in their proper places on the [assembly] floor."[92] This was three years before the league would leave Abyssinia in the lurch while Fascist Italy, also a member state, bombed African cities and occupied African territory.

In the early years of the league, when Bunche was still a university student in California majoring in international relations, he had contemplated "this Parliament of Man" as the guarantee of a future international peace, and "the people of the world inextricably bound together by bonds of common interest which make imperative an effective, active, international organization."[93] Bunche, the *ingénue*, imagined the unification of the Thirteen Colonies into the United States as the model for the transformation of the world's many states into a "*universal political society*" populated by a "*universal, rational-minded citizenry*." In this new world, "each nation would retain its individuality, its nationality, if you please; extensive freedom of action and autonomy within its own domain; yet maintaining, withall, an abiding consciousness of membership in the more significant international society."[94] The motto of this vision of an international society was conventionally enough "*a spirit of World Brotherhood.*"[95]

As Bunche advanced his academic career, he found new ways of conceptualizing the motivations of international society. He argued that the anthropology of Franz Boas and new psychological and sociological research proved that individuals were at their core indefinitely "plastic" and "modifiable" and shaped by the dynamic forces of history and society—in effect an environmental theory of human nature that competed with as popular contemporary theories of biological determinism. We have seen that in the 1920s Bunche would have not been alone in his vision of an evolving international society comprising popular transnational networks of sociability as well as the league's own civil servants and delegates.[96] Even in the 1930s, without the drawback of hindsight, Bunche was able to enjoy the league not only as a place where human nature might continue to be modified, but also as the forum in which the famous Haitian orator and league delegate Dantès Bellegarde had so dramatically alerted the world to episodes of exploitation and violence against colonial peoples.[97]

Bellegarde's own league career is a useful indicator of the political hopes for an internationalized public sphere that the international organization was able to sustain among its anticolonialist membership. In 1922, when the South African government, led by the liberal hero of the league, Jan Smuts, used aerial bombing to quell a revolt by the Bondelswarts in the South West African mandate, killing more than a hundred men, women, and children, Bellegarde used the floor of the league assembly to rail against the massacre and bring it to international notice.[98] In 1930, as a member of the temporary Committee on Slavery and Forced Labor, a position he took up against the wishes of the American-controlled Haitian authorities, Bellegarde used the league as a platform for exposing the sale of children in Haiti. Although his demands for a "coloured" delegate on the mandate committee were unsuccessful, the speech he delivered in the General Assembly attacking the de facto imperialism exercised by the United States through its economic control of countries such as Haiti made headlines internationally. The irrepressible Du Bois, who had met Bellegarde at the Paris Pan-African Congress, named him the "international spokesman of 'black folk.' "[99]

Du Bois regularly presented petitions and suggestions to league committees and the ILO, at the same time as he continued to organize gatherings of the Pan-African Congress, in London, Paris, and Lisbon.[100] Back in the United States, African American newspapers such as the Chicago-based *Defender* and *The Crisis* kept a close eye on developments in the work of the league on behalf of "all black humanity."[101] Marginalized voices lacking delegates in the league's General Assembly also found a vehicle in the league's Minorities Commission, which could receive petitions. Studies show that the commission preferred to not table those it felt used excessively violent language in the presentation of their case.[102] The commission's timidity did not put off the leader of the Cayuga Indian tribe in Canada. He made the journey to Geneva twice in order to argue that the Iroquois Six Nations minority was a sovereign "organized, self-governing people" and that the league should recognize it as a "confederacy of independent states."[103] Around the same time, an Australian Aboriginal, Anthony Martin Fernando also tried to petition the league. He argued that the only way that the "just future of the Aboriginal race" could be assured in Australia was if the league transformed reserve lands in Australia into mandates governed by Switzerland or the Netherlands.[104] Inevitably perhaps, neither man was successful in having their demands recognized by the Minorities Commission.

The Permanent Mandates Commission was as unreliable in its response to petitions. Nevertheless it too acted as a powerful magnet for complaint and resistance among the colonial subjects of mandate powers. The extensive correspondence between Geneva and the South West African communities of Rehoboth, Windhoek, and Pretoria illustrates how the mandate concept actually raised the expectations of the league among colonized communities, even though the league had little actual say in the administration of mandate territories.[105]

The political and moral power of the league's role in Africa was precisely what Bunche set off to study after his visit to Geneva for his Harvard doctoral thesis in political science. Bunche was conducting a comparative analysis of conditions in the French mandate territory of Togoland, on the one hand, and its neighboring colony Dahomey, a regular French colony with no league oversight, on the other, in order to understand the relative benefits of the mandate system. His conclusions were sober regarding the league's inability to directly improve the everyday lives of Africans. Local populations often were given little information about the existence of the league or their mandate status, and the French hardly differentiated in their approach to their mandate and nonmandate territories and subjects. Yet Bunche concluded that the fact of the existence of the league, despite its lack of authority, mitigated imperial behavior in mandate territories.[106] Taking a similar view, historians have since argued that the publicity given to the Bondelswarts massacre by Bellegarde in his league speeches made the South African government more cautious about dealing with other communities in its mandate of South West Africa.[107] This did not mean that the league was able to prevent empires or mandatory powers from doing what they wanted, or even that the Permanent Mandates Commission was willing to be critical of the colonial powers. The Mandates Commission was after all dominated by the colonial powers themselves. When, in 1925 and 1926, the French government bombed Damascus, the capital of its Syrian mandate, torched villages, and tortured and shot rebels with no concern for international opinion, the league criticized the mandatory power but was able to do little else. In 1927, the Mandates Commission actually encouraged New Zealand, the mandatory power in Western Samoa, to shoot the unarmed local leaders of a nonviolent protest.[108]

From its early days, the League of Nations provided a crucial site for vocal criticism of the very powers and world order it had been expected to defend. The league's drafters were more than aware of its potential in this respect. In 1919, Lloyd George was adamant that the structure of the league should prevent "propagandist associations and societies from all over the world" flooding the League of Nations with their complaints. He had in mind the impact of minority rights on "the very litigious" Jews.[109] To be sure, when the League commissions failed their petitioners, they sought other related international outlets. Bellegarde put to use the transnational networks and international associations that had become the mainstay of league supporters and a broader international society. He founded a Haitian chapter of the International League for the Rights of Man and was associated with the Bureau

International pour la Défense des Indigènes, the Inter-American Bar Association, and other Latin American leagues. He was involved in the Pan-African and the Pan-American Congresses, as well as the International Congress of Philosophy (which Haiti then hosted in 1944). Bellegarde utilized all these connections to promote, in his own words, "Western values and Christianity." He also worked for more specific national ends: a French rather than American destiny for Haiti.[110] Cuba's delegate to the league, Aristides de Aguero y Betancourt, spoke six languages, which he made use of through the offices of the ILO to advance a Cuban nationalism explicitly opposed to American intervention in Latin America.[111]

Women involved in anticolonial organizations as well as international feminist movements vested in colonialism were among the league's keenest advocates and persistent petitioners. Their stories can be traced along equally familiar trajectories of new opportunities exposed, ambitions curtailed, enthusiasm and disillusionment, intended and unexpected consequences.

Given the postwar reaction against women's participation in the public sphere, feminists had applauded the inclusion of a clause in the league covenant advocating equal employment opportunities for men and women within the organization itself.[112] Over the twenty years of the league's operation, however, women made up only 1 percent of the employees in the administration's First Division level; most years it fell below that mark.[113] Women were best represented as interpreters and translators in the Précis Writers Service or the Children's Information Service. If women did the same jobs as men, they were, as national conventions dictated, paid at a lower level. When (British) Nancy Williams, the de facto chief of the Personnel Office, was replaced by a (Czech) man, the post was elevated to director, although the tasks stayed the same. To the extent that women found a home in the league's upper echelons or political structures, it was usually exceptional or by default. British-born Rachel Crowdy, the only high-ranking and perhaps best-known woman in the league administration, owed her position, as did many men, to a connection with Drummond.[114]

There was the rare woman too who was granted a glimpse of the internal workings of the league as a member delegate. The appointment to the Permanent Mandates Commission of the Swedish-based Norwegian lawyer Anna Bugge-Wicksell came about because of the Swedish government's relative disinterest in its position as the one nonmandatory power. (The four mandatory powers had named prominent male politicians or former colonial governors.) But, as an unintentional result, an important precedent of appointing women as league delegates was established. In 1928, Bugge-Wicksell's successor was Valentine Dannevig, one of the founders of the Norwegian WILPF and director of a Girls School. Like Bugge-Wicksell, Dannevig was an abolitionist even as she was convinced of the civilizing potential of colonial trusteeship.[115]

Helena Swanwick's stint at the League of Nations Assembly in 1924 was brief by comparison, as a replacement delegate for Britain. Even so, her time in Geneva reminded her of the extent to which in this new era of internationalism "men were in all places of power. They alone were diplomats and foreign ministers and financiers and the manufacturers of munitions and editors and leader-writers." She recalled in her memoirs: "I was to feel at Geneva the enormous pull that the majority of men in public life have over women. . . . It seemed to me that we were artificially handicapped in all ways: bodily by our clothes and customs, mentally by the denial to us of sources of information and conditions of development open to men as men."[116]

As we have seen, for Alice Hamilton, a founding member of the American Woman's Peace Party and the WILPF and first woman professor at Harvard Medical School, the actually existing league had failed the test set at its inception. Then there had been talk of women's claims to equality and self-determination as an international concern, a league-sponsored annual "International Women's Conference," and a separate International Women's Organization that would correspond to the ILO.[117] Despite her criticisms of the league's shortcomings and the effects of the "victor" peace on the populations of the defeated nations, Hamilton agreed to take a position as the only woman on the League's Health Committee (1924–30). The committee met twice a year to decide the new League Health Organization's work program. An epidemiologist with public health expertise, Hamilton would have been aware that this program had already taken the league into the territory of population transfers, managing the spread of diseases on the frontier between Greece and Turkey as bewildered refugees fought smallpox, cholera, and typhoid epidemics.[118] She was one of many Americans who joined the league even while the U.S. government remained officially aloof, and one of the many women who saw opportunities to achieve their social, political, or personal ambitions under its auspices, regardless of the fact that women remained rare at the upper echelons of the organization.[119]

Hamilton's role in the league's continuation of the late-nineteenth-century international coordination of disease prevention is further evidence that the organization's significance in this period exceeded its official arrangements and personnel. Yet there were still disappointments at the scope of the league's interests. In 1920, Elizabeth Shepherd was so confident that the status of women was a league priority that she took the bold step of writing to Eric Drummond requesting the organization assist her with the publication of an important new study, *Woman's History of the World*, in exchange for which she would give advice on "an underlying philosophy of the World State."[120] Shepherd stressed her credentials as a member of various international organizations and her capacity as a widow to travel freely, "so that I am not in any way restrained from freedom to go to any quarter of the globe for material."

Drummond had no intention of taking Shepherd or her project seriously. But her typed request, with its official letterhead announcing the intellectual bearing of her project—*Woman's History of the World*—still sits in the league archive, evidence of the history of women's engagement with the world implications of this new internationalism. As state governments drove women out of the public sphere of work and politics they had temporarily occupied during the war, when men were in short supply, women's international organizations turned even more ardently toward the political and social work on offer in the precincts of the league.[121] It was more common, as Swanwick lamented, to find female delegates and lobbyists relegated to the work of the Fifth Committee's Social and Humanitarian Questions Bureau under Rachel Crowdy's administrative supervision. This committee tackled moral reform causes: "Opium, Refugees, Protection of Children, Relief after Earthquakes, Prison Reform, Municipal Cooperation, Alcoholism, Traffic in Women."[122] The international women's organizations that gained affiliate status (such as the WILPF) took the bureau's work in legal directions, drawing international law into the question of the national citizenship of women. The league, with the ILO, was not able to force states to enact any of this legislation, but its commissions did develop a repertoire of gender-specific international norms, including the right of married women to their own nationality, at the time still denied them in most Western European states.[123]

Throughout the 1920s and 1930s, the league inspired the support and dedication of women and men who took on the organization's promotion as their career, often from a distance and unpaid. The spread of League of Nations unions, associations, and societies in this second golden age of international organizations reflected a popular, mainstream fascination with international sociability and international minds, often alongside expressions of national patriotism and/or imperial efforts. In 1928, the British League of Nations Union boasted 650,000 members. The same year, individual membership of the French League of Nations Association (Association française pour la Société des Nations) was 3,200 (in 1927 it had been 8,500); its group membership, constituting other peace societies and interested collectivities, was an impressive 750,000.[124] The French association was made up of individuals with backgrounds that varied across generations and classes, but the typical member was male, was middle class, and represented an intellectual and political elite with moderate political views ranging from the socialist to the center-right. The French Foreign Ministry regarded the work of the league association as so much a branch of its own state propaganda it even provided them with their main source of funding, although international bodies such as the Carnegie Endowment for International Peace also chipped in.[125]

Retired league officials, diplomats, and consultants eventually left Geneva and ended up advising on or running these national league societies. Ishii Kikujiro became the president of the Japanese League of Nations Association, Nansen was president of the Norwegian League of Nations Society. The American League of Nations Association was assembled by Raymond Fosdick, a veteran of the American delegation to the 1919 peace conference and, thanks to his connections with Drummond, briefly an employee at the league itself (he left once it was clear that the United States had no formal future in that organization).[126] Back in New York, working as a lawyer, Fosdick founded the league association. He regularly took his vacations in Geneva, visited Drummond, and brought back news of the league. It was through Fosdick that the Republican John D. Rockefeller, Jr., who would eventually donate the land for the United Nations building in New York, became a supporter of the league.

Anita McCormick Blaine, the U.S. philanthropist who had closer links to Woodrow Wilson, spread her message through the League of Nations Non-Partisan Association.[127] The Unitarian Florence Kitchelt traveled to Geneva in 1925 and 1927 as a peace organizer, convinced that the league was the key to a pacific future. Her work was focused on persuading others of the same view, and she took her message to local women's clubs, civic associations, and schools. In 1928 she spoke to one hundred and nine gatherings, in 1929, seventy-nine. Kitchelt also worked the radio and organized World Court Committees in five American cities.[128] Harry Kessler, the head of the League of Nations Union in Germany, was born in Paris in the mid-nineteenth century, worked as a curator and diplomat, and was committed to bringing Germany into the league (it gained membership finally in 1926). Kessler saw the league as the first step to an international society based on international organizations rather than states. In 1933, the same year that Hitler came to power and pulled Germany out of the league, Kessler fled Nazism and took the league union with him.[129]

Inevitably, there was also the international organization that represented these national associations. In 1919, around the same time as the peace conference was convening in Paris, another conference had been taking place, the first gathering of the inter-Allied societies in support of the League of Nations. In attendance were a large number of British subscribers, fewer French, and six Americans, five Italians, a Belgian, a Romanian, a Serb and a Chinese enthusiast.[130] Some of them counted as their friends delegates to the official league proceedings nearby, including Bourgeois, Lord Robert Cecil, the British under-secretary of state for foreign affairs, the Belgian minister Emile Vandervelde, and the Italian senator Vittorio Scialoja. These personal networks made it almost inevitable that the national and international league societies had connections to the League of Nations and that their international alliance imitated the league's own form.

The International Federation (or *Union*) of League of Nations Associations, created at the end of 1919, comprised societies from forty countries. They were not all European, but all their conferences were held on the Continent, the first in Paris, others in Prague, Warsaw, and Bratislava, the better-positioned London, Geneva, and The Hague, as well as smaller Western European towns, like Aberystwyth, Folkestone, and Montreux. The International Union had its own General Assembly and Council. Its administration was organized much like a shadow cabinet, with commissions on education, labor, economic and social questions, law and politics, and minorities. It boasted a Secretariat with an elected president, and vice presidents and secretaries. The first French-language general secretary of the Federation was Theodore Ruyssen, who shared his new international position with English- and German-speaking secretaries.[131]

In contrast with the relative conservatism of the governments of the league member sovereignties and, in some cases, league functionaries, the league societies appear as an embryo international civil society taking positions on international questions and questioning government interpretations of national interest and prestige.[132] League associations also had as their focus, to a greater extent than the league itself, the evolution of mentalities and the role of education. Some society members retained their faith in the international organization despite its structural limitations. Others, particularly the French "militants," felt their expectations had been left unfulfilled. Where was the international organization that could boast an elected body of individuals not just states, or military clout? Where were the regional federations that might include not only Europe but also Latin America, and China, and that could be made the administrative building blocks of international government? Célestin Bouglé, professor of social economy at the Sorbonne, wrote that "we had dreamed more and better"; if the league failed its peace objectives it would be because its potential had not been embraced.[133] Their mood was not improved when a delegation from the Fifth International Congress of the International Federation of League of Nations Associations being held in Geneva in 1921 asked to be received by the league's Secretariat, and Drummond sent in his place his otherwise invisible wife Lady Drummond (Angela Mary Constable-Maxwell).[134]

The life of Raymond Watt, secretary of the Australian League of Nations Union, is testimony to just how irregular, deflating, and antiheroic the experience of career internationalists inspired by the league could be. A Genevan culture of conferencing and local tourism—a kind of education in cultural difference and exchange—may have been forming among an intellectual and political elite involved in the official work of the league, or attempting to influence that work through the International Union of League of Nations Societies from a geographical proximity. In Australia—a relatively new (federal) nation-state built out of the ethos of its "whiteness" and "Britishness," and governed by the "tyranny" of its distance from the northern hemisphere— league supporters worked through more local networks, always capitalizing on the momentum of the sociability within their reach. These networks were as likely to traverse membership of the English Speaking Union, the Student Christian Movement, the Town Planning Association, and the Racial Hygiene Association. The Melbourne-based Victorian Bureau of Social and International Affairs brought together the local League of Nations Union, local branches of the Institute of Pacific Relations, and older liberal internationalist groups connected to London, particularly the Royal Institute for International Affairs and local branches of the imperially minded Round Table. In Sydney, the Australian League of Nations Union ran membership campaigns, gave out badges, encouraged international pen friends, organized car treasure hunts and international balls, sponsored singing, set off fireworks, and, in 1936, sent members to the Brussels World Peace Congress. It also targeted a younger generation through schools. Children were invited to dress in national costumes expressive of the world's cultural diversity and to "imagine Geneva."[135]

Many of these campaigns, including "imagine Geneva," were the work of Raymond Watt. He was of the generation born in the last decades of the nineteenth century and dominant in the ranks of league patriots. His attraction to the league came about not from any vague notion of internationalism but what he generously thought of as its experiment in "a new 'technique of government': deliberative and representative."[136] This experiment was accompanied, he argued, by the new scientific ways of understanding the psychological, rather than moral, roots of the world's problems. Yet his own league-focused activities netted mixed results.

As one historian of the Australian League Union has noted, even in quieter years Sydney alone hosted more than two hundred lectures.[137] The impact was significant enough to attract the attention of the Australian government, which despite its own formal membership of the league, viewed the League Union's internationalism with suspicion. In 1938, when there were more pressing ideological challenges in the world for a liberal-democratic state, the government-funded public radio station terminated a women's talk show because of the airtime it was indirectly giving the League Union's views.[138] Although membership of the League of Nations Union was spread evenly among men and women, and, as with its sister societies in Europe, it peaked in the early 1920s, in 1927, and again in 1938, the momentum was difficult to sustain regardless of the campaigning. At the outbreak of World War II, the Union's popularity suddenly declined, and it was reduced to redundancy by the disappearance of the league itself. Watt's career ended in penury, and he was reduced to selling encyclopedias door-to-door, while his brother, who took the conventional international route of a diplomatic career, rose in the ranks of Australian foreign affairs.

We know too well the intersecting story of the League of Nation's institutional failures in the face of the political challenges of the later 1930s, including the depression, the rise of fascism, and the regular resort by member states to violence rather than arbitration. Until the early 1930s, however, transnational networks built up through intellectual and political affiliations continued to inspire the social and sociological motifs of the new internationalism. We might not be surprised to find that in 1927 the Australian H. Duncan Hall (who identified himself as a "British subject") reported for the Institute of Pacific Relations *News Bulletin* from the United States—where the first ever Model Assembly of the League was being held at Syracuse University in New York—that these were "the opening years of the new International Age."[139] In 1930, Willoughby Dickinson, a British liberal and former president of the International Federation of League of Nations Associations devoted to the ecumenical side of internationalism, told a League of Nations Union meeting in the working-class London suburb of Tottenham that if there was one lesson that the great war had taught, it was that the various nations of the world were so inextricably connected, "if once we allow war to break out between two of them the others are inevitably drawn in."[140] Logically then, state sovereignty could no longer be the core principle of international affairs.[141]

As the decade dragged on, the League of Nations was less and less at the center of influential internationalist initiatives. Pacific region international-ists such as Mary Woolley began to feel that Geneva might be too far away anyway.[142] Writing in her memoir, Helena Swanwick repeated the claims of prewar internationalism, that "the idea of a nation-state is, at this stage of European history, not only impossible of realization, but meaningless."[143] She was not as willing to announce that the objective facts of internationalism had surpassed those of nationalism; rather, "international organization" and the "international administrator, a newcomer among mankind," were only just beginning to take their place "in a world of nation-states." Rabindranath Tagore reflected that the league was only one of many forces at work, and not even "the most instrumental for the readjustment of international rela-tionships," although "somehow or other, the expectation of understanding and fellowship is in the air."[144] There was, he argued, still a need for a "new psychology," as well as personal adjustment to "the new necessities and con-ditions of civilization." Tagore argued there were other non-European tradi-tions to explore in meeting this challenge, including the example of the early nineteenth-century Indian liberal politician and thinker Raja Ram Mohan Roy: "He came from an orthodox Brahmin family, but he broke all bonds of superstition and formalism. He wanted to understand Buddhism, went to Tibet, studied Hebrew, Greek, Arabic, Persian, English, French, traveled widely in Europe, died in Bristol. . . . He realized that a bond of spiritual unity links the whole of mankind and that it is the purpose of religion to reach down to that fundamental unity of human relationship, of human efforts and achievements."[145]

By the late 1930s, world government and world citizenship were the call-ing cards of smaller scale albeit resilient international activism focused on in-stitutions and law as well as an international mind, mostly out of the league's sight. Rosika Schwimmer, a Hungarian and Jewish feminist who had worked at Jane Addams's side in the Hague women's peace congress and with the WILPF, outlined her Campaign for World Federal Government in 1937 from an American base, together with her close friend Lola Maverick Lloyd.[146]

Schwimmer's motivation was in part the statelessness of a new flood of Jewish migrants from Europe, and in part her own statelessness at the hands of the American legal system. Schwimmer, who had been active in the feminist international movement during World War I, was also briefly a Hungarian diplomat. When the liberal Hungarian government that had appointed her the world's first female plenipotentiary was overthrown by a communist revolution, she found herself in political exile and stateless. She fled to the United States, where she was repeatedly refused citizenship on the grounds of her pacifism and suspicions that she might also be a socialist—despite her anticommunism and devoted Wilsonianism.[147]

Around the same time as Schwimmer began her World Federal Government movement, Anita Blaine shifted her attention to the creation of a World Citizens Association that could foster discussion of world problems from a global perspective. Its membership grew quickly to include intellectuals, politicians, and journalists of the caliber of Quincy Wright, Adlai Stevenson, and Edward Mowrer.[148] Wright, a political scientist at the University of Chicago, was also on the World Citizens Association Central Committee, which harnessed the view that international political and legal structures came after international society, not the other way around.[149] If he could have looked forward into the 1940s, he would have seen that the intellectual and political networks built up by "World Citizens" like himself underwrote the aspirations of the league's successors, particularly UNESCO, an organization he would eventually advise.

By this time, the league's operations were increasingly compromised by its undemocratic member state governments. To some degree, the cachet of internationalism drew the curious fascination of the German and Italian fascist regimes, which, like their liberal counterparts, recognized the political utility of international organizations and networks.[150] The International Education Cinematographic Institute in Rome, a partner organization to the Institute for International Intellectual Cooperation in Paris, was harbored by the Fascist Italian government, even as, in Geneva, Fascist Italian delegates and appointees grew more brazen in challenging the legitimacy of the league's pacific mission.[151] The Italian under-secretary general who replaced Nitobe, Marquis Paulucci di Calboli Barone, formerly of Mussolini's cabinet, was known for encouraging all the Italians at the league to undermine the secretary-general.[152] Liberal Japanese intellectuals disillusioned with the league's feeble racial politics supported Japan's departure from the organization, and their country's retreat to a pan-Asianism focused on a "Greater East Asia," which would embrace the Philippines, Burma, Thailand, the provincial government of India, the Nanking government of China, and Manchukuo.[153] This was certainly Nitobe's attitude after retiring from the league and assuming the chair of the Japanese Council of the Institute of Pacific Relations. Nitobe continued to espouse among his countrymen "the imponderable advantages" of Japan's presence "in that parliament of the world."[154] Yet, like many Japanese politicians, he was left regretting the "myth of universality" and the league's preoccupation with European problems and issues.[155]

The League of Nations was always more and less than the sum of its institutional parts and limitations; certainly contemporaries counted on its cultural and moral capital, the communities it helped constitute, even when they were more imagined than real. Over the period of its existence, the status of international political realism had itself changed. With Europe once again consumed by war, the league's community was stretched beyond its conventional borders into relative ignominy. The remnant administration in Geneva was left to the controversial leadership of Joseph Avenol, a French diplomat who in 1940 voiced his admiration of Hitler. Avenol reluctantly oversaw the exile of the league's treasury, Court of International Justice, and High Court of Refugees to London and its economic and finance staff to Princeton University, while the ILO workers, many of them wanted by the fascist and Nazi governments, fled to Montreal.[156] In the midst of a new crisis in world affairs, and the uncertainties of the future, few looked back.

Chapter 3

The Apogee of Internationalism

The creation of the United Nations at the end of World War II confirmed the curious paradox of the twentieth century's progress. During the world's darkest hours, the popularity of international solutions surged. British surveys of postwar attitudes toward "world government" announced that being "internationally-minded" was a dominant trend, "somewhere between a large minority and a substantial majority, depending upon how the questions are phrased and upon the images associated with the poll."[1] In the United States, anxious government public opinion polling recorded similar inclinations. Of those surveyed, 60 percent had heard or read about plans for an international organization, and 81 percent agreed that America should join a world organization with the authority to police world peace.[2] In France too, government bodies monitored the influence of women on the molding of opinion in favor of internationalism.[3] In places and cases where there was no such polling, we have the evidence of many more voices, white and black, calling for a new geopolitical order grounded in the precepts of progress and democracy. The largest American movement for racial justice, the National Association for the Advancement of Colored People (NAACP), worked with the India League and other anti-imperial forces to impress "the will of colonized and dispossessed people" on a future form of international government.[4] On the eve of the 1945 San Francisco conference that drafted and adopted the UN Charter, Mohandas Gandhi announced his support for "a world federation of free nations [that] would ensure the freedom of its constituent nations."[5]

If the end of World War I was the apogee of nationalism,[6] then World War II was the apogee of twentieth-century internationalism, when "international government" renamed as "world government" was a rhetorical commonplace. The significance of this apogee lay not in its utopianism but in the fine gradations of political realism inspired by the vogue for being internationally minded.

Histories of modern internationalism that begin with the story of the UN, and histories of the UN that emphasize the leadership of the United States or the ideological burden of imperialism, or, alternatively, the un-ruffled utopianism of a select few, have forgotten the complex and dynamic social and political context of the midcentury. Black internationalists infuriated by the colonial powers' conscription of African men and resources into the battles of the European mainland and defense of their empires called on the Allies to make good the 1941 Atlantic Charter's promise of a new era of internationalism that would ensure political, social, and economic rights for the world's disenfranchised populations through national independence.[7] Gandhi's anticolonialism envisioned a "world federation" as the means to specific ends: "the prevention of aggression and exploitation by one nation over another, the protection of national minorities, the advancement of all backward areas and peoples, and the pooling of the world's resources for the common good of all."[8] To be sure, the Atlantic Charter was also the model for the Great East Asian Declaration, signed by Japan and its satellite states in November 1943. Its author, the Japanese Foreign Minister Mamoru Shigemitsu, may have been alone in hoping that a victorious Japan would lead a postwar international community emanating from East Asia, at the heart of which would be a new international organization. But the language of the Japanese declaration spoke too to the valuable currency of the vocabulary of "world peace," "mutual assistance and amity," "cultural intercourse," the "abolition of racial discrimination," and "the Progress of mankind."[9]

The focus of this chapter is on the 1940s debates about world citizenship, human rights, and economic development that circled the establishment of the United Nations and its early years of operation. This was the stuff of intellectual and political dispute that became elemental to the teachers who found themselves in UNESCO-led Adelphi seminars on Long Island. The emphasis in these debates was on international law, pacifism, federalism, social and economic justice, individual and minority rights, and the relevance of sociability and cultures of communication and exchange. Their breadth suggests important intellectual and institutional continuities with the prewar period, back to the international turn of the early twentieth century. What set mid-twentieth-century internationalism apart however was the extent to which, for a relatively brief moment and among a considerable swathe of mainstream and marginalized public opinion, the discarded utopian precepts of the earlier period suddenly took on the semblance of political realism.

World Citizens Out of the War

In the last days of World War II, talk of a new international organization resonated the repertoires of political, social, and economic rights. Equality of all kinds was at the forefront of deliberations on the institutional and legal foundations of a new international world order, including the issue of race equality that had been rejected by the American president Wilson in 1919. Once again, W. E. B. Du Bois, now sprightly in his seventies and returned to the NAACP, warned against the preservation of a color line that left most of the world's population, including American "negroes," without representation and rights.[10]

Du Bois took his critical cue from the "Conversations on World Organisation" agreed between the governments of the United States, the United Kingdom, and the Soviet Union at Dumbarton Oaks in Washington, D.C., in 1944, and their failure to address the status of colonies or racial equality, despite prodding from the delegates of Kuomintang China.[11] In response, he insisted that two world wars and the insidious race ideas that continued to underwrite the domestic and immigration policies of the major powers had robbed Europe of its civilizational claims and its moral stature. "Henceforth," Du Bois proclaimed, "the majority of the inhabitants of earth, who happen for the most part to be colored, must be regarded as having the right and the capacity to share in human progress and to become co-partners in that democracy which alone can ensure peace among men."[12]

What kind of democracy was that to be? And what was the role of international institutions? The pull of the Soviet Union, with its committed victory over the German forces and its embrace of modern social planning and industrial progress under the aegis of economic equality, exerted a redoubtable influence on demands for fundamental political change. Demoralized intellectual elites with no interest in class revolution felt emboldened to reconsider the political capacities of twentieth-century internationalism as an antidote to the accruing evidence of the atrocities committed on the grounds of theories of a "master race" and legitimated by nationalism. In 1919, Arnold Toynbee was among the British historical experts who had privileged nationality as an elemental psychological manifestation of modern civilized selves that required political borders (at least outside of Britain). In 1945, Toynbee advocated rethinking political sovereignty, whether as small city-states or new federal conglomerates. He had in mind, as the locus of these alternative polities, not the British Empire but the Balkans and Central Europe, where, he argued, the imposition of the principle of nationality had led to the transfer of populations and the exploitation of minority politics by aggressive nationalist governments.[13] A. J. P. Taylor was still a teenager during the 1919 Paris peace conference, but in 1945 he too took his lessons from that same past and heralded the international city as the solution to endemic nationalisms and "one symbol of the way things are going."[14] Their compatriot E. H. Carr captured the midcentury zeitgeist by arguing, as if it had never been argued before, that "the tradition which makes the drawing of frontiers the primary and most spectacular part of peacemaking has outlived its validity. . . . The urgent need now is to alter not the location but the meaning of frontiers."[15] In *Nationalism and After* (1945), Carr even predicted a decline in the number of sovereign states and the rise of "functional" internationalism. He was confident that after nationalism came internationalism focused on the "sovereignty" and security of individuals rather than states, and overseen by functional international organizations. These would attract the loyalty previously granted to the nation-state because of the functions they served and needs they met.[16]

Carr's "functional internationalism" was of a specific antifederalist kind rooted in the political thought of David Mitrany, a Romanian historian who had reinvented himself as British and who also influenced Hans Morgenthau's conception of internationalism as the product of networks and institutions. But the general internationalist mood also spurred federalist reconsiderations of sovereignty that suddenly seemed much less radical than they had at the end of World War I. Often the stimulus for these visions, as in the case of the Balkans, was specific and pragmatic. In post-Fascist Italy, for example, intellectuals and activists previously silenced or exiled for their liberalism or socialism anticipated postwar territorial disputes involving their own regions by pondering a federal Europe. The Italian historian Gaetano Salvemini returned to the urgency of a European experiment with American federal-style open borders, such as those in the tristate area of Connecticut, New Jersey, and New York, where he had waited out his self-imposed exile. The professor of statistics at the University of Trieste, in the thick of contested claims to the city's place on either side of a border separating a new British and American-backed Italian republic and a Russian-backed communist

Yugoslavia, proposed to the readership of the *Times* the "abandonment of the old idea of borders: a border should no longer be considered an impassable wall, fixed for all times to come."[17] From his perspective, a regionally autonomous territory centered on the port city of Trieste, linked by internationally supervised connecting roads and overseen by a world organization, seemed the better option. Then there were the ideological intentions of Triestine anarchists, who took courage from the moment and assembled one thousand strong in the tradition of their ideological forebears throughout the previous century. Their aim was to prepare for the revolution that would do away with "borders, political parties, and all other forms of organization."[18]

In a range of European ideological and national scenarios, state sovereignty was once again being tested by the idea of the international, and larger political communities were proposed as the only means of reconciling the imperatives of liberty, security, and peace. Even the imperial idea returned as a useful political model. Hans Kohn, an expatriate of the Austro-Hungarian Empire, and one of the earliest historians of nationalism, advocated the return of an enigmatic "ancient" concept of empire that would afford to all peoples the equal protection of a common citizenship and of a rational law. "This Empire," he argued, "would mean the end of all imperialism, it would be the consummation and the justification of the best tendencies inherent, though not realized, in the liberal imperialisms of the nineteenth century."[19]

René Cassin, the French jurist and future framer of the UN's Universal Declaration of Human Rights, was more concerned with empowering a new international organization with the legal authority to protect the rights of the individual irrespective of state sovereignty. In the interwar period, Cassin had made the cause of the League of Nations a priority of his own war veterans organization; he had participated as a member of the French delegation to the International Union of League of Nations Associations six times, even as he subscribed to and followed the French-based International League for the Rights of Man.[20] In the 1940s, as an inside member of the new French postwar government advising Charles de Gaulle on the international future, Cassin returned to the *droits de l'homme* (rights of man) tradition initiated by the French Revolution of 1789. He also considered empire a valid cosmopolitan political setting for these rights unprejudiced by race or religious chauvinism, in which Jews, such as himself, and Muslims, white and black, found politico-cultural convergence as French citizens and patriots.[21] In this vision of international community, unlike that of Carr or Mitrany, he felt keenly (like other pacifists and lawyers before him) that the historical example of the "true" French state and empire was one to follow rather than reject—despite the complicity of the French Vichy regime with Nazi anti-Semitism and in the murder of his own family.[22] Cassin saw no contradiction between his confidence in a particularly French rights of man tradition and the French Empire, and his emphasis on the need to establish the international right of refugees to traverse state borders and demand asylum over the rights of states to refuse them.

A similar combination of imperial and international thinking underwrote the ideas of H. G. Wells, whose competing reputation as the "father" of the UN's 1948 Universal Declaration of Human Rights went back to his compilation of a charter on the Rights of Man during World War II.[23] Wells represented in many ways the legacy of the long nineteenth century of a mind-set both antiracist and antinationalist, convinced by the objectivity of science, yet captured by the imperial platitudes of civilizational difference. Wells, who had been part of the Universal Races Congress scene, described himself as "a Cosmopolitan patriot" who celebrated the civilizing mission of God's Englishman and, in his case, the British Empire.[24] Regardless of such paradoxes, Wells retained his status as the spokesperson of a progressive internationalism. As he saw out the end of the war, a frail invalid living in a small London apartment, among his final visitors was Du Bois, who came to pay homage.[25]

It was not only the principles of an internationalized future that were under discussion, but also its institutions. The surviving representatives of a progressive past in imperial Japan looked to a tradition of support for institutional internationalism as a means of resuscitating the liberal pulse of national politics.[26] National and international archives overflow with letters penned in the 1940s by individuals, men and women, proclaiming their specific support for the creation of a world organization, albeit of varying political and cultural shades.[27] They provide a crucial reminder of the popular flavor of the apogee of internationalism, and of the extent to which Americans in particular thought of the new international organization, the United Nations, as their own, a perspective shared on Main Street as much as in Manhattan and the White House.

Exemplary of the crooked historical, geographical, and ideological trajectories of this mid-twentieth-century internationalism, and its shared world orientation, was the political and geographical journey traveled by the phrase "one world." In 1940, one world was the slogan touted by the Republican candidate Wendell Willkie in his presidential campaign against the incumbent

Franklin Delano Roosevelt, who would be lionized as the hero of the United Nations Organization, even though he died on the eve of its formation. When Roosevelt won the presidency, he sent Willkie on a world tour as his emissary to spread the one world message of international cooperation and the end of imperialism on his behalf. Willkie's travel diary, also published as *One World*, was translated into numerous languages and sold three million copies. It introduced its readers to a world brought into intimate connection through technological innovation and modern air travel, which had allowed Willkie to circumnavigate the globe in *only* 160 hours.[28] Echoing select internationalist refrains of the earlier twentieth century, *One World* declared the need to match the new technologically supported social and economic facts of internationality with an international program that included an integrated global economy and the need for a Declaration of *Interdependence*.

"One World" was certainly not a concept that eradicated nations or states or would have reassured Du Bois that change was at hand for the U.S. "negro." After all, many of the states that composed this one world and had a dominant role in determining the shape of the new international organization that would replace the League of Nations remained empires with vested interests in their economic influence over colonial territories or vassal states, and commitments to race-flavored citizenship and immigration policies.[29] For the leader of the Indian independence movement, Jawaharlal Nehru, however, "one world" was a useful trope for contextualizing the relevance of India's national "unification." India was carved out of the political, religious, and cultural diversity of the South Asian subcontinent, and its national self-determination would prove the viability of the unification of the world's nations.[30] After independence, as India's first prime minister, Nehru continued to espouse "real internationalism" as a form of world federalism that mimicked national unification (he did not mention the tragic religious partition that delivered Indian nationhood). Internationalism was the freedom for each national unit "to fashion its destiny according to its genius but subject always to the basic covenant of world government."[31]

World government was as ambiguous a concept as it had ever been. At times it was interpreted in ways that echoed the drafts put before the peacemakers in 1919 for a League of Nations on the federal model of Switzerland or Germany. At others, it resuscitated the interwar projections of a federal Europe, in which even Richard Coudenhove-Kalergi, the man most associated with a pan-Europe ideal, celebrated the United States as the template for a United States of Europe.[32] (Frederick Jackson Turner had made the same point in 1919 to Wilson about the United States as a federal model for Europe, but Wilson had ignored him.) When, in 1939, the American journalist Clarence Streit, a veteran of the league, published his oft-read and -quoted *Union Now*, urging the creation of a "Great Republic" on the American model, it may have seemed a propos. The only difference with Streit's "Atlantic" republic was its idiosyncratic detail: citizenship, defense, customs, and monetary union would be shared across the United States, British dominions, Canada, France, Benelux, Switzerland, and the Nordic states.[33]

In the 1940s, the building blocks of world government were more conventionally imagined as regional federations—European, Pacific, Asian, African, and Middle East economic and political communities. The Institute for Pacific Relations veteran Ken-Sheng Chou took the idea of a Regional Pacific Association of Nations, with its own administrative council, judicial system, military staff, and armed force, to the UN Charter–drafting conference in San Francisco in 1945, where he represented Kuomintang China.[34] The Australian (Labor Party) foreign minister and jurist H. V. Evatt attended that same conference as the delegate of an anti-Chinese white Australia, but he too saw in Pacific regionalism the future of international politics.[35] Ralph Bunche—who was involved in the Institute for Pacific Relations' famed wartime conference at Mont Tremblant in 1942 and at Hot Springs, Virginia, in 1945—brokered U.S. discussions with Great Britain, France, and the Netherlands in regard to the formation of a regional Caribbean Commission. He hoped the commission would act as a regional political authority coordinating economic and social programs for the good of its colonized territories.[36]

At the center of debate about the conceptual and practical bases of a new kind of internationalism that did not elevate the state above the individual, or beyond the collective good of humanity, was the individual imagined as an international or world citizen. The concept of "world citizenship" was burdened with an even longer historical pedigree, as the literal translation of "cosmopolitanism." Some of its wartime popularity was the consequence of the publicity garnered by Gary Davis, an American bomber pilot who, in 1942, renounced his national citizenship, produced his own "world passport" (taking a trick from Nansen's international passport), and dubbed himself the "First World Citizen."[37] In effect, by reducing himself to statelessness, Davis constantly risked imprisonment. It is a sign of the temper of these war years that a stunt that in another period might have been dismissed as crackpot was admired by mainstream politicians such as the Australian Evatt. In the final years of the war, the left-wing English writer J. B. Priestley proposed an Order of World Citizenship in support of Davis.[38]

On the American side of the world, Anita Blaine's World Citizens Association was transformed from a pariah organization harboring the politically disaffected to one of many federalist organizations that now stamped every serious intellectual and political actor's curriculum vitae.[39] The association's founding members, including Edgar Mowrer—a Pulitzer Prize–winning war correspondent and adviser in the U.S. Office of War Information—were very clear about what world citizenship now intended: a new international institution with a democratic General Assembly and a Security Council without a veto.[40] Sixty-year-old Ely Culbertson, the Romanian-born, Sorbonne-educated, polyglot American citizen and inventor of contract bridge, also advocated international peace through world federation.[41] In his monograph *Total Peace* (1943), Culbertson elaborated a structure made up of eleven smaller federations of nations, with a police force with eleven national contingents and a multinational one commanded by the world federalist government.[42]

In the desperate years of the 1940s, then, as the accumulating horrors of World War II were compounded by a looming threat of atom-bomb-induced annihilation, the resolve for international change was trumpeted as "world" oriented, and the term "internationality" rarely appeared. Instead, the idea of world government, like the equally popular world citizenship, stood for a conception of international politics as a sphere in which international organizations would represent the political ambitions of the world's population for equality, progress, peace and security, and democratic representation. In order to trace the relative significance and disappearance of many of the expectations that attended the popular trend for being internationally minded in this curiously utopian period, we need to return to the scene in San Francisco, in the spring of 1945, as political delegates negotiated their way through and around popular and more radical visions of an international future. As with the history of the League of Nations, understanding the significance of the United Nations in the history of twentieth-century internationalism requires attention to the plans and possibilities abandoned at the doors of renewed international enthusiasm as much as the international program that the victor governments eventually ushered through.

Drafting the UN Charter, 1945

The United Nations Conference on International Organization (UNCIO) held between April and June 1945 announced the mass scale of the newest experiment in twentieth-century internationalism. The U.S. and San Francisco authorities recruited 2,262 military, 400 Red Cross, and 800 Boy Scout helpers as well as an army of 1,000 volunteers to stage and service the event. Armies of "independentistas" and lobbyists insinuated nongovernmental agendas, alongside the 282 delegates from fifty-one countries bringing with them staff that amounted to 1,500 people (the American delegation alone added up to 174). The representatives of 250-odd international organizations were in attendance.[43] Never mind that, unlike Willkie's circumnavigation ideal, it took the French contingent more than two weeks to get there—nine days by boat from Glasgow to Halifax and five days by train across Canada on to Oakland.[44] When they arrived, a combined press and radio contingent of 2,636 were churning out between a quarter of a million and two million pages of news stories daily. Plenary sessions were held at the San Francisco Civic Opera House, requisite for its 3,300-seat capacity. At any one time there were up to twelve committees in session, as well as unremitting press conferences, incessant telegramming, and parallel public meetings.[45]

The sheer size of the San Francisco conference was enough to earn it the tag "the most important human gathering since the Last Supper." Or, if you were the reporter Edgar Mowrer, with a determined sense of the democratic objectives of this internationalism, "nothing ever was staged in this generation on such a scale of mass hypocrisy and global double cross."[46] The city's more celebrated drinking holes were awash with rumors and resentments that stood in for news in an age of proliferating mass media and movies. Political delegates had cornered all the swanky suites in town, while the better-known celebrities of the stage were politely asked to vacate their hotel rooms for the momentarily more famous. (Hollywood had its revenge when the UN created a special envoy to lobby for bit parts for the UN on the big screen.)[47] It was perhaps inevitable that in the course of two roller-coaster months of meetings and discussions the conference lost some of its sheen, leading Hedda Hopper, Hollywood's infamous gossip columnist, to complain, "My dear, if this thing doesn't pick up pretty soon, it's going to be the dullest clambake ever held."[48]

The progress of the San Francisco conference, slow as it was, drew the crowds. Men and women from around the globe, whether from old league societies, or the Institute for Pacific Relations, or world citizenship associations, or anti-imperialist organizations, came to promote their versions of inter-nationalism. In the three months of the San Francisco conference, the U.S. delegate Virginia Gildersleeve, the dean of Barnard College, received 65,000 letters, 82 percent of which she calculated were from women, and 95 percent of which advocated specific additions to the plans for a new international organization that would promote international cooperation.[49]

Discussion of the new institution and its mission was much more radical and diverse than historians have remembered. Correspondents demanded economic as well as political rights, animal as well as human rights. Student groups and political organizations from colonized African territories rallied to influence proceedings.[50] Du Bois worked his message of race equality and anticolonialism through consultants or lobbyists from smaller sympathetic nations such as Haiti, Liberia, Ethiopia, and Egypt. Some delegates supported the rights of individuals to move across state borders as well as claim asylum. It was widely anticipated that individuals, and not just states, would be able to petition the new organization, and even to claim representation within its ranks. The ambiguous signature phrase of the UN Charter's preamble—"We the Peoples of the United Nations"—was taken as a sign of a democratic in-ternationalism, albeit in the image of the United States.

For the delegates seated around the tables of the UNCIO, "United Na-tions" evoked the twenty-six Allied signatories to the Atlantic Charter led by the United States and Great Britain as much as a world union. The author of the phrase "We the Peoples" happened to be Gildersleeve. Trained as a liter-ary scholar, Gildersleeve was as opposed to the timbre of Jan Smuts's draft preamble as its moribund rhetoric. In Paris, in 1919, Smuts had been the liberal hero of the league's mandate system.[51] A quarter of a century later, Smuts's version of the new international organization attributed its authority to the same "High Contracting Parties" of the league covenant. Gildersleeve wanted the founding document of the UN to exude linguistic elegance and to deliberately echo the U.S. Constitution. From her point of view, invoking "We the Peoples" signaled the shifting moral and political center of the new world order, from Europe to America, and to a new era of political democracy and equality in America's image—reflected in her own role as a female U.S. del-egate at San Francisco.[52]

In San Francisco in 1945, there were undoubtedly more women with of-ficial positions than there had been in Paris in 1919, when there were none.[53] Yet for all the talk of equality among sexes as well as races that led up to 1945, apart from the delegates appointed by the United States, women were

sent to the UNCIO with full delegate status only by Canada, China, the Dominican Republic, Uruguay, and Brazil. Even then, as Gildersleeve also noted,
their scope of action in the UNCIO committees was relatively confined. The
British MPs, Ellen Wilkinson (of the Labour Party) and Florence Horsbrugh
(a Scottish Unionist-Conservative), came along as second-tier or "assistant"
delegates. Venezuela sent one and Mexico two "women councillors." Norway
and Lebanon some female "aides."[54] More strangely, the Soviets, who otherwise held to gender equality, were alleged to have rationalized the absence of
a female delegate on the grounds that "the flight over the North Pole might
have proved too strenuous for women delegates."[55] French women must have
appeared sturdier to their government, which nominated Elisabeth de Miri-
bel, a former resistance fighter who had been appointed to the cabinet of
General de Gaulle. But the French government fought hardest against any
agreement that made women's equal status a point of international principle.
Contrary to Gildersleeve's convictions, women's rights were still not easily accommodated in the context of internationalism.

The considerable public attention attracted by the appearance of women
in roles representing states attests to the problematic undercurrents of wom-
en's place in the new world order.[56] *Free World*, a "non-partisan magazine
devoted to the United Nations," reported the exasperated refusal of Gildersleeve, Horsbrugh, and Wilkinson "to be confined to the 'woman's field,' their
interests are global."[57] For her part, the Brazilian delegate Bertha Lutz resented
the Anglo-American trio's furtive attempts to silence discussion of women's
rights by the San Francisco committees.[58] Her friend, the upper-middle-class
Jessie Street, a "consultant" controversially attached to the Australian delegation, felt that the international scope of the conference made it entirely appropriate that women, workers, and indigenous populations demand their share
of universal rights there and then. Despite Street's relative lack of influence,
after she left San Francisco and en route to Moscow via London, she broad-
cast to an Australian audience her vision of one of the most important events
in modern history. As she put it, public opinion could now affect the international sphere, just as it did national life.[59] In hindsight, the problem was that
not everyone agreed on *which* opinions accurately reflected the interests of
either a national or international public. Indeed, women's groups in Australia
regularly distanced themselves from Street's more radical views.

Race equality had relatively more legitimacy in the San Francisco environment than in 1919. But in this case too the UNCIO soon exposed irreconcilable differences of opinion, much as Du Bois had feared.[60] When the

Philippine delegate General Carlos Romulo demanded a voice for the millions of unrepresented colonized individuals and the right of independence,
the British delegate Lord Cranborne responded with an unflinching depiction
of a world divided into "peoples of different races, peoples of different religions, and peoples at different stages of civilization," "from the most primitive
areas in the Pacific and Central Africa to such highly civilized countries as
Ceylon, Malta, and Java."[61] Cranborne's speech took his audience deep into a
familiar imperial past in which empires helped "non-self-governing peoples"
move up a ladder of self-government. He maintained that the differences of
these peoples in their position on this ladder imposed on colonial powers "a
duty . . . to train and educate the indigenous peoples to govern themselves."
This, in essence, was the concept of trusteeship that was to the UN what mandates had been to the league.

After a war fought against the evils of racism, often by conscripted colonial troops, a cloud of complaint hung over the continuing colonial control
of swathes of the world's territory by Britain, France, the Netherlands, Belgium, Portugal, Spain, South Africa, Australia, New Zealand, and Denmark.
It was all but inevitable that colonial controversy would make its way into the
meeting rooms of San Francisco. The trusteeship formula that was settled on,
however, was as much a practical response to the legacy of mandates and the
fate of the colonies of the Axis powers as the manifestation of egalitarian or
democratic idealism. With the league now defunct, the still-existing mandates required the question of their sovereignty resolved. During the league's
lifetime, some class A mandates had become independent, including Syria,
Lebanon, and the Trans-Jordan, but class B and class C African and Pacific
mandates remained under the authority of imperial powers, and these were
now the focus of discussions, along with the colonies of the empires of Germany, Italy, and Japan.[62]

The contradictory responses to the conditions of trusteeship enshrined
in the charter are indicative of the mixed expectations attached to the creation of the UN, especially when imperial delegates celebrated trusteeship
as less liberal than the league mandate system. The Dutch reported with not
little satisfaction that the obligations and responsibilities of trusteeship did
not suppose "interference in domestic affairs."[63] Smuts enthused that trusteeship established the kinds of international standards of colonial governance
that he had originally hoped for from mandates in 1919. But his spin was
hardly any more disinterested. As prime minister of South Africa, he wanted
to prevent international interference in a national policy of discrimination

against Indians, and to force the illegal absorption of the mandate of South West Africa into the South African state.[64] No one ventured that trusteeship heralded the end of colonialism.

The UN Charter agreed in San Francisco renamed the old mandates "trust territories", a category that drew in the colonies of defeated Japanese, Italian, and German empires, and any colony volunteered by an imperial power. Hopes of a new era were pinned on chapter 11 of the charter, which outlined the principles of "trusteeship" relevant to all "dependent peoples" in all "Non-Self-Governing Territories" (the euphemistic name for colonies that would not be transformed into trusteeships). All the world's "dependent territories," trust and non–self-governing alike, were to be governed as "a sacred trust" on behalf of the interests of the inhabitants. Those interests included the development of free political institutions, but only "according to the particular circumstances of each territory and its peoples and their varying stages of advancement."[65] As with mandates, there was no timeline for self-determination built into the concept of trusteeship. Instead, the terms of trusteeship were to be individually negotiated in each territory between the UN and the trustee, that is, the appointed colonial power.

The trusteeship system also created a third category of strategic areas of specific significance to the security interests of their trustees. These areas within trust territories were subject only to the limited oversight of the UN's executive arm, the Security Council, which did not need to divulge information about their condition if it was felt to compromise the security interests of the trustee.[66] In all other cases, the administration of trust territories was to be overseen by the Trusteeship Council operating under the authority of the General Assembly. Even then, the UN's oversight was limited to the drawing up of a questionnaire on the political, economic, social, and educational advancement of the inhabitants of the territory, periodic visits, the reading of reports, and the examination of submitted petitions in consultation with the trustee. The "sacred trust" was handed over to the trustees, whose international responsibility lay in answering the UN questionnaires and submitting reports.[67] Of the eleven trust territories that eventuated, only one had not been a mandate, Italian Somaliland. The trustees too remained the same: Britain, France, Belgium, Australia, New Zealand, and Italy; only South Africa resisted the transformation of its mandate, South-West Africa, into a trust territory.

The final terms of trusteeship seem to tell a predictable story about the failure of the UN to live up to the anticolonial expectations of internationalism launched during the final years of the war. But did the new UN augur a world government as beholden to race and empire as the league? If we turn to the part played in the history of trusteeship by Ralph Bunche, an African American inspired by his experience of the league, the story becomes more usefully complicated, a question once again of the finer gradations of political idealism. Not only was Bunche credited with the drafting of the charter's chapter on "Non-Self-Governing Territories," he was also appointed the first director of the UN Division of Trusteeship, within the Department of Trusteeship (the administrative arm of the Trusteeship Council), headed by its insouciant Assistant Secretary-General Victor Hoo.

The participation of men such as Smuts and Cranborne in the drafting of the UN charter reminds us of the generational continuities between 1919 and 1945, and the persistence of liberal imperialism in the conceptualization and implementation of mainstream twentieth-century internationalism and its institutions. By contrast, Bunche's formal role at San Francisco, and then at the UN, is evidence of a cohort of international actors, and specifically international civil servants, black as well as white and critical of colonialism. As we saw in Chapter 2, in the interwar period Bunche had built an academic career as an interdisciplinary social scientist, drawn to the methods of anthropology for his comparative political study of colonies and mandates in French West Africa. In the 1930s, as depression gripped the world, Bunche conceptualized *A World View of Race*, on the basis of a Marxist analysis that understood race as a category produced and manipulated by capitalism to divide the shared class interests of workers everywhere.[68] By the 1940s, however, Bunche decided that given the cost to the black race if "unscrupulous demagogues" such as Hitler were victorious, the relatively benign liberal democracy of the United States deserved his support.[69] During the war, he lent his African expertise to the newly formed American intelligence bureau, the Office of Strategic Services (OSS). At the end of the war, he was one of many OSS employees involved in the creation and operation of the United Nations. In San Francisco, he was a technical adviser and backroom negotiator, and the only black member of the American delegation.[70]

Bunche did not take a lead role in the discussions of trusteeship in San Francisco, and his influence on the drafting of chapter 11 of the UN Charter is attributed rather than proven. The story, when it is told, has him secretly handing a draft of the Declaration on Non-Self-Governing Territories to the Australian delegation, who use it to establish their international credentials in opposition to the imperialist position taken by Britain, even though they simultaneously defend their state's right to uphold a "white Australia policy."[71] Bunche's willingness to pursue trusteeship in the postwar period as a means of colonial reform brings us back to the history of the United Nations as an institution that in 1945 sat at the intersection of competing international aspirations and expectations of political equality and social change. As an anticolonialist, Bunche embraced the right of self-determination articulated in the Atlantic Charter, but he had no specific attachment to the nation-state as a requisite form of self-determination. His attention was consistently on the elements of active citizenship—social and economic as well as political rights—whether in respect to the United States or colonies. He argued that "the peoples of colonies and overseas territories" should have direct representation in the international sphere by "freely chosen representatives."[72] Consequently, he was a staunch advocate of the right of individual petition in the UN, particularly in matters of trusteeship.

The repeated emphasis of the theme of individual petition in discussions of the new international organization and its absence in the final version of the UN Charter exposed awkward gaps between the versions of democratic international government circulating around San Francisco and the institution that was actually created. In the context of the scenarios predicted before and even during the San Francisco conference, the biggest loser was the individual. The biggest winner in the new structure was the sovereign state, or more specifically those states with a place on the Security Council.

The UN Charter gave the international organization the overarching objective of permanent peace. But whereas the league had sought permanent peace by collapsing social justice into a focus on the principle of nationality or labor, the UN Charter famously confirmed the "fundamental freedoms without distinction as to race, sex, language, or religion" and introduced a human rights orientation to the concept of social justice.[73] "International problems of an economic, social, cultural, or humanitarian character" became the UN's raison d'être, even as the scope of the UN's capacity to address these problems was subject to continued negotiation and controversy within the structural confines also determined by the charter. The UN's principal organs were the Security Council, General Assembly, Economic and Social Council, Trusteeship Council, and International Court of Justice. The United States this time around took up its permanent seat in the Security Council, along with Britain, France, the Republic of China, and the Soviet Union. The Security Council also had eleven nonpermanent members elected by the General Assembly on two-year rotations, each of whom could vote. However, as analysts soon discovered, the voting principle of unanimity effectively gave the permanent members veto power.[74]

Membership of the UN was open to all "peaceloving states," and the charter protected domestic or national sovereignty from infringement by its own creature, even where abuse of its international principles was concerned. This was an overriding condition of the new international order introduced and fought hard for by Evatt, the Australian erstwhile admirer of world citizenship and determined advocate of an international court for state-based disputes. (He eventually was elected by member states as the third president of the UN General Assembly [1948–49], after Brazil's Oswaldo Aranha and before the Philippines's Carlos Romulo and India's Vijaya Lakshmi Pandit.)[75]

The UN system of these early postwar years was more than its Security Council, or even its Trusteeship and Economic and Social Councils. It also comprised autonomous agencies responsible for specialized activities. These included older nineteenth-century public international unions such as the International Telecommunication Union, the Universal Postal Union, and the World Meteorological Organization, and the league's ILO, newly renovated as UN agencies. The significance of the ILO's social justice business had been reaffirmed in the Philadelphia Declaration of 1944, which added human rights and international economic planning to the ILO's brief. Then there were the completely new bodies: the Food and Agriculture Organization with its headquarters in Rome, the International Bank for Reconstruction and Development (later the World Bank) and the International Monetary Fund in Washington, D.C., the World Health Organization in Geneva, and the United Nations Educational, Scientific, and Cultural Organization (or UNESCO) in Paris.[76]

Despite the concerted efforts of some of the UN's architects to quash the memory of the league, that earlier organization's legacy was absorbed into lessons learnt from the past. The creation of the UN's Economic and Social Council consolidated what had been two league departments and reflected the new centrality of economic and social questions. The Information Office was expanded to foster public awareness and support for the UN's international mission. Both initiatives were the result of recommendations of an internally sponsored review of the league's shortcomings, the so-called "Bruce Report," chaired in 1938 by a conservative former prime minister of Australia, Stanley Bruce.[77] As for the institution's representativeness, it was once again invested in the General Assembly as a forum representing the world's internationally recognized states, and in international civil servants like Ralph Bunche who staffed the UN administration but this time around swore a loyalty oath and carried UN passports.[78]

The specific concepts of "international territory" and "international citizenship" resurfaced too, as in the past, in unresolved territorial disputes. So, when a UN-led Boundary Commission could not agree on the principles or location of the border that was being contested between Italy and Yugoslavia (around the port city of Trieste), the administration of the Trusteeship Division, led by Bunche, revived the option of international territory under international supervision. The Free Territory of Trieste, as it was known, was mapped out in 1947 with a Free Territory flag, citizenship, and economy. Like its interwar league versions, the Free Territory barely had time to catch its breath, a demise this time overdetermined by the creeping Cold War divisions within the Security Council, the members of which could not agree on the Free Territory's governor. In this Cold War environment, local preferences for an elected governor could not even be contemplated.[79] Meanwhile, the attempts by Emily Greene Balch, the American feminist and economist (and 1946 recipient of the Nobel Peace Prize), to petition the member-state delegates of the Trusteeship Council on behalf of the internationalization of the polar regions met with such obstruction that by 1948 she gave it up as pointless.[80] By then, one of the few places in the world to be organized around the principle of international territory was the New York headquarters of the UN itself, not yet on its iconic Manhattan site, and not yet known by the symbol of its own distinctive light blue flag.[81]

Within a few months of the ceremonial signing of the UN Charter, the Allies' resort to the dropping of atom bombs on the Japanese cities of Hiroshima and Nagasaki threw a shocking pall over preparations for the international machinery that was intended to usher in a new international era of peace. For the elderly and experienced Du Bois, disillusionment had set in even earlier. Du Bois was less convinced than Bunche that the UN would be able to represent the interests of the colonized or the racially disenfranchised.[82] The UN, he railed, had "disenfranchised 750 million persons living in colonies because the international organization could not interfere within domestic matters." Alienated even from Bunche, Du Bois started planning another pan-African conference in protest against the trusteeship system, this time in Manchester. On his return to New York, he sent each of the U.S. delegates to the San Francisco conference copies of *Color and Democracy*.[83]

Ironically, the international feminist lobby was also galvanizing its forces at this time in the belief that race was getting all the attention and women none.[84] In January 1946, Emmeline Pethick-Lawrence, the celebrated suffragist and socialist, now eighty years old, was sent to the first General Assembly and Economic and Social Council meeting of the UNO, held in the central-city precincts of war-ravaged London. Her task was to warn ECOSOC's president, Ramasamy Mudaliar, a British-appointed pre-Independence Indian delegate to the UN, that "the problems which concern displaced persons, persecuted Jews, and economically exploited races are so immediate and so urgent that matters concerning the status of women will inevitably fall into the background and be lost sight of."[85] It was in this same period, a year after the San Francisco conference, when the sixty-five-year-old Albert Einstein added his voice, as an American citizen and NAACP member, to the clamor for a world government empowered to resolve conflicts between nations by judicial decision. Einstein joined the intellectuals and scientists demonstrating in New York and elsewhere to demand the internationalization of atomic energy or risk mass annihilation. There was no shortage of reminders of the range of practical hopes that still clung to the message of one world, even after the disappointments served up by the United Nations Charter.

Human Rights, 1946–48

Preparations for the first gathering of the UNO's General Assembly in January 1946, in London's Westminster Central Hall, gussied up with a coronation-style light blue chair for every delegate, proffered further evidence of the staying power of an older European-centered order, which, given the material and moral damage inflicted by the second total war within a generation, had otherwise seemed so unlikely. Lord Gladwyn Jebb, the acting UNO secretary-general and executive secretary tasked to lay the bureaucratic foundations for the new body, was a proponent of four power hegemony on a nineteenth-century model. Jebb's perspective set a peculiar tone for the mock rehearsal of the anticipated meeting: he elected himself "president," and appointed fictional representatives of Patagonia and Antarctica to make moving speeches about the misfortunes and ambitions of penguins.[86] On Jebb's view, there were only two tones for the impending historical event: satirical and mendacious. He blamed both on the lingering memory of the league, which undermined any "'mystical' faith in the Parliament of Man." He also conceded that optimism was the business of Americans warming to their new role on the world stage. It was Americans, Jebb claimed, who insisted he cease his flippant references to the UNO and use the more serious-sounding "UN."

Given the tenor of the London meeting, it is difficult not to see the decision to locate the UN's permanent headquarters in New York as an acknowledgment that the center of world economic, military, and cultural dynamism now lay across the Atlantic. The specialized agencies that were the economic engines of this new internationalism—the International Monetary Fund, which was to bankroll the stability of international trade, and the International Bank for Reconstruction and Development, which was meant to stabilize Europe—were both given homes in the U.S. capital. History, even the history of internationalism, is often an accident that only in hindsight can be imagined as inevitable. The decision to name the new international organization the United Nations was only a last minute compromise—the "Latin nations," according to Gildersleeve, "objected strongly to a plural form. They wanted some collective noun like 'league' or 'union' or 'association.'"[87] The New York headquarters option, as we might expect, was as unpremeditated.

If the traumatic memory of the league counted against a UN based at Geneva's Palais des Nations, until John Rockefeller offered a gift of land in Manhattan's midtown as home for a new UN building most bets were on less obviously American-identified locations: Navy Island near Niagara Falls in Canada (on the border with the United States), or even Paris.[88] For a while San Francisco was under consideration because of the UNCIO precedent and its proximity to the important Pacific region. All but the best-heeled of delegates invariably grumbled that New York was too expensive for UN workers and visitors. Then there was the absence of an existing infrastructure and the "enormous" distances between the makeshift Long Island and Manhattan campuses that constituted the headquarters of the early UN. Nevertheless, in May 1946, an initially skeptical René Cassin arrived in New York from war-ravaged Paris to take part in a new United Nations Human Rights Commission and was quickly convinced that New York was a fitting home to the new international organization after all.

From his refuge in the art deco tower of the Waldorf Astoria—the hotel of choice for visiting UN diplomats and politicians—Cassin contentedly contemplated the luxury of his enormous bath, the height of new-fangled skyscrapers, the disorienting traffic below, and the novelty of traffic lights regulating the movement of people and cars. Daily, he ventured forth from Fifth Avenue to the temporary UN administration at the Bronx campus of Hunter College (built, like the Waldorf, in the 1930s). "I have the impression," he wrote to his wife, that "it is a world apart from our own. New York is very cosmopolitan."[89] That impression was formed not in his visits to the Bronx or the journey through Harlem that Jebb's assistant, the young Brian Urquhart recorded,[90] but at the coiffeur in the Waldorf's lobby. Here, among employees and clients, Cassin described all the possible "types" of the descendants of Europeans on display. All in all, he concluded, having the UN in New York might augur well for the future. Like other dignitaries and bureaucrats, Cassin soon adapted to the transatlantic internationalism and travel itineraries that linked the UN in New York to UNESCO in Paris and to smaller UN outposts at the league's former home in Geneva.

For the earlier years of the UN's operations, its most utopian age, we need to imagine the makeshift settings stretched out across the Bronx, and (by 1947) capaciously filling the former munitions factory site on Long Island with its prefabricated, alternately sweltering and freezing, open and noisy office suites, at the optimistically named "Lake Success." After 1952, when the UN moved to midtown Manhattan, Alfred Hitchcock exploited the organization's new modernist spaces and sculptures, and its idea.[91]

For delegates based downtown, the sheer size and bustle of the modernist metropolis of skyscrapers was, at the least, time-consuming to negotiate. New York certainly avoided the much-panned parochialism of the Geneva spirit, but not all new UN employees benefitted from New York–style cosmopolitanism. Ralph Bunche moved to the UN expecting a refuge from race-segregated Washington, D.C. He quickly discovered that the UN was involved in a major housing project that excluded its "Negro members." The result was, as he complained, "many delegates from abroad, as well as members of the secretariat, have been genuinely surprised and not infrequently shocked at anti-Negro and anti-Semitic attitudes and racial discrimination practices observed in this country."[92]

UN employees were as liable to express discriminatory attitudes, in spite of a declared inclination to being internationally minded. Walter Crocker, an administrator on the Trusteeship Division's Africa desk, was among the international civil servants appalled by the local discrimination shown to black UN workers and delegates—including the barbers who refused to cut their hair.[93] Adelaide born, Oxford and Stanford educated, and a self-identified "internationalist," Crocker had worked in the British Colonial Service. A term in Nigeria had made him a vocal critic of the incompetence of British rule. But Crocker was as vocal a critic of the UN's New York location because of the city's messy mixing of races and classes, and the influence that he believed it gave the city's Jewish lobby during delicate international negotiations over the status of Jerusalem and Palestine. He was as quickly disillusioned with his supervisor, Wilfred Benson, the director of the division of the Trustee-ship Department that oversaw "Non-Self-Governing Territories" (alongside Bunche's Trust Territories Division). Benson, a Fabian and formerly with the ILO, was too anti-imperial for Crocker's liking. When Bunche was awarded the Nobel Prize in 1951, Crocker seethed with competitive resentment at the "black man" who had risen, he argued, on the stocks of his race rather than ability.

Crocker was no more a disinterested witness to the UN's early history than René Cassin, or Bunche himself. His approach to trusteeship and to his coworkers, is proof that questions of race as well as empire—Du Bois' color line—were still at the core of conceptualizations of internationalism. In contrast to 1919, however, both racism and imperialism were also increasingly difficult to justify given the UN Charter's emphasis on "human rights."

The preferred French translation of human rights as *droits de l'homme*, the rights of man, rather than *droits humains*, spoke to a long tradition of political thought, reaffirmed in various declarations by European antifascists during the 1930s, and popularized during the war by H. G. Wells and others. The familiarity of this tradition also implied a general consensus about what such rights might include, and how they could be implemented. Although historians since have noted that human rights was not a familiar concept in the mid-twentieth century,[94] the incorporation of human rights in the UN charter also immediately translated into a flood of demands for international attention and intervention. By the first meeting of the member-state delegates to the Human Rights Commission, and long before any formal agreement was reached on the scope of human rights, the new UN Human Rights Division was inundated with examples of the violations of such rights. At the Human Rights Commission's opening session held at Lake Success in 1947, Henri Laugier, the assistant director-general of the Social Affairs department under which the administration of this Human Rights project sat, described the "great wave of confidence and hope" that ran "through the whole world" on the new understanding "that no violation of human rights should be covered up by the principle of national sovereignty."[95]

There may have been a rhetorical flourish to Laugier's description, but he was not alone in his impression that human rights were being celebrated as the international antidote to the absolute authority of the sovereign nation. René Cassin, for example, argued that *droits de l'homme* was the best legal

basis for ensuring the right of the new international organization to intervene not only in humanitarian crises but also where the rights of individuals
were under threat from states.[96] At the front of his thinking was the league's
infamous inability to protect the victims of anti-Semitic laws in the 1930s. As
the UN human rights commissioners deliberated a legal framework for a new
convention on human rights, they also gave rise to questions about the func-
tion and the authority of the Human Rights Commission itself: Should individuals have the right to directly petition international organizations? Should
the Human Rights Commission comprise appointed individuals rather than
nominated state delegates? Should the UN have the power to prevent the
transgression of human rights? Should member states be legally obliged to
uphold and protect human rights?

Cassin's own answer to these questions was invariably yes. In the various
UN debates on human rights leading up to the signing of the 1948 Universal
Declaration on Human Rights, however, he commonly found himself posi-
tioned between a conservative portrait of human nature and humanity put by
the Belgian delegates and a relatively radical cosmopolitan vision of the history and significance of human rights proposed by the representatives of new
postcolonial states. Although Cassin took credit for naming the Declaration
of Human Rights "universal," the adjective was proposed by delegates from
the new Haitian republic that had thrown off the government backed by its
American occupiers.[97] When Cassin resorted to renditions of the European
roots of *droits de l'homme*, the Kuomintang Chinese delegate on the Human
Rights Commission, Peng-Chun Chang, replied that the eighteenth-century
Enlightenment philosophers of the rights of man had borrowed their ideas
from a Confucian tradition.[98] Carlos Romulo, who like Chang had been educated in North American universities as well as institutions in his own country, appealed to the drafters on behalf of the Philippines and "the vision of
World Government which the implementation of the proposed international
bill of rights will doubtless require in some degree, and of which, as a matter
of fact, it will be the cornerstone."[99] He also presented the cultural "cosmopolitanism" of the Philippines as exemplary of that vision, and of the need
for "a rational bill of rights that will take into account all the different cultural
patterns there are in the world, especially in respect to popular customs and
legal systems."[100]

The distillation of a list of universal human rights out of the world's diverse "cultural patterns" was easier said than done. There was not only the
problem of religious and ideological differences but also the question of race

and sex difference that some delegates believed were fundamental determinants of human inequality. For Belgium's delegate, the *fact* of sex difference established the *fact* of race difference, and rendered both a fundamental qualification of any universal application of human rights.[101]

Cassin's most compatible ally on the Human Rights Commission was India's representative, the feminist anticolonialist Hansa Mehta. "Black-eyed, soft spoken,"[102] Mehta was a supporter of Gandhi and had built her anticolonialist career resisting the intrusion of foreign clothing and liquor into Indian life, and, consequently, had spent some of the war incarcerated by the British for her views.[103] Once India became independent and its new Prime Minister Nehru chose his own UN delegates, Mehta took her place alongside Vijaya Lakshmi Pandit, Nehru's sister and Institute for Pacific Relations veteran, and Lakshmi Menon, a colleague in the feminist organization, the All India Women's Conference.[104]

On the eve of the first gathering of the Human Rights Commission, Mehta's instructions from Nehru were in keeping with his pronouncements on "one worldism," "the interdependence of world problems," and the inevitable advance to "the realization of a world order and a world government."[105] She was directed to take a stand on "the equality of opportunity for all peoples and races," while dealing with human rights in "its broadest aspects and not consider particular cases."[106] As on many other points, Mehta was happy to pursue her own views on human rights in the commission, including the particular cases of the vulnerable Indian minorities in Smuts's racializing South Africa, as well as the peaceful federation of religious differences in the secular Indian state.[107] She was so convinced that human rights would be literally interpreted according to its French translation as "rights of *man*" that she supported the establishment of a separate human rights commission for women.[108]

In 1946, against the better judgment of Eleanor Roosevelt, who argued that segregating the office of human rights would reinforce the marginalization of women, the UN Economic and Social Council created the Sub-Commission on the Status of Women, as part of the Human Rights Commission.[109] The sub-commission soon won the status of an independent body, as the Commission on the Status of Women. The rights it promoted were concretely juridical and borrowed heavily from the unfinished work slate of the Social Questions division of the League of Nations: equality in marriage, monogamy, nationality, property, and guardianship of children, social and economic equality, equal opportunity in the domain of education, and the prevention of slave trafficking.[110] But the rights invested in the Human Rights Declaration adopted in December 1948 by the UN General Assembly gave credence instead to historically specific gender norms, particularly in regard to the place of men and women in families.[111]

There were other disappointments in store for the enthusiasts of an international human rights regime. The Universal Declaration of Human Rights that was passed in the UN General Assembly effectively rejected all the innovations that Cassin and Mehta thought crucial to the creation of an effective body. That the text on universal human rights was even accepted by the UN's constituents after two years of deliberation was the result of the scaling back of its ambitions for a legally binding document to a moral "declaration." As significant, the Human Rights Commission itself could not field individual petitions, receive nonstate delegates, or do more than monitor human rights.[112]

There was little place in this new international regime for storing a memory of the breadth of the vision of human rights in the early years of the UN. Contemporaries, however, found it difficult to ignore the vitality of interest aroused by the human rights idea. The evidence of that interest lies not only in the surging notes of Laugier's self-consciously public address to the Human Rights Commission but also in the private correspondence of the Oxford Colonial Administration scholar Margery Perham, a member of the same British Fabian Colonial Bureau that counted among its reform-minded members Wilfred Benson and the black West Indian economist Arthur Lewis. Perham was one of the few female academics drawn into government advisory positions during the war, in her case valued for her knowledge of Africa. By the 1940s, Perham, a devotee of colonial reform, was a convert to the Christianizing mission of colonialism. In 1947, as director of the Oxford University Institute for Colonial Studies, she wrote to her old friend Crocker, bemoaning the interference of the UN: "I must say my British gorge rises against the malicious depreciation of all colonial achievements by Ukrainians, Haitian and South American small fry. I wish I could think it did not matter, but I fear it does with American opinion, and U.S. negroes shouting out on platforms and in the press all round your assembly rooms and offices. What say you?"[113]

Whatever the intentions of its framers, the UN was in practice turning into that "debating club" that long maligned its reputation as ineffective. However, as Perham's comments suggest, the vigor with which colonial subjects debated was evidence of the vitality of the UN's role in the firming up of an international public sphere. Like the league, the new international organization and its numerous agencies gave few direct rights of representation to individuals, but it did provide platforms for the colonized and smaller states and for competing international images of political, social, and economic order and equality. And not everyone was happy.

UNESCO, Cosmopolitanism, and the Cold War

While the new UN comprised a myriad of committees, commissions, and agencies, each of which owed their existence to the ambitiousness of mid-twentieth-century internationalism, UNESCO was the special bearer of the cultural concerns attached to that internationalism. As the preamble to UNESCO's Charter (drafted in London in November 1945) recorded, the organization would work on behalf of "One World in the things of the mind and spirit" on the grounds that "wars begin in the minds of men, it is in the minds of men that the defences of peace must be constructed."[114]

Until the late 1940s, the "world"-oriented motifs of the 1930s and wartime internationalism were woven into the fabric of UNESCO's identity. Jean Thomas, a French philosopher and director of UNESCO's Cultural Activities, thought of UNESCO more technically as the world's "switchboard," in the vein of H. G. Well's fictional world brain.[115] He echoed India's pre-Independence UNESCO delegate, the philosopher and statesman Sarvepalli Radhakrishnan, who spoke out at the First UNESCO General Conference in 1946 on behalf of "the development of what one may call a world brain, a world mind, or a world culture, which alone can be the basis of a world authority or a world government." Radhakrishnan had in mind a commonwealth of free nations.[116] Walter Laves, a U.S. delegate to San Francisco, and UNESCO's deputy director-general, claimed that the one world motto was premised on either an attitude that encouraged friendliness toward the people of other nations or "a sober comprehension of the behaviour of other peoples whether friends of enemies."[117] UNESCO's first director-general, the British naturalist Julian Huxley, drew on the older Enlightenment stagist view of the inevitability of internationalism, with a self-consciously Darwinian and scientific spin: mankind, Huxley maintained, was naturally evolving toward larger-scale, more efficient, scientific forms of social and political organization.[118]

UNESCO itself stood for something more international and "world"-like than had ever been seen. Early visitors to its first headquarters at the Hotel Majestic just off the Champs-Élysées commented on the Babel-like babble of languages, the representation of "as many races, complexions, and national backgrounds as you can imagine," and the "air of constructive international geniality."[119] The media as eagerly reported on Huxley's cosmopolitan credentials—by which they meant he had a Swiss-French wife and threw entertaining cocktail parties.[120] The new organization was also the object of bemusement, obvious in the fairly standard joke that Huxley was most fitted for his UNESCO position by his time as director of the London Zoo. The American columnist who reported literally on "Doctor Huxley's Wonderful Zoo" depicted the cafeteria as a surrealist symposium "where men and women of white, brown, black and yellow skin talk shop in terms of terms."[121] He took similar delight in describing the earnest men and women of good will, foreheads furrowed from much thinking, who populated the cold former bedrooms and parlors of the Majestic, most recently the headquarters of the Nazi occupiers of Paris, another popular joke.

At the heart of UNESCO's mission was the reconciliation of "cultural diversity within an advancing world civilization," concepts that its detractors believed to be irreconcilable and that echoed the tensions between nationalism and internationalism. Huxley brought to this conceptual challenge his evolutionary outlook; just as biological evolution required a diversity of species, the evolution of a "world"-scale functional internationalism required the protection of cultural diversity. Huxley's self-styled "scientific humanism" translated genetic diversity into a question of the species survival of national cultures (which also explains his abiding eugenicist perspective on "morons," and his "personal aversion to aliens").[122] UNESCO would simultaneously promote this ambiguously national cultural diversity and prevent "the separateness of nations from increasing."[123]

While Huxley's religious colleagues, especially the political scientist Sir Ernest Barker, were concerned with the survival in Huxley's mooted world culture of a Christian-centered worldview that left such matters to God rather than international organizations, it was the status of nations in this new "One World" that troubled most of UNESCO's delegates and financers. As chair of the 1945 London Conference that drafted UNESCO's Charter, Ellen Wilkinson, a former trade union radical and feminist newly installed as British minister of education, gave voice to a significant strand of thinking about UNESCO's work, when she reminded her committee of state delegates, "We here could not be interested in international work if we were not firmly rooted in our national loyalties."[124]

The emphasis on the cultural diversity promoted by UNESCO as specifically national was dictated by the governments of member states seeking reflections of their national selves and national conduits of influence in the international organization's administrative structure. As with the league, this led to concerns about equal representation in UNESCO. And like the league, UNESCO, despite the image of a zoo-like institution, was deemed a failure. Huxley often found himself on the offensive, throwing off relevant national data: The Education Division was headed by a Chinese, with senior staff comprising a "Brazilian, Dane, Englishman, Frenchman, Haitian, Mexican Woman"; Natural Sciences had an English head, and senior staff comprising "Chinese, French, Russian woman, and an Indian."[125] Other statistics, however, detailed that in 1947, of the 557 posts in the UNESCO Secretariat, 514 were held by French or English nationals.[126] By contrast, the UN in New York had a Secretariat of around three thousand, 50 percent of whom were North American; six of its nine assistant secretary-general posts were held by Europeans.[127] Around 7 percent were from Asia and the Far East (a category that included Australia and New Zealand), 7 percent from Eastern Europe, 4 percent from Latin America, and less than 1 percent each from Africa and the Middle East. Needless to say there were no specific tallies of women, who had no presence in any of the executive levels of any UN organization until 1949, when Alva Myrdal was appointed a "top-ranking director." Nor was there an accounting of the "citizens of the One World of the human mind" identified by Huxley as crucial to the UN and UNESCO's success.[128] The only difference between the Paris and the New York operations was the respective organization's size and the bearing of its immediate surroundings on its employment pool.

It is easier to understand the conceptual status of nations in UNESCO's mission if we consider the influences at work at the organization. Huxley, for example, brought to bear not only his background in the natural sciences but also his experience on the Board of Trustees of Gilbert Murray's Council for World Citizenship.[129] The UNESCO "Tensions" program, like the work of the league's International Intellectual Cooperation, which Murray had chaired, rehearsed the traditional pacifist belief that peace could be achieved through "international understanding."[130] UNESCO programs that invited students and workers on exchanges, or teachers to international seminars on history and geography, or "world citizenship," brought to fruition the ambitions of the league's International Committee for Intellectual Cooperation. UNESCO's targeted cohort was updated—Americans and Russians, businessmen and members of the Communist Party, Roman Catholics and Muslims[131]—and the methods made more self-consciously scientific. Huxley dedicated a "ways of life" project to the preparation of monographs on different national cultures that would be translated into numerous languages.[132] There were also committees for textbook revision and—one of Huxley's favorite projects—the writing of a "world history." The problem of the political resuscitation of specific nations from their authoritarian and racist pasts, also led UNESCO staff into field work in postwar Germany and Japan. While these efforts were concentrated on Germany, Japan proved the greater long-term success. There, old-school liberal internationalists cooperated with conservative nationalists to reimagine Japanese education, culture, and history through the UNESCO intervention.[133]

If there were echoes of the international mind in the charter's version of one world, and in the focus on cultural contact and communication, UNESCO also operated in the context of mid-twentieth-century developments in the social sciences, including the dominance of psychologists and anthropologists. Tolerance was to be fostered not only through the practical opportunity for "sociability" but also through directed psychological studies run by UNESCO's Social Sciences Department.

Under Otto Klineberg, a psychologist at Columbia University, the Social Sciences Department investigated "techniques to change psychological attitudes" as well as the psychology of national character. The favored techniques were "neo-Freudian" and anthropological.[134] When the Chicago sociologist Edward Shils was brought in to devise the tensions project, he outlined studies of psychological predispositions, patterns of culture, and ruling groups, using the methods of dynamic psychology in combination with historical biographical data.[135] For the first time in history, Shils explained, scientists would probe the causes of nationalist aggression by studying the insecurities and deprivations of infancy and childhood. They would examine group images of "the self and the Other," survey public opinion polls, play out psychodramas; they would link psychology to economics, discover the techniques of attitude change, and foster international unity among social scientists themselves.

UNESCO epitomized the changing theories of human nature and methodologies that coincided with and consolidated the rise of the social scientist—the league's International Intellectual Cooperation program had been run in the main by historians and literary specialists and focused on elites. The contrast was too clear for Gilbert Murray, who had led the interwar approach. Writing to Huxley in Paris from his home in Oxford, Murray warned against UNESCO's "excessive emphasis on the international, the democratic, and the immediately useful" and its lowering of "the intellectual and imaginative standard of education."[136] Murray's disapproval provides a useful measure of just how differently culture was thought of in this mid-twentieth-century experiment in internationalism, despite the intellectual and institutional legacy of the preceding decades.

Murray attributed the fall from high culture to UNESCO's flagship program on illiteracy, "Fundamental Education." He might have sniffed out that Fundamental Education also involved health, methods of agriculture, techniques of labor, and "better methods of making money."[137] Through Fundamental Education, UNESCO civil servants banked on peace by means of raising the standard of living in a world economy.[138] UNESCO's Fundamental Education program not only brought science firmly into the domain of culture, and engaged culture in the name of the challenges of social justice that were the UN's brief, it also anticipated the UN's gradual deployment of the phenomenon known as Technical Assistance, which became, in turn, development.[139] In practical terms, this program made UNESCO the first of the new UN institutions to appoint natural and social sciences and economics experts to help emancipate colonial and postcolonial societies from their "backwardness," newly defined relative to their technological and economic rather than biological or "civilizational" status.

Again, Huxley's intellectual and political networks, and his personal history of travel, were crucial to the purpose and location of the Fundamental Education experiment. In the 1930s, Huxley participated in the Colonial Office Advisory Committee on Native Education to East Africa. During the war, he was a vocal member of a Fabian intellectual network that included Benson and favored the development of international standards and oversight of colonial administrations.[140] As director-general of UNESCO, Huxley invited into his organization British colonial expertise. He began by placing John Bowers, the former director of the British Colonial Film Unit, at the head of Fundamental Education.[141] He also worked with the British Colonial Office to bring Fundamental Education to British-administered East Africa, specifically the UN Trust Territory of Tanganyika (later Tanzania) and the Protectorate of Nyasaland (later Malawi). In the Nyasaland project, a Danish agricultural economist was appointed to advise on the development of secondary-level agricultural education programs in a traditional African village. The bolder project was in Tanganyika, where UNESCO was to collaborate with the British government on a scheme that would, it was claimed, modernize agriculture in practice, not just theory. In 1947, Armando Cortesao, UNESCO's external relations officer, and a former Portuguese colonial agronomist, presented the project to the UN Trusteeship Council as "an interesting experiment in building up an *ab initio* of a complete new African society."[142] Cortesao was personally so taken with the idea that he complained in private about the priority given to the British and urged UNESCO to develop similar projects in Belgian and French African colonies.

From the British perspective, UNESCO's involvement in a business venture prompted by the United Africa Company (a division of British Unilever) would kill two birds with one stone—provide postwar Britain, and Unilever, with sorely needed oils and margarines, and ward off any potential criticism of Britain's "sacred trust" with evidence that it was advancing the well-being of colonial populations.[143] UNESCO's role was to recruit thirty thousand selected Africans from several tribes and educate them in industrial agriculture, planting, and harvesting "groundnuts."[144]

The story of Fundamental Education in East Africa is better known as the groundnut fiasco, and UNESCO's role has been forgotten in the larger picture of economic waste and environmental destruction. Bulldozers shipped in at great expense became stuck in the unnavigable roads leading inland from a distant port; no one had bothered to consider the lack of accessible drinking water for the workers who also had to be brought in. When the modern technology did arrive, the stubbornly resistant soil thick with baobab tree roots hacked back at the bulldozer blades and left a ghostly landscape strewn with broken bits of machinery. A project that had set out to cultivate 150,000 acres of scrub in six years ended with barely a quarter of that amount cleared and most of it rendered a dust bowl, including the devastation of land traditionally used for ancestor worship. The cost to the U.K. taxpayer was £36 million, the effects on the local populations unaccounted.[145]

The end of the groundnut scheme coincided with the premature termination of another Fundamental Education project, in Haiti. At its outset, the Haitian endeavor had augured well, in part because it was established through local initiatives. The remote Marbial Valley was chosen as the experimental site on the initiative of the new Haitian government.[146] While UNESCO awaited the report of the anthropologist Alfred Métraux on a culturally appropriate approach to the extensive local problems of soil erosion and tropical disease, local Haitian-based experts and institutions laid the groundwork for the arrival of technical assistance. Oral histories and photos suggest that the even the local villagers were excited at the prospect of the program.[147]

UNESCO's focus on Haiti was the work of its lone black Fundamental

Education employee, the Haitian educationalist Emmanuel Gabriel. Twenty years later, Huxley complained that he had felt under pressure to appoint "a coloured man on the staff" at UNESCO in order to stress the organization's "universal character."[148] Although Huxley did not name him, the man Huxley had in mind must have been Gabriel. The Haitian's path to UNESCO had been similar to Huxley's own—the serendipitous auditing of the 1945 UNESCO planning meeting (Gabriel was in London at the time on an international fellowship studying at the Institute for Education). Gabriel was fluent in Creole, French, and Spanish, was "fair" in English, and had knowledge of Latin, and he was an open enthusiast of UNESCO's institutional cosmopolitanism, which he described as representative of *"tous les citoyens du monde."* More than that, he believed that Fundamental Education could be utilized to do something concrete about the high rate of illiteracy in Haiti, and the generally "pitiful" conditions of villagers and city slum dwellers.[149] When the Marbial venture failed, it was despite Gabriel's efforts to cling on to the day-to-day running of the various projects in small-scale production and education that he had initiated.

Fundamental Education in Haiti fell victim to a combination of factors, including the extreme challenges of its location, UNESCO's limited budget and preparation, and the lack of coordination among UNESCO, the World Health Organization, and the Food and Agriculture Organization, each of which wanted a controlling stake in the program. Gabriel was effectively sidelined and underfunded. What remained of the endeavor was a series of Creole primers written by Gabriel, and the nostalgia of the local community for a period of international intervention that contrasted strikingly with the unfinished large-scale, debt-laden, and environmentally suspect developmentalism that was to come in the darker dictatorial days of the Haitian republic.[150] After Gabriel's contract was terminated, he returned only briefly to UNESCO as a Haitian delegate, and within a few years died in mysterious circumstances.

Although the history of Fundamental Education had no happy ending, it offers another poignant reminder of the social and economic expectations generated by mid-twentieth-century internationalism, at its center and on its margins, and the UN's symbolic status as an instrument for leveling up global living standards and opportunities. Fundamental Education preceded and competed with the UN's Technical Assistance program, formulated in 1948 with the General Assembly's approval of a major initiative providing technical knowledge and aid for economic development.[151] In January 1949, the American president Truman's Point IV program, with its call for "techni-cal assistance" led by the United States, gave "TA" the imprimatur of realpo-litik legitimacy. From the perspective of the United States, TA was the "rest of the world" corollary to the European-focused Marshall Aid program, of-fering similar opportunities for tactical advantage in the Cold War. From the perspective of members of the UN Secretariat in New York, and UNESCO in Paris, it was the culmination of its own work.[152]

Even before the floodgates of development opened, representatives of non-European states and colonies were generally keen to divert to their own countries the resources of the UN that had until then been concentrated on Europe.[153] At a 1946 meeting of the General Assembly's Economic and Social Committee to support Technical Assistance programs in Asia and the Ameri-cas, Brazil's ambassador explained that his own country had, for two years, given nearly 1 percent of its national income to the UN's refugee program "for war-ravaged Europe."[154] Jamaican Henry Fowler could barely contain him-self when he heard that UNESCO was bringing "Fundamental Education" to Haiti and tried unsuccessfully to get the (British) director of education in Jamaica to consider the project for his own country.[155] Among UN civil servants, Technical Assistance corresponded to the influence of social justice imperatives.

As we have seen, mid-twentieth-century internationalism was fashioned out of a conception of economic progress and opportunity for economic eq-uity and democracy in the image of modern industrialization. As director of Trusteeship, Ralph Bunche focused his administration, and the Trustee-ship Council's oversight of eleven trust territories and twenty million trustee subjects, on what he termed the "Problems of Colonies and Underdeveloped Areas" (borrowing the term "underdeveloped" from his colleague Benson, who had coined it). The intention was to improve access to education, health, and housing and thereby address the growing restiveness of colonized popu-lations and the allure of nationalism, as well as the racialism that had infested colonial practices.[156] Bunche thought of this as a practical internationalism.

Similarly, for the Swedish feminist Alva Myrdal, the only woman to scale the heights of the UN and UNESCO in these years, the real challenge to world peace and security was not a lack of cultural understanding but, rather, the alarming inequalities between European and colonized societies. During her short tenure as acting "top-ranking director" of the Division of Social Affairs at Lake Success (1949), Myrdal brought to the UN and its agencies a perspec-tive informed by her feminism and social welfarism, and her friendships with

Bunche—who had cowritten *The American Dilemma* with her husband Gunnar Myrdal—and Huxley—her colleague in population concerns. One of the architects of Swedish social democracy, Alva Myrdal was convinced that the Swedish model of progress from rural to modern society could be adapted in colonial settings through "planned social development."[157] From Myrdal's perspective, the Swedish precedent had shown that giving women as well as men a greater stake in the improvement of quality of life had, in the course of half a century, led that country out of its feudal past into a more democratic and modern future. She was inclined to see the potential of the UN's Technical Assistance program in places such as the Near East in similar terms.

Myrdal's arrival at the UN coincided with the surge in the UN's Technical Assistance initiatives, backed by the American president's announcement that the U.S. would work with the UN and NGOs such as the Rockefeller and Ford Foundations. Between 1950 and 1956, eighty countries pledged the UN $142 million to help 131 countries and territories. Newly configured UN bodies—the Technical Assistance Committee of ECOSOC and the Technical Assistance Board made up of representatives of UN agencies (including UNESCO)—sent out more than five thousand experts and awarded eight thousand training fellowships.[158] At the same time that the UN was revamping its economic policies around technical assistance, Myrdal also turned her attention to "development."[159] She described her typical day when the UN was in session, in the Economic and Social Council "just glued to my seat in order to demonstrate the interest of the Department of Social Affairs in the development of under-developed countries."[160] She also insisted that UN experts needed to understand the societies they were helping to industrialize, and advocated "balanced modernization."[161] Myrdal believed that the Department of Social Affairs brought a whole repertoire of accumulated social welfare expertise to the TA agenda, and that TA should take account of housing, the maintenance of standards of living, social welfare services, the prevention of crime, social care of immigrants, and the status of women.

After 1950, Myrdal's prioritization of the social ended up having more of an influence on UNESCO's program, where she was now director of the Social Sciences Department. By this time the Mexican educationalist Jaime Torres Bodet had succeeded Huxley as director-general, but Huxley's research agenda still decided the organization's priorities. Huxley had repeatedly refused UN requests to take on the problem of discrimination against women and directed the Social Sciences Division to focus on the UN-determined priority of "questions of race," including the dissemination of scientific information on race and the preparation of educational campaigns "based on this information."[162] The culmination of the antiracism campaign coincided with Myrdal's arrival.

In July 1950, a *New York Times* headline read "No Scientific Basis for Race Bias Found by World Panel of Experts," crediting UNESCO.[163] The panel was Huxley's idea: a team of anthropologists, psychologists, and sociologists instructed to define the concept of race and issue a formal statement. Coincidentally, the UNESCO statement on race ended up echoing the arguments of Huxley's own 1936 antiracist tome, *We Europeans*: "That all men belonged to the same species, Homo Sapiens; that national, cultural, religious, geographical, and linguistic groups had been falsely termed races; that it would be better to drop the term and use 'ethnic groups' in its place; that the 'race is everything' hypothesis was untrue."[164] Myrdal's problem was managing the criticisms of the UNESCO statement by scientists who had been left out of the panel. Effectively, at a time when the discovery of DNA was rendering race a redundant scientific category altogether, UNESCO had rekindled scientific controversy over its definition. Myrdal, whose own antiracist views had been schooled during her years in the United States in the company of Bunche and other progressive social scientists, was forced to accommodate a second declaration scrutinized by nearly one hundred anthropologists and geneticists who agreed only on the lack of proof that race was more a social myth than a biological fact.[165]

The confidence with which race returned to the international stage at the beginning of the 1950s was not all the work of Huxley or UNESCO. The Cold War view of the world asserting itself across the Atlantic had in its sights the specter of internationalism and the reputed cosmopolitanism of the UN and its agencies. In 1950, the British ambassador to the Soviet-backed Central European state of Czechoslovakia wrote in dismay to the secretary for Britain's National UNESCO Commission that "at one time the 'new democracies' pointed with pride to their professed interest in cultural exchanges as a proof that they were decent internationally-minded people." That had all changed with the Soviet Union's campaign against cosmopolitanism.[166] Russia labeled UNESCO (which it joined only after Stalin's death in 1953) a front for American attempts at world domination. Tito's Yugoslavia, which had broken from the Soviet Union by then to travel its national road to socialism, attacked UNESCO for its antinationalist and anticommunist "philosophical Esperanto."[167] Even as UNESCO cut ties with communist-linked groups such as the World Federation of Democratic Youth, the U.S. government began its own campaign branding UNESCO both cosmopolitan and communist. Nationalism was now the least suspicious political and cultural objective—regardless of political ideology.

In 1949, the year when Myrdal arrived at the UN as top-ranking director, the UN was a sizable town-like structure numbering (with all its related agencies) around ten thousand employees, with its own internal economy and transport, ferrying staff and visitors in shuttle cars across its campuses on the half hour. This was the organization that the American Federal Bureau of Investigation began to monitor as the site of communist threats to the state, alerted in the first instance by the alleged radicalism of the Trusteeship Division. At the same time, U.S. government agencies began exerting pressure on the organization, "to make clear that promotion of international understanding did not mean support of world government."[168] The mood reached Paris, where Jaime Torres Bodet turned from advocating world citizenship as "an ever vigilant critical spirit and a bond of sympathy making each man feel with his fellows in their suffering, joy, disaster or success," to emphasizing that it had *never* been UNESCO's purpose to turn citizens from their national loyalties (which was in fact true).[169]

The serious purging of the UN began in January 1953, when President Truman signed an executive order requiring the investigation of the national loyalty of all Americans working for international organizations—even as the United States took the lead with international development. McCarthyism cut as deep into the UN as the rest of the United States. Within a few months the U.S. Senate Internal Security Subcommittee called upon Bunche (already a Nobel Peace Prize winner) on the grounds that he was a founder of the National Negro Congress (even though Bunche had exited when it turned communist), and for being more UN than U.S.[170] That same year, the U.S. delegation to the UNESCO General Conference in Paris declared its intention of staying on to assess the charge that the organization was "under Communist control," and that it "advocates a political world government."[171]

UNESCO now stood accused of seeking "to undermine the loyalty of Americans toward their own government and toward their own flag, and to substitute for that loyalty one favoring a political world government." The means of this alleged subterfuge was UNESCO's commission on the rewriting of history textbooks in order to highlight the history of peace rather than war, and of humanity rather than nations, revisions that allegedly would indoctrinate American schoolchildren and teachers with ideas contrary to American national traditions.[172] The delegation's findings, not guilty on all counts, suggest that its members might have been as keen to use the inquiry to clear the air of suspicion surrounding UNESCO as to condemn the organization.[173] Regardless, UNESCO never recovered its "one world" momentum, as national and imperial as it had sometimes been.

What had happened to the prevalent popularity for being "internationally minded"? The answer depended at least partly on where you lived. In the postwar period, the transformation of League of Nations Societies into United Nations Associations was relatively painless in the United States, where it took place under the mentorship of Eleanor Roosevelt, and in Britain, where it was backed in 1946 with government funding of £34,000. The British United Nations Association had built on the success of the League of Nations Union and boasted seventy thousand "contributors" and 572 local sections. By contrast, the French version barely kept afloat. It was still run by the interwar generation, many of whom were now in their seventies and eighties, and faced with a disinterested postwar government doling out meager funding scraps.[174] In 1946, a new international body was organized with the help of high-level Americans in the UN and UNESCO administrations to bring these associations together. The World Federation of UN Associations was presided over by Jan Masaryk, the Czechoslovak foreign minister. It had regular meetings and drew the support of twenty-six countries and thirteen international organizations. It also had consultative status at the UN. But by the late 1940s, it was difficult for any of the national associations to summon the same levels of activism and enthusiasm that even the wounded league had managed.[175] The attention of French "militants" moved instead to the federation of Europe, and Europe became the locus of competing visions of universalism, including human rights.[176] The Council of Europe's adoption of a separate convention of Human Rights (1950), the creation of a European Human Rights Commission (1954) and a European Court of Human Rights (1959) had awarded to Europeans the authority to take action on human rights questions—an authority that the UN Human Rights Commission did not have, despite the efforts of Mehta, Cassin, and others. The progenitors of these European-based human rights instruments were conservative European politicians, but from Cassin's perspective, the new European institutions empowered individuals against states and authorized international intervention in human rights abuses everywhere.

In that year for turning, 1953, Cassin assumed that the French had forgotten why the United Nations was created and out of which desires.[177] His own disillusionment was provoked by the shifting framework of debate in the UN Human Rights Commission, with its new emphasis on collective rights and national self-determination, as well as the demands made on him by the French government to contradict his universalist human rights convictions in those debates by arguing for cultural relativism.[178] To top it all off, he was briefly detained at Victoria Station by British police, who seemed to have the same memory loss. They were puzzled both by his UN passport (which he should not have been using to attend a meeting in London of the International Institute of Administrative Scientists) and by its description of him as a delegate to the Human Rights Commission. They kept asking what human rights meant.[179] When she heard of the incident, Alva Myrdal wrote to Cassin in sympathy.[180] A few months earlier she had been detained by customs officers on her arrival in the United States. While traveling on a UNESCO mission on her way to the UN, she was refused a visa. In her case, the rumor mill blamed her estranged son's communist affiliations.

In the mid-1950s, Myrdal gave up UNESCO for a posting as Swedish ambassador to Nehru's India—a keen contributor to the UN's coffers and supporter of the social and economic bent of Technical Assistance. By then there was a long-accruing list of abandoned international ambitions and forgotten institutional memory, including the idea that social justice and disarmament were the core missions of international government. Myrdal's time at UNESCO had been spent trying to shift attention away from psychological studies (with which she largely sympathized given her own background in child psychology) toward applied welfare and development programs and understanding the impact of industrialization on human communities. In the end she decided she could be more effective as a diplomat than international civil servant.[181] When eventually, in the 1980s, she too won a Nobel Peace Prize, it was for her diplomatic work on disarmament. By then political theorists were reinforcing the idea that diplomacy, within a state-based international system, was the only realistic way of forging an international society.

These later developments place into even more striking contrast that curiously utopian moment of the mid-twentieth century, the apogee of internationalism, with its multiplicity of interpretations and expectations of "the international," encouraged by the language of world citizenship and human rights. Cassin had thought in terms of a long French tradition of universal rights, Bunche and Myrdal had been recognizably practical and nonhistorical in their approach to internationalism. When, in 1947, Bunche's fellow Howard sociologist E. Franklin Frazier—a Myrdal appointee in UNESCO's Social

Sciences Department (1951–53)—had put into writing his commitment to "A World Community and a Universal Moral Order," he drew on the resources of a twentieth-century tradition of political thought. Frazier articulated a vision of international community that stuck to the script of the international turn, dressed in what were then the new fashions of the midcentury: he spoke of a world community where nations as much as people had been brought into intimacy through modern technology, and economic ties, and empires; he rejected "a shallow cosmopolitanism" and proposed "human equality, freedom of person, and a minimum standard of living" as the "universal values" on which to base a "world culture."[182] Frazier's explanation for the absence of consensus on this world culture also looked forward to the themes that would dominate later-twentieth-century iterations of internationalism: the xenophobia of nation-states, their control of "channels of communication," and, as he put it in 1947, the new "cartels and other economic organizations that transcended state boundaries" and that "were hardly invested in a universal moral order."[183]

The purging of the UN and the attacks on UNESCO's cosmopolitanism that took place in the 1950s are useful markers both of the shifting winds of international politics and of the 1940s as distinctively international years. Brian Urquhart, who built a career in the United Nations working first for Gladwyn Jebb, then for Bunche, finally taking on Bunche's job after his death, would describe the difficulty of recapturing "the freshness and enthusiasm of those pioneering days. . . . We were all optimists and regarded the occasional cynic or 'realist' with contempt. I have since wondered whether in 1945 we were exceptionally naïve, in the company of many others who believed in the possibility of organizing a peaceful and just world."[184] But the question of "realism" was as significant for Urquhart, as he also recalls in his autobiography: "I was a determined internationalist, and saw our work as a mission to bring objectivity and common sense to bear on problems of peace and war, as a national civil service does in a well-organized state."[185] The Cold War placed in sharp relief the extent and range of those earlier conversations on the need for new forms of international government, and even state sovereignty, and what might lie ahead in the future. It also helped later generations forget just how central to those conversations the claims of realism, objectivity, and pragmatism were.

Chapter 4

What Is the International?

A quarter of a century after the apogee of internationalism, through a window of Cold War détente, the world took on a global hue. The viewers of American television, and its global affiliates, could watch Henry Kissinger, the period's ubiquitous American statesman, speak of "an extraordinary opportunity to form for the first time in history a truly global society, carried by the principle of interdependence."[1] Readers of social scientific literature could find the same view corroborated by Harvard professors such as the political scientist Stanley Hoffmann, who tendered that a new language of internationalism was needed to describe the exercise of international power by "non-state actors," "multinational companies, international organisations, and the like."[2] Since then, the historian Akira Iriye has recovered the 1970s as a decade that witnessed "a definite phase of globalization, a process that was to continue into the subsequent decades" and aided the emergence of "a genuine world community."[3] In the context of the longer history of twentieth-century internationalism, the conceptual materials of this new "global" era look remarkably familiar.

The 1970s were a curious combination of the old and the new, not least because of the simultaneous pull of the universal and particular, the international and national. Kissinger, for one, hedged his bets, warning that the seventies would be viewed in retrospect as *either* "a period of extraordinary creativity or a period when really the international order came apart, politically, economically and morally."[4] Daniel Moynihan became as convinced during a stint as ambassador to the UN that even if the talk was all global villages and spaceship earth, something closer to regression was taking place; the world was relapsing into a timeless mode of tribal fragmentation and strife.[5] It was not only the foundations of empires that were vulnerable. The seventies saw Pakistan violently splinter to form Bangladesh, Cyprus sundered into a Turkish north and Greek south, and the Arab-Israeli conflict spread, taking as its emblematic hostage that cosmopolitan city, Beirut. There was no shortage of "peacekeeping" for the UN, as the organization now turned to the task of stabilizing the conflicts that continued to erupt across the globe and utilizing in new ways the international military force that had been dreamed of half a century earlier.

How we understand the seventies as a transformative decade depends on setting and perspective. While most studies of the period place events at the United Nations offstage, in this chapter I look at the international organization as a compelling theatre of competing narratives of a twentieth-century internationalism imagined in the language of a "truly global society," and the fragmentation of existing states into smaller nations. The UN was the forum for economic claims so unprecedented that they profoundly troubled American diplomats while cheering the delegates of new postcolonial states. As a result, in the same decade that some historians argue a truly international human rights agenda was born, Western governments began to disown the international organization at the symbolic center of the modern experiment in institutional internationalism. In addition, the drama of empire and race played out at the UN in the 1970s directly influenced Western scholars of race and nationalism, and indirectly affected new theories of international politics that wrote the UN into the margins of the present and the past, where historians long managed to leave it.

By placing the UN at the center of the decade's contradictions and changing theorizations of the international, we get a much clearer impression of the apotheosis of a globally oriented internationalism in the first half of the 1970s, and its contorted demise. It is a history that usefully reminds us of the extent to which, even at the end of the twentieth century, definitions of the "international" remained as contested and crucial to the progress of collective politics as the question "What is a nation?"

Third World UN

At its beginning, the seventies ushered in a self-conscious internationalism in the language of globalism. As with the apogee of internationalism, and before then the international turn, the new global era was replete with descriptions of international-scale intimacy and identification shaped by expanding technologies and networks of communication and commerce. In reality, over this same period, the progress of economic globalization had been as unpredictable as that of international institutions. The seventies felt more global because the structural globalization that had stalled during the 1930s into economic deglobalization suddenly restarted.[6] We might imagine the shifting tides of world trade like currents forcing the ebb and flow of the "global mentality" talk that was the seventies version of being internationally minded. But trade and talk were not the only factors determining global perspectives. The space race, stories of the Russian Sputnik satellite and televised images of Americans planting their flag on the moon, and satellite imagery itself fundamentally altered the ways in which "international society" was imagined, now in technicolor visions. On the cusp of the new decade, the UN's first "Third World" secretary-general, the Burmese U Thant, specifically called for "a new quality of planetary imagination" that could match "the realities of the present-day world."[7]

Employees attached to the UN Secretariat and Economic and Social Council were particularly fond disseminators of global terminology. The council's administrative head, the under-secretary general for economic and social affairs, Philippe de Seynes, propagated "globalism" as the "functional expression" of the increasingly prominent notion of the "world as a whole."[8] The rare scholarly commentary on the "facts of international life," or the sentiment of internationalism, might claim that population growth in combination with "easier than ever" communication across nations, the spread of industrialization, and international institutions ("the most essential prerequisite for the growth of a widespread sentiment of world citizenship and loyalty") had led to a corresponding reduction of the "disparate nature of the cultural values held within the world community."[9] But the language of world citizenship and community seemed bland and even old-fashioned in comparison with the new globalism.

More common from outside the UN was the view that UN agencies and the UN General Assembly had a diminished role in these global developments.[10] Political scientists sympathetic to concepts such as interdependence, which conventionally implied relations between sovereign states, lit on a new term, "transnational," which, like "international regime" and "nonstate actors," put a spotlight on the unprecedented growth in international organizations other than the United Nations.[11] Between the late 1960s and early 1980s, the number of these nonstate actors doubled to nearly eighty thousand (compared to the double digits of the 1890s).[12] Each of these often had multiple domestic or national branches, adding to the sense that they were everywhere.

If we think back over the twentieth century, the role of nonstate actors dominated as the subjects and objects of observations of the sociological dimensions or "objective facts" of a new internationalism. These had included not only early institutions such as the Universal Postal Union, but also the Cercle International of the Hague Peace Conference, the international women's organizations lobbying the league, and the NAACP's efforts on the sidelines of the San Francisco meeting that drafted the UN Charter in 1945. The UN Charter, like the league covenant, was intended to avoid an international government by individual plebiscite. The drafters, though, gave in to some of these actors' demands by granting consultative status to any international organization that had approval from the General Assembly and that was not itself the product of an international treaty. The charter also formally introduced into political parlance a new noun, "nongovernmental organization," or NGO.[13]

From the 1940s until the 1970s, the story of the international sway of NGOs was still as much about the UN. There were forty NGOs in the first group to be given access to the Economic and Social Council.[14] Most were already well-established transnational ecumenical, legal, worker, and commercial bodies, whether trade union federations, internationally organized employers, or women. They included late-nineteenth-century organizations such as the International Law Association (1873), the International Cooperative Alliance (1895), and the International Council of Women (1888); and common issue alliances formed in the interwar period such as the International Chamber of Commerce (1919), the Christian-democrat-oriented World Confederation of Labor (1920), the International League for Human Rights (1922), and the International Federation of Business and Professional Women (1930).

The UN's recognition of the "NGO" also breathed life into a new postwar generation of international institutions, which sought to influence national policies: from the Coordinating Board of Jewish Organizations and the Consultative Council of Jewish Organizations (which René Cassin helped establish) to the International Federation of Agricultural Producers, the International Organization for Standardization, the United Cities and Local Governments, and the All Pakistan Women's Association. Not all these interests had the same claim to status within the UN. Diverse women's groups were told they had to coalesce to gain recognition; the Bahá'í International

Community, which registered with the UN in 1948, was not granted consultative status until 1970.[15] The multiplication of NGOs in the 1960s was also spurred by the popularity of development and modernization schemes in postcolonial states. By then too the UN, and its place in a broader constellation of international power and authority, had taken its own global turn. As the political scientist Leland Goodrich observed, the United Nations had grown into an organization that participants at its founding 1945 conference (including himself) would have found difficult to recognize.[16] From his perspective, the difference was less a matter of the proliferation of international institutions and a "global consciousness" and more a matter of the delegates of new postcolonial nation-states crowding the corridors and assembly halls of the UN.

At its outset, the UN had comprised 51 member states, of which the large majority were countries of Europe, including the Soviet Union, the Americas, and the "White Commonwealth."[17] When the People's Republic of China was admitted to membership in December 1971, there were 132 member states (in 2010 it had 192), the majority postcolonial. In the interim, at least thirty had claimed their independence from the British Empire alone—including India, Pakistan, Burma, Ceylon, Israel, Sudan, Ghana, Malaya, Nigeria, Cyprus, Tanzania, Sierra Leone, Uganda, Jamaica, Trinidad, Kenya, Zanzibar, Malta, Malawi, Zambia, Singapore, Gambia, Botswana, Lesotho, Barbados, Guyana, Aden, Mauritius, Swaziland, Fiji, and Tonga. The appointment in 1961 of U Thant as UN secretary-general—successor to the Swedish Dag Hammarskjöld,[18] who succeeded the Norwegian Trygve Lie—was a striking symbol of how anticolonial the tenor of UN-centered internationalism had become. For Thant, a former headmaster and UN diplomat, the "question of colonialism" was at the heart of the UN's work.[19] This was also a period, needless to say, when the UN-sanctioned language of non-self-governing territories and trusteeship faded into irrelevance.

Thant was hardly alone in his priorities. Already in the mid-1950s, American and Russian strategists were transforming the "question of colonialism" into the substance of Cold War strategy.[20] At the same time, the ongoing UN discussions about a binding convention or bill on human rights began to feature the "self-determination of peoples."[21] The shift was as noticeable in the Human Rights debates at the UN, as the commission worked on the transition from the 1948 declaration to justiciable covenants. From the 1950s, the new discussion of human rights turned on the separation out of civil and political rights from economic and social rights, and the inclusion of the "self-determination of peoples" as a human right. Meanwhile, the expanding General Assembly began throwing its own weight behind the national ambitions of colonized societies by adapting the techniques of international law to the cause of decolonization rather than empire.

In 1960, the UN General Assembly passed the Declaration on the Granting of Independence to Colonial Countries and Peoples. The following year, it created a Special Committee on Decolonization to monitor and make recommendations on the application of the declaration. While existing international laws of state succession imposed on any new state the maintenance of colonial obligations—including the concessionary rights given to trading companies to exploit natural resources—the General Assembly devised its own principle of self-determination. It deemed "the right of peoples and nations to permanent sovereignty over their natural wealth . . . in the interest of their national development and the well-being of the people concerned."[22] In 1966, the same principle of popular and national sovereignty over natural wealth and resources was codified in the International Covenants on Human Rights, alongside the now universalized right of peoples to self-determination. The UN had effectively made control of natural resources a defining aspect of national sovereignty for new postcolonial states.

As in the past, there was little the General Assembly could do to enforce its declarations, covenants, or resolutions. Nevertheless, its efforts were crucial to perceptions of the UN's changing international constituency and the effect on the balance of power within the organization.[23] There was not only the pressure of new member states weighing in but also the expansion in the UN's admission of NGOs.[24] During the 1970s, the NGOs granted consultative status tripled to nearly six hundred, comprising institutions from a broader geographical and cultural spectrum than ever before, such as the World Muslim Congress (founded in 1949), the Muslim World League, the Afro-Asian Peoples' Solidarity Organization, the Arab Lawyers Union, the Organization of African Trade Union Unity, and the Anti-Apartheid Movement. The UN also provided, in a more old-fashioned way, the opportunities for sociability that gave birth to a range of associations and agencies engaged with postcolonial nation building. The offices and meeting places of the UN were the congenial setting for the creation of the Group of 77 coalition of "Third World" member states, and the Conference on Trade and Development (UNCTAD), established to promote "the development-friendly integration of developing countries into the world economy."[25]

U Thant's two terms as secretary-general (1961–71) also coincided with

the first Development Decade. This was no lone UN agenda. It was backed—
like Thant's own appointment—by the Kennedy-led U.S. government, and
powerful American philanthropic organizations such as the Ford Foundation, in the context of the Cold War struggle for colonial hearts and minds.[26]
From the perspective of the UN's Secretariat, of course, the concept of development had specific institutional roots, nurtured in experiments in Technical
Assistance (which, as we have seen, also capitalized on personal connections
with colonial reform movements, and the Cold War concerns of the new superpowers). These experiments were now increasingly oriented around population planning. In the 1940s, Huxley had supported a population program
at UNESCO on eugenicist grounds, with little success; in the 1950s, Myrdal
was intent on population planning on feminist grounds, and knew Huxley
through their shared enthusiasm. By 1960, population was a mainstream
political as well as welfare topic. Its place in "development" programs was
ensured by the conceptualization of population control as a solution to Third
World poverty, and by the encouragement of postcolonial leaders who saw
in population planning a technology of modern government and state building.[27] At the 1960 UNESCO General Conference British and American figures, from Norman Angell and Bertrand Russell to Dean Acheson, Archibald
MacLeish, Arthur Schlesinger Sr., Eleanor Roosevelt, and Sumner Welles,
signed off on a statement of conviction about overpopulation. This insisted
on the importance of birth control as well as "social and family stability" for
raising living standards and achieving international peace.[28] By 1968 the UN
had declared "family" planning to be a human right, and in 1974 it held the
first World Population Conference under its auspices.[29]

Not everything about the economic and social motifs of globalism was
new. The global turn of the seventies can also be read as another chapter in
twentieth-century narratives of internationalism as the means to economic
and social as well as political progress. The creation of the ILO by the "great
powers" in 1919, for example, and its evocations of "social justice" had recognized the threat that the determined clamor for economic rights and equality
posed not only to peace but also to the political integrity of existing empires
and states. The motifs were repeated through the crisis of World War II,
and the drafting of the UN Charter; we can hear them as loudly in Gandhi's pointed recitation of the aims of the Indian anticolonial movement.[30]
The claims for social justice are audible too in the UN's accentuated social
and economic program, on the advice of the 1939 Bruce Report. In 1955, the
same motifs were rehearsed "offshore," as twenty-nine new African and Asian

national governments seized the opportunity to gather in the old colonial plantation resort city of Bandung, in Indonesia's West Java province. During the 1945–49 Indonesian independence battles, most of Bandung had been purposely destroyed by the Dutch; now it was a provincial postcolonial capital transformed by the noise of modernizing industry. And playing a key role at the 1955 Asian-African Conference, as it was known, was the Indian prime minister Nehru, who had invested so heavily in the one worldism of the early UN. At Bandung, Nehru turned to the creation of a new Non-Aligned Movement, distanced from the Cold War machinations of the United States and Soviet Union that were taking their terrible toll on the worldly status of internationalism and the UN itself.[31]

In the "Asian arena" of the 1950s, the motifs of economic and social progress were deployed in two distinctive intersecting versions of internationalism—a twinning that rehearsed in historically specific ways the themes of the new internationalism, and Nehru's own 1940s Indian internationalism. As the historian Sunil Amrith has described them, one version "drew on a language of global citizenship and rights, rights which locked into a common struggle the 'wretched of the earth', the recent and current victims of racism and colonialism"; the other conceptualized "the international system as a source of strength and support for state-directed programmes of national development," including "a belief in the international circulation of 'governmental technologies.'"[32] In the narrative of internationalism that framed the Non-Aligned Movement and the Bandung program, the two versions were inextricably intertwined: peaceful coexistence through the implementation of human rights; the equality of all races and nations large and small; development and the inviolability of state sovereignty, with attention to natural resources. By the 1960s, this intersecting nation building and economic and social justice international agenda had made its way back, via the Third World member states of the UN, to the UN General Assembly.[33]

Despite the longer history of internationalism as the means to economic, social, and political progress, and the persistent importance of the UN to the political changes of the postwar period, the UN was not the only international game in town. Scholars of the international took note, preferring to study transnational phenomena and "nonstate actors" that were not in the orbit of the UN, including multinational corporations (Frazier's "cartels") exerting their mysterious and unaccountable influence on international trade, and humanitarian NGOs that advertised their causes with "no borders," Amnesty International (1961), the aptly named Médecins sans frontières (1971), and the champions of environmentalism, Greenpeace (1971).[34] The origins and physical headquarters of these later now well-known NGOs tended to be European, but their agents were willing and able to exploit new media technologies to attract mass support for humanitarian intervention. Some historians consider these organizations the successors of the Christian missionaries of the nineteenth century.[35] Others categorize them in more contemporary terms, as the core of a new "global civil society," mirroring the civil society movements that also took hold in the 1970s in communist Eastern Europe, whether Charter 77 in Czechoslovakia or "anti-politics" in Hungary.[36] As the characteristics of this new international society unfolded, the critical question for contemporaries was as much *whose* interests they represented.

The answer to that question, like the problem of determining the nature of changes to international society in the 1970s, depended significantly on perspective and perceptions. The UN's landmark 1970s international meeting, the Stockholm Conference on the Human Environment, is a useful case in point. Attended by 113 state delegates and four times as many representatives of nonstate actors, all gathered under the UN's auspices, the conference announced environmentalism as a newly globalized issue on the international scene. Its concluding Declaration on the Human Environment set the goals of sustainability and equity and international scientific research that would inform international discussions and action on environmental issues such as endangered species, air pollution, and the ozone layer into the twenty-first century.[37] It also inadvertently confirmed that international politics remained ideologically fractured along an older imperial color line— newly identified as North and South—as much as the East-West tracks of the Iron Curtain.

When the Stockholm Conference sent out the message that industrialization was the cause of environmental degradation and global ecological disaster, it brought to the surface of global life evidence of a deepening division between the perceived international interests of the already industrialized world or "North," and those of the "developing" world, or the "South" or "Third World." The place of the UN on this new ideological, and moral, map was at times ambiguous. From the perspective of the UN's under-secretary general for economic and social affairs, the Conference on the Human Environment signified the conceptual distance between the development focus of "traditional internationalism," on the one hand, and globalism, measured in a new ambivalence toward technology, on the other. Philippe de Seynes blamed technology for "the degradation of the environment, the destruction of ecological balances, the limited capacity of the biosphere, the possible depletion of natural resources, the population explosion, the finiteness of the planet, and perhaps even the finiteness of knowledge."[38] (This was certainly a million miles from the suggestion made by Julian Huxley as UNESCO director-general in the late 1940s, that exploding an atomic bomb in Greenland could create a useful global warming effect that would transform icy climes to arable farming.)[39] From the perspective of many postcolonial member-state representatives, the environmental challenges that had brought them to the Stockholm Conference were the responsibility of the industrialized North whose wealth was built on an accrued environmental debt. They argued the conference-sanctioned view that any global remedy should not be at the cost of the new nation-states' equal right to economic development (and prosperity) through industrialization.

Over the next few years, these conflicting North-South perspectives came to a head in the precincts of the UN General Assembly.[40] Fueling the conflict was the instability inflicted on the balance of international economic power by the discovery by oil-rich Arab states that they could exploit the control of oil prices.[41] In 1973, while Egypt and Saudi Arabia were embroiled in a war with Israel, OPEC, a new ostensibly intergovernmental organization made up of states pursuing their common interests, mobilized an embargo on oil supplies to the United States, which it also demonized as a supporter of Israel.[42] The OPEC states simultaneously agreed to cut back on oil production and to raise oil prices. The result was an oil crisis felt most acutely by the industrialized North, even as it "greatly encouraged" the assertion of collective cultural and economic claims by the South.[43] For Joseph Nye, an American political scientist, it felt as if international politics was no longer determined by the dominant powers. Instead, there was the influence of "transnationalism," a term he coined to capture the processes of negotiation in which organizations such as OPEC and the Non-Aligned Movement wielded power in competition with the individual superpowers, NGOs, and the UN.[44]

The crucial year proved to be 1974, when the UNCTAD, on the urging of the Non-Aligned Movement (led at the time by Algeria, a member of OPEC since 1969), put its proposal for a New International Economic Order, or NIEO, to the UN General Assembly. Like the Bandung communiqué, the NIEO program emphasized the disequilibrium between developing and developed parts of the world, illustrated in the worsening gap between North and South living standards. And like the UN adopted Charter of Economic Rights and Duties of States (also promulgated in 1974), the NIEO affirmed

the role of international law and new economic principles as tools for legiti-
mating the self-determination of peoples, state sovereignty, and the national
significance of industrial development. It also reinforced demands for national (and nationalized) control of local natural resources, now expanded to
the right of all states to restitution and compensation for the past exploitation
and depletion of those resources by colonial powers and foreign companies.[45]
The NIEO provoked an uproar among the states that had most to lose from
these demands. It is worth noting, however, the mixed response of UN civil
servants and NGO workers, many of them citizens of the developed world,
and some of whom supported the core demands of the NIEO, if not always
their methods, and established networks across the North-South divide in
order to press for their adoption.[46] UN secretary-general Kurt Waldheim
(whose personal links to the race crimes of the Nazi period had not yet been
exposed) celebrated the new economic agenda as "a historical moment in the
life of the United Nations."[47]

From the international organization's perspective, the NIEO was only
one component of a resolve to affect international social justice, summed
up in the report "A New United Nations Structure for Global Economic Cooperation." The mooted structural changes involved a strengthened General
Assembly and ECOSOC, streamlined UN operations, and the creation of a
second director-general for development and international cooperation.[48]
As Ronald I. Meltzer noted in the UN-friendly journal *International Organization*, the report was evidence of "a basic structural trend towards a more
centralized and integrated UN system, after more than a decade of rapid organizational growth and uncoordinated institutional pluralism."[49] The retired
U Thant glossed that the NIEO was one component of "a bridge" that was
being built between the North and the South, and "of a community of interest and recognition of interdependence."[50] De Seynes argued "it was always assumed that . . . these changes would help in relieving the rich of a
sense of guilt toward the two-thirds of mankind living in poverty, disease,
and ignorance."[51] Formerly a French bureaucrat, as a top-ranking UN civil
servant, de Seynes interpreted the demand for economic equity as an international accounting of the ongoing effects of colonialism: even after having
given up direct political control in Africa and Asia, colonizing countries were
maintaining their economic dominance in formerly colonial regions to the
advantage of their own economies and disadvantage of local populations.
Stanley Hoffmann wrote that "the concern for a world system both less brutal
and less unfair than that of the past" supported a solution that maximized

"interdependence."[52] Even Ivor Richards, the U.K. permanent delegate to the UN, ventured that the NIEO would not go away since "'interdependence' is not merely one of the empty platitudes of United Nations rhetoric, it has become a fact of world trade."[53] As it happened, the facts of trade meant that it was not long before the South's oil leverage dissipated and the NIEO program and most of the planned structural changes to the UN were also laid aside. Historians have argued since that although the NIEO did not achieve its aims, it did encourage the IMF to introduce compensatory financing facilities and to increase its credit to the South.[54] Its other more palpable effect was to feed contradictory perceptions of power and authority at the UN.

The demands made through the NIEO reinforced a perception that Northern dominance of international affairs had finally declined with the help of the very international institutions established principally by the West. The defeat of the NIEO economic agenda, in turn, exposed the relative weakness of the South's hold on the General Assembly, UNESCO, and the ILO, compared to the international clout of the North-controlled International Monetary Fund, the International Atomic Energy Agency, and the Security Council.[55] In 1975, Harvard alumnus and Lebanese delegate to the UN Charles Malik was careful in his assertion that "Western causes have no chance of enlisting a majority in the UN today."[56] He tempered his claim with an acknowledgment of the predominance of Western causes through the exclusive right of veto in the Security Council enjoyed by "three Western powers." John Reginald P. Dumas, a diplomat from Trinidad and Tobago at the UN, observed, "The whole affair was largely a question of perceptions: How the U.S. perceived itself, how it and other western countries perceived the Third World (and vice-versa), how the various elements of the Third World perceived themselves."[57] The *perception* of the race dimensions and possible economic consequences of a new balance of power was potent enough to stimulate widespread debate about the renewed significance of an international color line. UN secretary-general Waldheim remarked, "Some people were shocked to see the U.N. reflect the 'entirely new balance of power in the world,' as compared to the founding days of 1945."[58] But the basis of this balance in the statistics of UN membership was ultimately fragile. As the Indian economist Jagdish N. Bhagwati put it, by the late 1970s "the early post-OPEC Northern perception of Southern strength yielded to reality," and the "passionate Southern voice of solidarity and confrontation" had given way to "a frustrated Southern monologue."[59]

Global Shock as Culture Shock, 1970s to 1980s

The bold turn-of-the-twentieth-century assertion by W. E. B. Du Bois of "the problem of the Twentieth Century as the problem of the color-line,"[60] the Universal Races Congress of the pre–World War I era, the willful exclusion of racial equality from the League of Nations Covenant, and UNESCO's botched Statements on Race in the early Cold War, exemplify the persistent and troubled century-long awareness of the constitutive influence of race thinking on international politics and international society. Race-thinking was institutionalized in the mandate and trusteeship systems of the league and UN. It also mediated relations inside international bureaucracies and between international civil servants otherwise tasked with eradicating race discrimination. In the 1940s, Julian Huxley was behind the antiracist intentions of the Statement on Race project, but in the 1960s he bitterly recalled the pressure placed on him, as the director general of UNESCO, to appoint a "black man."[61] The first UN secretary-general, Norwegian Trygve Lie, behaved no better overseeing the organization's antiracist brief. Lie personally directed Ralph Bunche "to 'go easy' on colonial questions in the Trusteeship Department and to instruct the staff to press less hard on such matters as UN Visiting Missions to Trust and colonial territories."[62] Even if these actions can be attributed to the pressure exerted on Lie by the colonial powers that continued to dominate the Trusteeship Council and the Security Council, Lie's personal ambivalence toward the idea of race was as apparent in his ad hoc directives. When the parents of a boy from Norway complained to him because a black woman from the Secretariat, Edith Jones, was dating their son, he fired her.[63] It was only when Bunche confronted Lie that the dismissal was rescinded.

These small examples prove that it was impossible to predict the consequences of the UN's activities and spaces. Much depended on the individuals involved. In the early days of the Trusteeship Council, it received twenty-six petitions from inhabitants of trust territories, "twenty-three were from white residents (chiefly Germans and Italians) concerning their particular interests, and only three from natives."[64] However, from 1951, the Trusteeship Division took matters into its own hands, colluding with a coalition of the NAACP and a lone South African Anglican minister to expose South Africa's abuses in the Trust Territory of South West Africa (Namibia) and initiating what became a long-standing UN campaign against South Africa's apartheid race laws.[65] (This kind of activity was a red rag to the McCarthyist bull that was at this same time wreaking havoc on international morale at the UN, and particularly its Trusteeship Division.) Despite the conservative influence of the stacked Trusteeship Council, and misgivings at the limitations of the system expressed by Du Bois and others, the rhetoric of the UN Charter exerted power of another kind, as even the conservative weekly, the *Economist* conceded: "It hardly makes sense to repeat time and time again 'we support to the full your International Organization's desire to secure development—economic, social and constitutional—in Africa, but we cannot tolerate any inspection by you to see if our deeds match our words.' "[66] Trusteeship reports put pressure on Britain to abolish corporal punishment in Tanganyika, where it was used against the native African population, but not Indians or the British.[67] During Trusteeship Visiting Missions to the Cameroons in 1955, the organization received forty thousand petitions; in Togoland there were two hundred thousand petitions—mostly addressed to the General Assembly, not the Trusteeship Council. While the Trusteeship missions acted as catalysts to local political ambitions, and even the creation of nationalist political parties, the UN General Assembly, rather than the Trusteeship Council, was becoming the locus of decolonization and nation-building as an international cause.[68]

Although the General Assembly increasingly enacted resolutions, conventions, and programs directed at outlawing expressions of race discrimination in the laws and practices of states,[69] women still were not faring well in the international scene. In 1963, the Committee on the Status of Women proposed a Declaration on the Elimination of all Forms of Discrimination against Women, that it managed to have adopted in 1967, but the declaration was translated into a convention only in 1979.[70] All the attention was on race discrimination, as successive U.S. governments seeking the higher moral ground from communist foes faced the fallout from the de facto race segregation of UN worker and visitor accommodation in New York City.[71] By the 1960s, scholars of race politics observed that the relative empowerment of "black and brown people" within the UN, "where racism is universally condemned, and all the states are accorded the outward signs of equal status," placed into embarrassing contrast the situation in countries where those same people were subject to persistent race discrimination.[72] National civil rights organizations were quick to use the contrast to their advantage, whether in the United States—where the civil rights movements were gaining force—or in Europe—where cultural and physical confrontations were as obvious in the French *négritude* movement, in riots that pitted black youths and

police in the British metropole, and in Western European immigration policies that thwarted "colored" immigration and constricted citizenship on race
grounds.[73] In a 1969 article for *Foreign Affairs* (the journal that had begun
in 1910 as the *Journal of Race Development*), the American China scholar
Harold Isaacs painted an international landscape in which the "superstruc-
ture of beliefs about the superiority-inferiority patterns of races and cultures"
and the "white"-dominated power system were now in ruins. So sudden were
the changes that social scientists had been left stumbling blindly, "trying to
discern the new images, the new shapes and perspectives these changes have
brought, to adjust to the painful rearrangement of identities and relationships
which the new circumstances compel."[74]

One American political scientist was inclined to repeat a point made by
Alva Myrdal's husband Gunnar in the politically unpropitious year of 1938:
"'No one except in very thin intellectual strata, seems to have a working sentiment of identification with humanity or even western culture.'"[75] Isaacs's own
view was that matters of race and color (significantly, the terms were usually
interchangeable) were not any more important in world affairs than they had
been a generation earlier, "only the thrust and direction of their importance
have changed." The Chicago sociologist Edward Shils, previously the director
of UNESCO's "tensions" project, now emphasized the growth of modern society as the history of "attenuation and dispersion—with numerous relapses
into intensification and concentration"; "color" was the "major primordial
property" that had not yielded to such attenuation.[76] His sometime collaborator Talcott Parsons, professor of sociology at Harvard, similarly singled out
color as "the axis" of a new polarization of the world.[77]

In sight of these diagnoses of the international relevance of "color" was
the theatre of the UN, where, according to Harold Tinker, the changing profile of lead actors had made "startlingly clear" the impact of the national on
the international, and the importance of race in international conflict.[78] The
turning point, he explained, was in 1961, when "there were still 51 white
states, but the Afro-Asians totalled 53."[79] Like most of his peers, Tinker ana-
lyzed the transformations by color counting with attention to white and black
members of the UN, and without the early-twentieth-century obsession with
"yellow." In all these studies, Asian no longer connoted Japanese, or Chinese,
but rather the former colonial territories now named, "Afro-Asian." The West
Indian scholar Roy Preiswerk premised a color imbalance in international
relations whereby "the non-Whites of the world" "now hold the numerical
majority in the bodies of the world organisation."[80]

Preiswerk's not unreasonable analysis was that the cultural and psychological "revolution of the coloured people of the world," and "the transformation of a European-Christian-White dominated world into a pluralistic world—has not been understood or accepted in the centres of power": "The new nation-States [sic], representing difference races and religions, have been given legal equality, but no respect for their cultural and human identity."[81] The American scholar of Islam Bernard Lewis took a more cynical view of events: "The fashionable enemy in the West in our day is the racist, just as a few years back he was the communist."[82] It was an equivalence that in Lewis's eyes did no credit to the cause of antiracism.

The steadfast engagement of the UN with apartheid practices in South Africa led to that state's departure from UNESCO in 1957, with its membership of the World Health Organization, the Food and Agriculture Organization, and the International Labour Organization following suit. In 1971, the United States too stopped paying its dues to the ILO (an organization that was to a significant degree an American invention) for ideological reasons.[83] As we have seen, the race and political controversies of the Arab-Israeli war split the North and South even further. The UN General Assembly now invited the oppressed people of South Africa to take "guerrilla action," and gave observer status to the Palestinian Liberation Organization—even after the PLO had taken responsibility for the murder of Israeli Olympic athletes in "the Munich massacre." When the UN General Assembly targeted Israel as a supplier of arms to the South African regime, it brought the two issues too neatly together. The defiant culmination of this new internationalism was a 1975 General Assembly resolution declaring Zionism "a form of racism and racial discrimination."[84]

There is no doubt that that the problem of racism within member states and within the UN had become highly politicized. In 1974, the Australian Senate was concerned enough at the possible implications of this "colour imbalance" to establish an official inquiry into "The Role and Involvement of Australia and the United Nations in the Affairs of Sovereign Australian Territories."[85] In particular, conservative senators were wary that a newly elected Labour government keen to make national and international amends for race-based Australian citizenship and immigration policies might lead to UN intervention in the region. Would the UN be allowed to pry into the embarrassing circumstances of indentured labor in the Cocos Islands under Australian administration, or the conditions of indigenous populations in Australia's Northern Territory? Would the UN bolster any territorial claims by the newly independent Papua New Guinea, a former Australian mandate and trust territory, over islands in their neighborhood? The Senate inquiry took little comfort from the expert witness, Mr. Bulbeck, the vice president of the United Nations Association in Sydney (and formerly a journalist in New York covering UN affairs), who described a UN whose members shared "a very high regard for newly emerging nations, and it is a fact of life that most of the new members have been black since 1945."[86]

In the circumstances it was hard not to hear the strains of alienation in the speech made to the UN General Assembly in September 1974 by the U.S. president Gerald Ford (hurriedly sworn in to replace the disgraced Richard Nixon), strongly cautioning the member states not to succumb to the "tyranny of the majority."[87] For some of those listening, Ford's speech was the product of a range of factors that had heightened the U.S. sense of international vulnerability: the oil crisis, a disastrous war in Vietnam, the Watergate scandal, and the Soviet Union's ideological maneuvers around these issues, even in a period of relative Cold War détente. Canadian and British diplomats and international civil servants wryly observed that the General Assembly had ceased to be "the moral conscience of the world" only when the American government was no longer able to control its voting.[88] Daniel Moynihan, the twelfth U.S. ambassador to the United Nations (1975–76), was convinced that the General Assembly was the pawn of trumped up postcolonial rulers inculcated with social welfarism (he liked to blame the intellectual influence of the London School of Economics on the new generation of British-educated postcolonial leaders). Moynihan's own as famous verdict to the UN was that it had been reduced to a "theatre of the absurd."[89]

Moynihan had come to diplomatic life as a political scientist with a reputation in the emerging scholarly field of ethnicity studies. That reputation was fired in the heat of debates in America about assimilation and integration, which he directly addressed with his coauthor Nathan Glazer in *Beyond the Melting Pot* (1963), and in his own government report, *The Negro Family* (1965). Although Moynihan presented ethnicity as a positive feature of postwar American culture, his work attracted controversy for arguing that the dynamics of "negro" American families were as responsible for their disadvantaged situation as structural socio-economic factors. When, in the 1970s, Moynihan began to focus more intently on the force of ethnicity in the international affairs of the modern world, he changed his mind about its virtues. During his diplomatic tenure in India, he had observed the effects of the violent breakaway of Bangladesh from Pakistan. Elsewhere, the partitioning of Cyprus and rise of national secessionist movements in Tito's Yugoslavia suggested that no state was immune from the destructive influence of ethnic politics. As he headed for the UN to take up his new diplomatic appointment, he took time out to teach a special Harvard seminar, "Ethnicity in Politics." The following year, in the book *Ethnicity in Politics*, Moynihan reiterated the view that ethnicity was a social category as important as social class for understanding the world.[90] For Moynihan, ethnicity described and explained what he saw as the increasingly dangerous and dysfunctional celebration of "black-white confrontation" in national politics and at the UN.[91]

The political significance of Moynihan's ethnic logic is easier to understand if we compare his conclusions to those of the aging and ailing Ralph Bunche. In the mid-1960s, still in his role as the UN's under-secretary general, Bunche looked on from his Manhattan skyscraper office as the ghetto riots spread destruction across the cities of the United States. He mourned the failure of integration in his own country and reluctantly sympathized the turn taken by some African American men toward the identity politics of the Black Power Movement. After the assassination of Martin Luther King, Jr., Bunche retreated even further from national politics to the relative antiracism represented by the UN's international profile. He began to openly condemn the common ground shared in the United States by white segregationists and black separatists. Both of them, he claimed, "reject integration and demand separation of the races; both are racist in their approaches."[92] The chronically ill international civil servant eschewed brotherhood as "a misused, misleading term": "I used to make speeches about brotherhood but I never mention it any more. . . . What we need in this world is not brotherhood but coexistence. We need acceptance of the right of every person to his own dignity. There are a hell of a lot of people in the world, black and white, that I wouldn't want as distant cousins, much less as brothers."[93] Moynihan's analysis of "ethnicity" drew on a similar revulsion of identity politics. However, within a few years of Bunche's death, in the context of the shifting balance of symbolic power at the international level, Moynihan used his influence to draw the United States away from the UN.[94]

Ethnicity, like color and race, was the underside of the global momentum of the seventies. The essentialist rumblings had begun before Moynihan's arrival at the UN and represented a diversity of international forces. In 1971, the famous French anthropologist Claude Lévi-Strauss launched the International Year for Action to Combat Racism at UNESCO in Paris by arguing a natural human propensity to cultural xenophobia.[95] His claim came as a

surprise to those who associated him with UNESCO's original 1950 Statement on Race. Lévi-Strauss now lectured the UNESCO audience against a
wrong-headed emphasis on cultural knowledge, exchange, and toleration.
Racism, he maintained, was the inevitable product of overpopulation fed by
"civilizing" development or industrialization policies, and which led to new
tensions between groups for survival. These tensions were fueled by environmental factors, including competition for natural resources. When, two
years later, the Nobel Prize for Medicine was awarded to three ethologists
from Austria, Germany, and the United Kingdom, who argued on the basis
of their study of insects and animals that humans had a genetic inclination to
violence, the notion that race discrimination might be ended and permanent
peace pursued through General Assembly resolutions seemed quaint to say
the least.

Meanwhile, other observers from within the UN noted that the actions of
its General Assembly could not simply be explained by resort to race, color,
or ethnic makeup. The Non-Aligned Movement active through the UN, for
example, included not only Afro-Asian states but also Yugoslavia, Argentina,
and Uruguay, and, at a distance, Sweden. The Trinidad and Tobago diplomat Dumas was as harsh on his Third World diplomatic colleagues who, he
claimed, used the appellation "the people" to mask elite undemocratic interest, rather than race or color or ethnic solidarity.[96] The historian Vijay Prashad has since concurred that this was the period in which the distinctive
social and cosmopolitan agenda of the "Third World" was lost to those elite
interests.[97] In other words, the concepts of race and ethnicity, as much as
class, were being manipulated for other reasons, much as they had ever been.

As nationalist Third World leaders maneuvered through the UN, a new
theory of international relations took a different toll on the status of globalism and the UN. Hedley Bull's extremely influential study *The Anarchical
Society* (1977) claimed that the real vehicles of international society were
not international organizations such as the league or the UN, but rather the
Westphalian state and its international legal and diplomatic norms. In *The
Anarchical Society*, Bull traced the maintenance of "order as it exists in world
politics" "to institutions of international society that arose before these international organisations were established, and that would continue to operate
(albeit in a different mode) even if these organisations did not exist."[98] On
this version of the past, there was no new internationalism, and the UN was
not the culmination of a nineteenth-century *esprit d'internationalité* tradition
of international law, or a conferencing system that had led to the formation

of intergovernmental international institutions. Instead, Bull's version of international society separated out the strands of the history of a liberal internationalism that worked through the conventions of state diplomacy, and the salience of state sovereignty. The UN, by contrast, was overstudied and a "pseudo-institution."[99]

Bull, an Australian academic based at Oxford, showed little explicit interest in the politics of race or color or ethnicity. Still, the events at the UN made a substantial impression on his historical and theoretical accounting of international society. Since then his collaborator Adam Watson has explained that Bull was made particularly uneasy by the new status of the "Third World" as "subjects and not merely objects in the international political process," and of the UN as a forum for "universally valid standards of human rights, democracy, the position of women in society, the protection of the environment and so on." According to Watson, even as Bull supported these standards, he believed it had thrown off balance "the relationship of the newly independent non-white world to Western values and standards of civilisation."[100] This was despite the fact that, as Bull and Watson acknowledged at the time, the economic and military dominance of the industrialized powers of the northern hemisphere continued unabated.

It was no coincidence that *The Anarchical Society* appeared at the same time as the "shock of the global" was reverberating in and through the social sciences. At the epicenter of this shock was the question of "multiculturalism," or as Bull also phrased it "cosmopolitanism": What constituted the international when states with non-Western cultural values exerted international political influence? The Bolshevik Revolution and the Cold War may have had a role to play in a decline in the "consensus about common interests and values within the state system," but the contemporary challenge, Bull argued, was more about "cultural differences" than ideological opinions.[101]

A later essay, "The *State's Positive Role* in World Affairs," suggests that Bull was as concerned with the impact on the "sovereign state" of the new international institutions that were proliferating alongside the UN in defense of human rights or "humanitarian intervention," in the name of a "globalist doctrine" that was "the ideology of the dominant western powers."[102] This doctrine, Bull claimed, was espoused by the "Western globalist" who "does indeed express, among other things, an exuberant desire to reshape the world that is born of confidence that the economic and technological power to accomplish it lies at hand." That desire was fed by "a feeling of impatience that the political and legal obstacles ('ethnocentric nationalism,' 'the absurd political architecture of the world,' 'the obsolete doctrine of state sovereignty') cannot be brushed aside."[103]

This discussion of humanitarian organizations is worth considering for the picture it draws of competing versions of the nature and point of international society, including the pending (if always delayed) obsolescence of the nation-state, the problem of cultural relativism, and the clues offered by human nature. Bull now argued against humanitarian international institutions on the grounds that they derived "wholly from the liberal, social-democratic, and internationalist traditions of the West," and took no account "of the values entertained in other parts of the world, with which compromises may have to be reached," or of the salience of ethnicity and nationalism.[104] Internationalism and universalism were reduced to Western bogeys undermining the values of cultural pluralism. In this case, Bull's equation of universalism with Western omnipotence resonated the efforts by colonial powers, and then postcolonial governments, through the 1950s and 1960s, to challenge the relevance of an international human rights regime in their colonial territories. A similar critique would echo through later assessments of the new international human rights and humanitarian institutions that pointed to their origins in the North, and operations in the South.[105] In all these cases, asserting the significance of cultural relativism or imbalance came at the cost of a longer history of internationalism, in which colonial subjects and anticolonialists defended the universalism of social and economic and even human rights, and invested (literally) in development and international organizations such as the UN.

Bull's theory of the "true" international society as beneficially "anarchic" reinforced the view that the Westphalian state and the legal and diplomatic instruments of the nineteenth century formed a tradition of international politics separate from the "Western globalist" internationalism manifest in the League of Nations, and then the United Nations. His dismissal of the United Nations, and of the new internationalism that paved its path, was on par with a more general intellectual preference by the end of the 1970s, among liberal international relations theorists at least, for studying anything rather than the UN system. At Harvard, Bull's friend (and Moynihan's colleague), Stanley Hoffmann, was sympathetic toward the ambiguous role of the UN in this state-focused international system, both as "a significant factor in establishing a world order based on the nation-state" and at the same time perpetuating a view of "the drawbacks of sovereignty." But even Hoffmann observed that internationalism was no longer associated with the "idealism that originally pervaded, guided, and at times distorted the study of international organization."[106]

The world of theory has always taken its inspiration from the world of policy and practice.[107] Looking back onto this period, Joseph Nye, the theorist of transnationalism, argued that by the 1980s there was a marked "change in psychology and mood" that could also be measured in the resurgence of realist analyses of power and the central role of the state in international politics.[108] The revival of realist political theory left the study of the mutually reinforcing relationship between what was happening and how it was being observed and talked about to the field of cultural studies. That was the context in which an American literary scholar, Edward Said, arrived on the international scene.

In 1978, Said published *Orientalism*, an account of the influence on international politics of cultural caricatures (or "fictions") of difference—specifically Western perceptions of Islam, the Arab world, and the East. Said explained that these fictions were cultivated in Western scholarship and disseminated through the hegemonic power of the Western media. His idea that conceptions of race and civilizational difference exerted substantial political influence in international affairs went back to Du Bois's depiction of a color line at the beginning of the century. In the early 1970s, this understanding of the relationship between culture and power inspired the UNESCO plan for a New International Information Order (NIIO) as the partner to the New International Economic Order. The NIIO was promoted by UNESCO as a corrective to the hegemony of Western media reporting of non-Western places and people, countering the race stereotyping that dominated representations of Islam and the Arab world in particular.[109] We can also hear the equation of culture and power in Dumas warning that events at the UN, including Moynihan's attack on the General Assembly, were being determined by "perceptions" of cultural differences and the past.

Nor was Said an impartial observer. A Palestinian exile with a Harvard Ph.D. in English literature and a tenured member of the English department at Columbia University, Said belonged to the Palestinian National Council at a time when Middle Eastern politics dominated the General Assembly's rhetorical and quasi-legal interventions on race discrimination. Yet his academic argument was convincing. It elaborated the extent of scholarly complicity in the production of knowledge about an Orientalized Arab Other reinforced in the context of the long history of Western imperialism. It would take a few decades for Said's theory to trickle through to the thinking of international relations scholars, but *Orientalism* made it impossible to ignore the power that could be exerted in international as much as national politics by reference to stereotypes of Arab, or Islam, or Eastern (and eventually Balkan) "Others." As important, Said's theory focused attention on the ways in which bodies of knowledge about differences (whether race or color or civilizational) were accumulated and deployed rather than the differences themselves. Read through the cultural precepts of *Orientalism*, the UN had become a battleground of competing representations of difference and ways of thinking about the relevance of difference to international politics, as well as about the relevance of the international past. As the UN had become more globally representative, its more representative fora were used to launch broad challenges to the imbalances of the existing cultural and economic international order. Paradoxically, the UN had also provided its newest state members with the opportunities for reasserting the rights and authority of nations over the claims of globalism.

If there was one episode that captured the paradox, and pathos, of the UN's situation, it was the General Assembly's "Agreement Governing the Activities of States on the Moon and Other Celestial Bodies," passed in the last days of the seventies without a vote. This agreement rendered the moon and its natural resources "the common heritage of mankind," and advocated "the creation of an international regime to govern the exploitation of the moon's natural resources not subject to national appropriation by any claim of sovereignty."[110] By this time, back on earth, the international significance of the North-South divide had temporarily receded as East-West antagonisms reignited. Entente was over, defense budgets were on the increase, and the two superpowers were stockpiling their nuclear arsenals.

Postinternationalism

When the extraordinary spectacle of the popular breaches of the Berlin Wall in 1989 brought a sudden end to the Cold War, as well as to the Soviet Union, it took with it any remaining traces of the class-based revolutionary internationalism that had sprung up in the mid-nineteenth century around the Communist Manifesto. The twentieth century had come to a close on an unexpected note of millenarian optimism and avowedly liberal internationalism. Nuclear war had been avoided (although the arsenal remained), and the prospects for being internationally minded had radically altered. A new Europe without borders was accompanied by the prophesy of the "end of history," that is, the resolution of the story of ideological struggle between capitalism and communism. The promise of a new era of permanent, possibly even boring, peace was in the air. Social scientists invented a new vocabulary to match the more optimistic mood. This time "postinternationalism" was to reflect the reality in which "more and more of the interactions that sustain world politics unfold without the direct involvement of nations and states."[111] The postinternationalism diagnosis was made in 1990, by James Rosenau, a political scientist who found himself on the liberal or idealist side of the divide that constitutes the study of international politics.[112]

There were though unavoidable and worrying signs that the end of the Cold War might have inaugurated a fourth age of nationalism (after 1815, 1919, and 1945), an inferno of violence, and some claimed genocide, sparked by the political destabilization of the Soviet Union and Yugoslavia, but as pronounced in the African continent, most notoriously Rwanda. Between 1991 and 1993, there was an eightfold increase in the number of UN peacekeeping troops and a fourfold increase in the UN's peacekeeping budget, as the UN stepped up to its remit for "crisis prevention, peace enforcement and the idea of humanitarian intervention in an on-going conflict."[113] The UN Security Council provided "safe areas" to protect the Kurds of northern Iraq and the Muslims of Bosnia. In Somalia the UN assumed responsibility for the deployment of forces under the authority of the Security Council in order to make peace-keeping possible. In Kosovo, the UN Security Council even gave retrospective backing for NATO's intervention in the conflict between Kosovar Albanians and Serbia.

The evidence of events was ambiguous enough to inspire some intellectuals to focus on the "unfreezing" of "the germs of European nationalism," while others pointed to the revival of an older tradition of liberal internationalism, with roots in the eighteenth century and an accent on the security of the individual rather than the state.[114] The diagnosis of "postnationalism" found support in studies that highlighted the new legitimacy of international intervention on humanitarian rationales.[115] The almost serial evidence of multilateral humanitarian interventions under the UN's auspices and the creation of UN-sanctioned International Criminal Tribunals to punish crimes against humanity and genocide in Yugoslavia (1993) and Rwanda (1994) were taken as signs of a new international solidarity among the UN member states. It was as if the end of the Cold War had inaugurated a new "solidarist" conception of international society that implied the natural and necessary solidarity of states. Solidarism, an idea that spoke to the influence of Léon Bourgeois and the internationality of the early twentieth-century international turn, lent moral authority to the legitimacy of international intervention in cases where the rights and lives of individuals were threatened by their own governments.[116]

Cosmopolitanism also returned, as the descriptor of a new kind of "international democracy" consciously evocative of Immanuel Kant's proposals for permanent peace, inviting reform of the UN, but favoring new international political and legal procedures over an emphasis on structural political power.[117] The creation of the International Criminal Court (1998), with its seat at The Hague, seemed to reinforce the continuous progress of international law and its conceptual relevance as a body of legal precepts and principles beyond the bias of state interests, except that the United States was among the more than seventy states that refused to recognize its authority.

Not everyone read the significance of the international conscientiousness of the 1990s in the same way. Some blamed the delay in international intervention in the war in Yugoslavia on prevalent Orientalist perceptions of the "Balkans."[118] The historian Jonathan Haslam has unsparingly documented how the Harvard political scientist Stanley Hoffmann reentered the fray in the 1990s in support of unilateral humanitarianism (later this approach was labeled "progressive internationalism"). Hoffmann urged the United States to go it alone "on moral grounds almost anywhere, regardless of security or material interests." As the remaining superpower, the United States did not have to wait for multilateral agreement.[119] Instead, it was obliged to act unilaterally in cases where human rights abuses, genocide, or ethnic cleansing were at stake because the UN could not be counted on to act. Haslam heard in Hoffmann's argument for American unilateralism historical echoes of late nineteenth-century British imperial folly.[120] But he did not have to look so far afield for these late nineteenth-century resonances. In 1999, British prime minister Tony Blair invoked the "Doctrine of the International Community" in front of an American audience at the Chicago Economic Club in order to urge the necessity of unilateral international intervention, and offering as his example British policy in Sierra Leone, where "democracy-building" was at stake.[121]

In hindsight, it is hard not to hear the paradoxical timbre of twentieth-century internationalism in the 1990s language of "postinternationalism," including the staying cultural power of empires and nations, much as Said had described them. By contrast, the term "human security" that came into common political parlance in this same period hearkened back to the well-rehearsed traditions of earlier twentieth-century internationalism, invested in social and economic prevention rather than military cures.

Human security was coined in the precincts of the UN's Development Program, during preparations for the fiftieth anniversary of the UN, and as part of a concerted effort to resuscitate the organization's relevance to the new plausibility of international solidarism. It came packaged in the seventies language of "sustainable human development" and presented as both a "complement" to state security and a basis for international intervention when the state was the culprit or lacked the means to protect its citizens.[122] Although the kinds of intervention it espoused were not military, they were fundamentally invasive of nation-state sovereignty. In conjunction with the rhetorical promulgations of a new World Social Charter, the UN conception of human security extended to the need for *international* minimum living standards. This would be achieved through programs supporting universal basic education, fair-trade markets to benefit the extreme poor, and universal access to basic health care by making generic medicines more affordable through the development of an efficient and equitable global system for patent rights.[123] On this economic social justice version of security, prioritizing health and education would equate to less risk of violence and conflict. The rationale was as familiar: the reality of the world's increasing "interdependence" witnessed in the challenges of environment, poverty, and conflict, the larger burden of which seemed to fall on women.[124]

These themes were reinforced in the companion concept of "responsibility to protect," formulated at the turn of the twenty-first century on the initiative of a Canadian government-sponsored independent inquiry, the "International Commission on Intervention and State Sovereignty." It held that "under certain circumstances, . . . state sovereignty could be set aside for the good of 'humanity.' "[125] Responsibility to protect (usually referred to as the acronym "R2P") constituted a more direct response to the contemporary challenges of genocide, ethnic cleansing, and war crimes. In 2004, the United Nations Office for the Coordination of Humanitarian Affairs (established in 1991) created a further bureaucratic node, the Human Security Unit. Its role was to resuscitate an interventionist conception of human rights and the relevance of an "international community" as a "value added" activity.[126]

For those who know their international history, internationalism has throughout the twentieth century been entangled in the strands of state- and individual-centered rights, and political, cultural, social, and economic methods. The conceptual roots of human security lay in specific moments of twentieth-century internationalism, when the prevailing view of political realism leaned toward internationality and being internationally minded. Even though there was little reference to the past in the presentation of human security, its tagline, "freedom from fear and freedom from want" rehearsed the words made famous in 1941 by Franklin D. Roosevelt as he convinced the U.S. Congress that it was time for the United States to intervene in the war on the principles of the "four freedoms" (the other two, freedom of speech and freedom of religion, were borrowed from the American Declaration of Independence).[127] These freedoms framed the 1941 Atlantic Charter and, consequently, defined the Allied cause; later, their significance and meaning were fought over in the drafting of the UN Charter and the Universal Declaration of Human Rights.

A traditional conception of the international domain of the league and the UN found its way into the long list of international human security priorities: the prevention of human trafficking (white slave traffic under the league), arms control and outlawing land mines (once disarmament), and upholding the jurisdiction of international law in international criminal courts (the old courts of international arbitration and justice). The key objectives of human security were normatively the protection and empowerment of those groups left the most vulnerable in the dominant nation-states system: the stateless and refugees, women and children, the subjects of discrimination. These same constituencies had been the drivers of the social portfolios of the league (the Social Questions bureau) and the UN (its refugee relief programs and more generally the activities of its Economic and Social Council). Similar ideas had percolated through aspirations for economic democracy in the 1920s and 1930s, including John Hobson's critique of the league's failures to implement the efficient distribution of the world's resources and wealth "assigned to the cultivation of the inhabitants of the various countries, according to their capacities, and supplemented where necessary by suitable drafts from other countries."[128] In the 1940s and 1950s, Alva Myrdal understood economic parity for women as well as colonial subjects as fundamental to peace and human rights. She had placed her faith in rationality and science, and in programs that measured quality of life outcomes rather than GDP. Despite the differences in methodology, her views on the significance of the "human" approach to development, and the internationalization of social justice norms in living standards, were uncannily akin to the priorities captured in human security and even its language.[129]

In the age of human security, economic parity through opportunity was tied more closely to the point of collective security rather than social justice itself. It was also premised on a new conception of the social roots of internationalism. Despite the lack of memory regarding these earlier endeavors, human security's UN architects presented the new concept as the antithesis of earlier top-down UN programs such as 1940s "Technical Assistance" or "Fundamental Education." Human security would work through the encouragement of simultaneously global *and* national efforts to empower people. Empowerment was a term that returned again and again, attaching to the particular status of women as well as sex-unspecified victims of conflict and poverty.[130]

In similar ways, the prospect of international intervention on the grounds of the security of the individual (R2P), along with the protection of individual rights, quietly reached back to the international aspirations abandoned in the constitution of the UN, and again in the seventies moment of global community. We might remember, for example, that the protection of the individual against state abuses and the rights of the refugee was on René Cassin's mind when he angled for *droits de l'homme* as the principle on which international intervention could be legally justified, and individuals might be granted representation on the Human Rights Commission, and the commission might be enabled to take direct action. Cassin had, in turn, honed those ideas in the interwar period in the social spaces of the International Federation of League of Nations Associations.

The critics of human security struck as familiar chords as the concept itself: human security presented a "conceptual overstretch," it lacked roots in any established tradition of realist political thought—at the forefront of which sat the state. On this view, there were two kinds of security, the hard or traditional security issues that were focused on the state, the human or soft security that enfolded in its definition issues of human rights and development. The overwhelming view was that "policy gains in the human security realm" were recent, from "the land mines convention, the International Criminal Court," to "the various international interventions to stem massive abuses, and the development of a range of human rights and humanitarian norms, especially the responsibility to protect."[131]

These thematic repetitions and rehearsals in both the embrace of internationalism and its critiques raise a number of important questions about how we understand the past, as progress or as change, and how we think about the twentieth century. Throughout the twentieth century, the pundits of internationalism negotiated the rights and role of the state, the pertinence of the nation, and the relative efficiency of empires. Their versions of twentieth-century internationalism, particularly those invested in sociological definitions of internationalism, and the political form of international government, were self-consciously "realist." "Real internationalism," as it was sometimes termed in the early twentieth century, or the "adult internationalism" of the UNESCO teachers gathered on Long Island in the summer of 1948, implied working with the state *and* understanding the political and economic limits of state sovereignty in a world where everyday life was shaped by the objective facts of internationality as much as nationality. Internationalism included economic and social programs because of this same sociological truth, and because political progress measured through the concepts of liberty and equality were understood as international as much as national goals.

The history of internationalism in the twentieth century is not a history of utopianism, but rather of the fine gradations of idealism that took on the urgency of political realism at specific moments of despair and illumination. What changed over the course of the twentieth century was the realist weight given to specific aspects of internationalism, what could count as realistic or not, particularly in relation to the relative realism of states, and states as nations. In 1951, Stephen Spender, an erstwhile "Unescan," recollected that after World War I, there were great expectations of the League of Nations, but few people were "prepared to abandon national sovereignty." By comparison, at the end of World War II, "a great many everywhere are prepared to sacrifice a great deal of nationhood and possessions which they formerly clung to, but they do not believe in the United Nations. The most important condition of change—a widespread realism—has been achieved."[132] Human security can be understood as a renewal of the invitation to an internationally constituted audience to reflect on the realist relevance of international organizations, international laws, universal rights, and state sovereignty, in the midst of general ignorance and mistrust of the UN itself.

The window that opened onto a humanitarian accented internationalism in the 1990s, and the millennial moment of post–Cold War optimism, as quickly closed at the turn of the twenty-first century. In 2001, a new global war on terror briefly united an "international community," then almost immediately fractured it along cultural fault lines reminiscent of the Cold War.[133] In 2002, the United States had effectively withdrawn from the UN, in order to enable it to meet the threat of international terrorism unilaterally. The descent of international politics into a civilizational struggle between Christianity and Islam brought an end, temporary or otherwise, to anything but the most superficial forms of multilateralism.

In 2003, a critically ill Edward Said revised the preface to *Orientalism*, singling out the ongoing relevance of his argument. This time a neo-Orientalist "imperialist war" had been confected "by a small group of unelected US officials and waged against a devastated Third World dictatorship on thoroughly ideological grounds having to do with world dominance, security control, and scarce resources, but disguised for its true intent, hastened, and reasoned for by Orientalists who betrayed their calling as scholars."[134] Said had in his sights, once again, Bernard Lewis, the historian whose dismissive response to the antiracism themes of the UN had given authority to Moynihan's own account of the UN as a "theatre of the absurd." From Said's perspective, Lewis had returned as an expert tilting the balance toward the demonization of Arabs. The only space of hope Said could find in the events unfolding around him was the United Nations World Summit on Sustainable Development in Johannesburg (a week before the 9/11 acts of terrorism on American soil). This gathering, he claimed, was evidence of really existing global interdependence, "a vast area of common global concern that suggests the welcome emergence of a new collective constituency that gives the often facile notion of 'one world' a new urgency."[135]

For the international lawyer **Martti Koskenniemi**, however, writing around the same time, twentieth-century-style internationalism had in its essence already disappeared. Since the 1970s, he argued, international law no longer addressed ideals "such as the eradication of poverty." Instead, "the vision of a single social space of 'the international'" had been replaced by "a fragmented or kaleidoscopic understanding of the world where the new configuration of space and time have completely mixed up what is particular and what is universal."[136]

Emma Rothschild has painted a more nuanced picture of internationalism at the turn of the twenty-first century, framed by the continued operations of an intrinsically vulnerable UN. **Rothschild concludes that "the UN and its constituent entities"** are "profoundly virtual—the most purely places of images, words, and precedents."[137] She offers that the relative success of words such as "sustainable development," "common security," and "the Human Development Report" is the result of the UN's so-called "'soft agendas,' including the United Nations Environment Program and the Stockholm Conference of 1972."[138] On Rothschild's accounting, even though the unilateral decision by the U.S. to invade Iraq in 2003 was taken as a sign of the UN's decline, the UN's legitimacy was in fact widely discussed and sustained in "public information about the law, in innumerable reports and series and digests."

She takes as evidence the French foreign minister Dominique de Villepin's reference, in the context of 2003, to the UN as "the place where international rules and legitimacy were founded."[139]

In the post-9/11 twenty-first century, it is as difficult to find scholarly or popular agreement on not only the UN, but also how the world we live in should be described, the extent of its globalization, whether it is more or less international, or even "postinternational." On the one hand, socially based international movements such as world federalism have lost their intellectual or social cachet. On the other hand, since the beginning of the new century, there has been a sustained revival of scholarly interest in humanitarian- ism, and in the history of international organizations. Even cosmopolitan- ism has returned as a term with some traction in the world of scholarship, drawing students of transnationalism beyond the boundaries of states, and toward counternarratives of the status of international imaginaries. The phi- losopher Jeremy Waldron's neat summation of cosmopolitanism as either "a way of being in the world, a way of constructing an identity for oneself that is different from . . . the idea of belonging to or devotion to or immersion in a particular culture," or "the substantive utopian ideal of a *polis* or polity constructed on a world scale, rather than on the basis of regional, territori- ally limited states," unintentionally sings to the forgotten refrains of "being internationally-minded."[140] And like the mid-twentieth-century accommo- dation of internationalism, cosmopolitanism is regularly validated through comparisons between good and bad versions. Descriptions of a good cosmo- politanism are still firmly anchored in the local and the national.[141]

One hundred years after the earliest predictions of a twentieth-century internationality, and more than half a century after the apogee of interna- tionalism, political, scholarly, and popular understanding of what is more or less possible, or realist, has significantly changed, even since the end of the Cold War. The UN continues its operations in peacemaking as well as peace- keeping and nation building; international lawyers continue to ponder the benefits and bases of international law, now of the environment as much as war crimes; nonstate actors increasingly occupy the spaces of transnational agitation (even though, as Jeremy Suri has pointed out, organizations such as al-Qaeda use international networks to enact terrorism);[142] and historians turn their attention to the traces of a world that went missing. But the kind of international organization that was central to the imagining of twentieth- century visions of international community is increasingly sidelined in the face of imposing world-scale environmental and economic challenges, in favor of nation-state-specific responses. Most fundamentally, the grand expectations of an epochal shift—whether the notion that familiarity (at the level of family, tribe, nation, or the international) breeds solidarity, or that humanity is progressing into ever-widening concentric circles of association, or that internationality is as realistic as nationality for determining political and social communities—are difficult to conjure. They sound more like extant voices from a foreign country, a place where they do things quite differently. If we are to believe Eric Hobsbawm, the very fact that historians are beginning to make some progress in the study and analysis of internationalism suggests that the phenomenon is past its peak. "The owl of Minerva which brings wisdom, said Hegel, flies out at dusk."[143]

Afterword

The National in the Age of Internationalism

Historians understand more than anyone else that there is no progress in history and no utopia in the past. But it is useful at times in trying to understand where we are, the world we live in, to come to some understanding of the world that we have lost. That world, I have been trying to argue, was one in which internationalism was an idea underwritten by an older story that imagined the march of humanity into ever-widening circles of association, nations as a historical pit stop on the way to somewhere else, and modernity and democracy as the engines and outcomes of this inevitable forward movement. It was the combination of those expectations in the context of a century darkened with threats of man-made destruction that, in the twentieth century, made the international as inexorable an imagined community as the nation.

Despite predictions that in the twentieth century the role of nationality as the driver of modernity and progress would be overtaken by internationality—as if the formation of an international community were the next stage in the social and political evolution of humanity—the national and international remained entwined as ways of thinking about the self and society, about the borders (and point) of political communities and government, and about liberty and equality. The story of that entanglement has not always been easy to tell, partly because internationalism, regardless of its content, has been tainted as utopian in ways that nationalism, regardless of its content, has not.

Bolstered by the political realism of the state, and the potency of state sovereignty, modern historical attention has attended to the unrelenting question "What is a nation?" and narrating national pasts to the neglect of internationalism. It did not help that when the history of internationalism was first broached, after World War I, like the history of pacifism and, later, human rights, it tended to be written as a history of political idealism above and be-yond the cynical practices of nation-states. In the 1950s, Theodore Ruyssen, who was by this time approaching ninety, put himself to the task of continu-ing the historical work begun by Christian Lange (Lange had only completed the first volume of his history of internationalism, which ended in the eigh-teenth century). The result was first *La Societé internationale*, which in effect concentrated on the conditions of internationality, described by Ruyssen as the "powerful movement" of his times that had brought nations into a com-mon field of cultural, economic, and political life. This was followed with *Les sources doctrinales de l'internationalisme*, a complementary study of the intel-lectual origins of internationalism and its sources in "Western civilization." Ruyssen projected a tradition of international thought backward through nineteenth-century international abolition, peace, and working-class move-ments to the ancient world, and then forward to the cultural politics of the new age. The propagator of internationalism's *mystique* argued that this his-tory proved that internationalism was an essentially Western phenomenon, by virtue of its modern manifestations, its basis in Christian universalist thought, and its practical spread through the expansive force of Christian missionaries and Western empires.[1]

Ruyssen's version of the history of internationalism competed of course with that of Cassin—who went to great trouble to emphasize both the in-trinsic Frenchness and Judaic attributes of human rights thinking—and Peng Chun-Chang—who attributed this "Western" tradition to the influence of Confucius. Ruyssen was also fighting against the disinterest of academic historians who ignored twentieth-century manifestations of international-ism on the grounds either that internationalism was irrelevant to the study of real (national) societies and even more powerful psychological (national) subjectivities, or that internationalism was a nineteenth century class-based political phenomenon that transformed into the international communist movement and antagonistic to liberal nationalism.

With the end of the Cold War, however, the balance of historical interest tilted increasingly in favor of the plausibility of an international past, and an "international turn" in the historical profession. This turn began with the cul-tural history of nonnational experience explored through the methodology of transnationalism and examples drawn from the geography of empires or the movement across national borders. As international intervention once again dominated discussion of international politics, historians became attracted to the study of humanitarianism and human rights, and more belatedly to international organizations as significant transnational sites. The new historical interest in the transnational and global has provided a congenial setting for historians, like myself, curious to understand the modern significance of the international as a political idea, international organizations as political spaces, and internationalism as an ideology that overlapped and intersected with, even as it ran counter to, the history of nations and nationalism.

The international turn in History has so far led to two dominant ways of thinking about the international past, particularly where the league and the UN are concerned: as evidence of a progressively accumulating actually existing cultural internationalism built out of the kind of "international living" that the teachers gathered under UNESCO auspices were intended to experience in 1948; or as proof of the tenacious hold of liberal imperialism, whereby internationalism replicated the race-based civilizational thinking that had girded the colonialism of the later nineteenth century.[2] The historical sources support both of these arguments. They also illustrate that internationalism cannot simply be reduced to either a more positive story of cumulative cultural progress or a purely cynical tale of imperial intentions, not if we take into account generational shifts in thinking about the purpose of internationalism and international institutions, or the voices of actors differently situated in the dominant national and imperial political communities, or the extent of political investment in institutional, "real," "objective" internationalism. Ultimately the history of internationalism travels along a characteristic narrative line from utopia to disillusionment, but no more than the tales that can be told of imagined national communities.

By contrast, historians of nationalism have kept themselves relatively aloof from the twenty-first-century international turn in historical scholarship. They rarely ask the question "What is the international?" If they did they might discover telling theoretical inconsistencies in the still predominating historical answers to the question "What is a nation?" These are inconsistencies that not only are pertinent to the historian's work but also beg other questions about the purpose of History and its power. My examples return us to the 1980s, a decade in which the historical study of nationalism suddenly took off, after a slow start in the ethnonational theories of the 1970s, and with a sharp turn in the direction of antiessentialist constructivism.[3] From the perspective of the history of twentieth-century internationalism, the historiography of imagined national communities and invented national traditions is fascinating because, first, it was attended by a self-conscious reduction of internationalism to the nineteenth-century story of Marxism, and, second, it unwittingly reprised the sociological theses of the early twentieth-century international turn, but now, as we will see, as the explanation for nationalism.

In 1983, the Southeast Asian scholar Benedict Anderson published *Imagined Communities: Reflections on the Origin and Spread of Nationalism*, perhaps still the most influential English-language historical account of nationalism. His argument has become so familiar that its title alone regularly stands in for the idea that nations are modern inventions, rather than the political artifacts of primordial communities. In *Imagined Communities*, Anderson accepted the view that nations exuded a "profound emotional legitimacy" and attributed their emotional hold to the impact of commerce and technology. Print capitalism, he proposed, had "made it possible for rapidly growing numbers of people to think about themselves, and to relate themselves to others, in profoundly new ways."[4]

The argument of *Imagined Communities* transferred the analysis of nationalism away from primal ethnic urges and onto the sociological settings in which subjective national identifications and imagined communities had come to the political fore since the nineteenth century. At the core of this history was the nineteenth-century "philological-lexicographic revolution," which had made print culture available to a wider group of individuals. The specific forms of that print culture were the novel and newspaper; their narratives, he argued, had inculcated a newly literate mass of readers with the experience of homogenous empty time or "simultaneity."[5] This meant that "the members of even the smallest nation will never know most of their fellow-members, meet them, or even hear of them, yet in the minds of each lives the image of their communion."[6] Reflecting on whether the same reading technologies might have made it possible to imagine larger as well as smaller communities than the nation, Anderson concluded that "the fatal diversity of human language" made the nation the most likely object of this social imaginary.[7] Language was crucial to this account of the social and cultural effects of the print revolution because it allowed for the more intimate origins of nationalism in patriotism, which Anderson understood as the inspiration of love through a maternal tongue: "Through that language, encountered at mother's knee and parted with only at the grave, pasts are restored, fellowships are imagined, and futures dreamed."[8] In *Imagined Communities*, national patriotism could also be a learned form of emotional subjectivity passed on through the family—much as the nineteenth-century proponents of linguistic nationalism Mazzini and Michelet had theorized.[9]

Imagined Communities was the product of Anderson's desire to understand the violent and authoritarian progress of nationalist politics in postcolonial Indonesia. Possibly because of that same Indonesian context, the internationalism Anderson did discuss was class focused and Marxist in origin.[10] When it came to the League of *Nations* (Anderson's italics) "from which non-Europeans were not excluded," internationalism was still not relevant since the league was exclusively the epitome of the new age of nationalism.[11] It was an institution to which, tellingly, even imperial powers came dressed in national costumes rather than imperial uniforms, and Anderson regarded it pointedly as part of the history of nationalism, rather than internationalism.

Eric Hobsbawm's slightly later classic *Nations and Nationalism since 1780* (based on lectures given in 1985) drew in a more partisan antinationalist reader—although Hobsbawm, like Anderson, did not bother with an index entry for "international."[12] Born to Jewish parents in Vienna at the eclipse of the Habsburg Empire, Hobsbawm wrote a history more attuned to the alternative conceptions of political community in the early twentieth century. His analysis of the cultural origins of nations and nationalism was also threaded with the muted traces of an underdeveloped story of internationalism. Hobsbawm tracked the late-nineteenth-century standardization of languages that contributed to the invention of national identities and the coinciding deployment of the universal "languages" of international telegraphic and signaling codes and attempts to "construct artificial world languages" from national "dialects." He also noted the international pretensions of the liberal ideology of "liberty and fraternity."[13] Nations were "part of liberal ideology," as Hobsbawm described, "because the development of nations was unquestionably a phase in human evolution or progress from the small group to the larger, from family to tribe to region, to nation and, in the last instance, to the unified world of the future in which, to quote the superficial and therefore typical G. Lowes Dickinson, 'the barriers of nationality which belong to the infancy of the race will melt and dissolve in the sunshine of science and art.'"

Despites these examples of their intersecting histories, in *Nations and Nationalism*, as in *Imagined Communities*, internationalism remained the story of Marxism, separate from the story of nationalism, and with its heyday either in the nineteenth century or in the Cold War context of decolonization, and nothing in between. Anderson linked the failure of Marxism to the limited capacity for imagining an international community and gave no place to the historical overlap of nations and the social and political investment by progressive (and conservative) liberals, and by the world's marginalized in international institutions, law and sociability characteristic of the international

turn earlier in the twentieth century.[14] In Hobsbawm's narrative, internationalism entered the main arena of political life only in the late twentieth century, as the context for "nation-building out of the fragments of post-colonial
territories."[15]

These constructivist explorations of nations as invented or imagined
hardly glanced sideways at how over the same period international communities were imagined in relation to national communities. Yet if we read them
in the context of the *longue durée* history of twentieth-century internationalism, regardless of the intentions of their authors, these histories illustrate the
historical overlap between imagined national and international communities.
Anderson and Hobsbawm's analyses of the mechanics of nationalism take on
an uncanny resemblance to the mechanics of internationalism emphasized
by witnesses to an early twentieth-century communications revolution.[16] This
is how, in 1906, John Hobson invoked the concept of *simultaneity* to describe
the possibility of internationalism and internationality built out of the society
of nations:

> The greatest thing which has happened within the last two genera-
> tions has been the practical enlargement of the world for all members
> of civilized communities. Everyone today as we say familiarly, lives at
> the end of a telegraph line, which means not merely that all the great
> and significant happenings in the world are brought to his attention in
> a way which was impossible a generation or two ago, but that they are
> brought at once and *simultaneously* to the attention of great masses
> of people, so that anything happening in the most remote part of the
> world makes its immediate impression upon the society of nations.[17]

Hobson repeatedly used variations of the same concept, describing "the immediate and *simultaneous* sympathy" aroused by new ways of communicat-
ing and traveling, and the "new element of sociality" it introduced into the
world, at least for "the mass of civilized mankind":

> You can book a passage by rail or sea in London or New York for any
> point in the civilized or uncivilized known world. You can transmit
> money from Philadelphia to any part of the civilized world, surely,
> securely, quickly and easily. We can read books, either in foreign
> languages—if we know them—or in translations, books, which put
> us in direct communication with the thoughts and feelings of distant

peoples. Many of us have friendships which bind us closely to members of various nations of the world.

These narratives of internationalism share with the constructivist historiography of the nation the concept of simultaneity; the new internationalism
was imagined as nationalism writ large.[18] In the early twentieth century, both
phenomena were understood to be the result of available technologies and
experiences that linked individuals and communities across expanses of land
and sea. The international mind and international man self-consciously com-
plemented scientized theories of national patriotism and national consciousness. We might remember that on the eve of World War I, Jean Claveirole, the
enthusiastic French law student, listed a similar set of seemingly miraculous
developments in internationality enabled by communication technologies,
and the new opportunities for travel within reach of the middle classes. He
also explained that these mechanisms of simultaneity and sociability emu-
lated the processes that had created nations, now on an international scale,
inventing and consolidating a consciousness of humanity.[19]

Across the twentieth century, invocations of nations and the international,
theories and histories of nationalism and internationalism, have turned on
the expectation that once political institutions were created, the relevant respective forms of social consciousness would take hold. Take, for example,
the making of the Italian nation-state. It is widely acknowledged that when
Italy was politically "unified" in 1860, its political elite accepted it was still
necessary to create an Italian identity (captured in the comment *Abbiamo
fatto l'Italia ora dobbiamo fare gli italiani*), rather than the other way around.
Modernist scholars of nations and nationalism (not only students of Italy)
acknowledge the controversies at their heart, including the question of what
comes first, the political nation or the cultural nation, the nation-state or the
desire to belong to and identify with the nation-state. Historians of nations
and nationalism are also able to maintain a double focus on the study of the
success *and* failure of nations as states or social movements, on what is popularly forgotten as well as what is remembered. But historians rarely extend
the same grace to the study of international subjectivities or international
imaginaries in nineteenth- or twentieth-century history, despite the existence
of the League of Nations, the United Nations, and innumerable movements
and stratagems for rethinking democracy, sovereignty, identity, and governmental internationalism.[20]

In the current historiographical segregation of the histories of nationalism and internationalism, there is no space for reflecting on early twentieth-century perceptions of national communities as less sociologically and economically realistic than the idea of an international community, even when both kinds of communities have been portrayed by their analysts as fictions. In 1916, Leonard Woolf thought the more you looked at nations the more you saw the interests of a specific elite represented, not "the people." Ellen Key regarded nationalism as more utopian than internationalism, in the sense of the unrealistic expectations of community it aroused.[21] At the other end of the century, in 1970, Stanley Hoffmann ventured a different take on the existence of the "fiction of a world community" based on "an image of the world that was at least as far removed from reality as had been the image of the original UN."[22] Hoffmann argued that this "image of a fictitious world community able and willing to make of the UN a force that would represent and expand the common interest of mankind" was precisely what had made it possible for "the organs of the United Nations to concern themselves with most of the important political and economic issues that agitate the international system." Bringing us back full circle to the 1980s, Said's *Orientalism* provoked his readers to reflect on the cultural power exerted by fictions of race and civilization on the UN's capacity to sustain its own fiction of a world community.

For the historian, or anyone who wants to remember the past, the challenge is quite specific: if, as Anderson argued, "communities are to be distinguished, not by their falsity/genuineness, but by the style in which they are imagined," then it is as relevant to ask, as individuals pondering internationality did throughout the twentieth century, what has been the place of internationally imagined communities in the intersecting and overlapping history of nationally imagined communities?

The point of juxtaposing descriptions of the sociological origins of internationalism and nationalism is not to argue that they cancel each other out, or that we have traveled from the international to the national and abandoned the international at the sound of the century's first bugle call to war. Rather, it is to illustrate that the history of internationalism maps profoundly onto the genealogy of nations and nationalism, that in the twentieth century the international and national shadowed each other as the object or method of political ambitions. Both histories are evidence of, and evidenced by, the cohort of women and men who often imagined their necessary and utilitarian complementarity. Early twentieth-century theorists of the sociological and therefore historical bases of internationalism such as Claveirole not only made the international crucial to the conceptualization of nations—their origins and purpose—but also to the sociological and historical explanations of the nation, at a time when determinist biological and psychological national imaginaries were on the ascendant. From our perspective, these intersections are also a useful reminder that, for better as well as worse, twentieth-century internationalism, like the UN, was composed out of a complicity as much as compatibility with nationalism.

A history of the twentieth century that takes into account the long past of international imagining and invention also has repercussions for other intersecting historiographies of development, democracy, liberalism, or human rights. In new histories of the UN, the organization is often the sum of liberal imperialism. In new histories of human rights, the 1970s are in effect the origins of human rights because, the argument runs, that was when the message and organization of human rights began to exhibit a social base, and began to be conceptualized in ways that fundamentally challenged the rights of states.[23] These narratives make little space for the social dimensions of internationalism, or for its returning significance as the focus of claim-making among the disenfranchised of nations and empires. They ignore the voices of the teachers reporting on UNESCO's efforts who maintained that internationalism always tackled sovereignty and the state in a willing embrace of distinctive proportions, or Hans Morgenthau's perhaps unintended message, that political realism was a question of perspective and historical moment, or women such as Hansa Mehta and Alva Myrdal, who tried to specify the gender dimensions of the political and social ambitions of internationalism, and ended up largely sequestered from the main story. In close-up, the history of the twentieth century, examined through the lens of a liberal internationalist tradition, suggests, as much as the history of liberal nationalism, a panoply of political possibilities continually delayed or delegated to the domain of idealism, even as they might later reappear on the realism side of the ledger of international affairs.[24] The progress of internationalism in the age of nationalism indicates that both histories are less meaningful and less true to the past when they are told as narratives of growth or decline rather than contingent, accumulating imperatives.

In the 1880s, the French philosopher Ernest Renan famously remarked, in answer to the question of the day "What is a nation?" that the authority and realism of national communities relied on forgetting the past as well as reinventing it.[25] Nations, he claimed, were obliged to forget traumatic histories of fratricidal conflict or risk fragmenting along lines of irreconcilable division. In similar ways, albeit for different reasons, forgetting has often followed the periodic shifts that mark twentieth-century internationalism, the forgetting of words, concepts, events, and experiences. After the failures of the league, forgetting gave twentieth-century internationalism a new lease of life in the form of the UN, a project that required the forgetting of counternarratives of international government and international selves; forgetting the popular enthusiasm for both organizations in moments of crisis was also their death knell. In the 1980s, when the question "What is a nation?" returned to prominence, a different kind of forgetting of twentieth-century internationalism and its relationship to nationalism took hold in the new stories that were told about the sociological origins of nations.

When at the end of the Cold War, the UN Evaluation and Communications Research Unit (a modern modification on its old Information Section) grasped the opportunity to survey "knowledge awareness" about the UN in twenty-eight countries, they found a mixed picture of remembering and forgetting.[26] Highest knowledge awareness, the survey reported, occurred in Jordan, then Norway, Austria, and Sweden. At the bottom sat Brazil and the United States, two of the countries that had played prominent roles in the debates over the UN Charter and Human Rights. In 1945, the United States was under the spell of an extraordinary public interest in the new organization; nearly fifty years later, few Americans knew what it did or why. In the 1950s and 1960s, American public opinion of the UN had exhibited "more positive evaluation than negative"; in the 1970s and 1980s, under the influence of the oil crisis and the "dominance of the Third World" in the UN, the United States had "net negative" poll ratings. Attitudes had shifted to a small degree after 1989, but even fewer people could name the secretary-general (the Peruvian diplomat Javier Pérez de Cuéllar) or a UN agency. The greater success of the UN among Scandinavian publics was attributed to the fact that they were taught about the UN at school and their states had personnel in the UN peacekeeping forces in the period of the survey. When it came to the more negative assessments in English-speaking nations, the explanation was that representations of the UN in major Western news gathering institutions were often the only source of information on the organization and its international purpose, and they continued to "convey negative impressions of underdeveloped nations."[27] The memory sites of internationalism in the new postinternational age were still few and far between.

Memory has long been as important to the study of nations as forgetting. It was the project of memory that Jean Claveirole clung to in 1910 as he launched into his study of internationalism. He began with his own memory of the thirtieth anniversary of the Universal Postal Union and the "world celebration" that took place in Berne in 1904. Staged at the Swiss Federal Palace, the anniversary was attended by representatives from "all the states of the world" on the invitation of the (no doubt politically savvy) Swiss government. The event was crowned with a competition for the design of a suitable monument.[28] In 1909, when the completed winning design was finally unveiled, Claveirole imagined the monument as a testament to the realism of contemporary internationalism: the earth's globe embraced by the figures of five women representing the world's "race" regions, passing on letters, one to the other, as if linked in a dance.

A hundred years later, the enchantment of international post barely lingers as an emblem of an international present, let alone its past. If, as Pierre Nora has argued in respect of national remembering, the concept *lieux de mémoire* signifies a community that has lost "an immense and intimate fund of memory" and survives "only as a reconstituted object beneath the gaze of critical history,"[29] then a critical history of internationalism might also take as its task the reconstitution of international *lieux de mémoire*, in the interest of contemplating the relevance of twentieth-century internationalism in the twenty-first century. This repertoire of international *lieux de mémoire* takes us comfortably from the neo-Renaissance red-brick solidity of the Vredespalais—the Peace Palace built in The Hague on the instructions of the 1907 peace conference with the funding of the Scottish-American philanthropist Andrew Carnegie—to the expansive crumbling modernism of the Palais des Nations on Geneva's calm shores. In 2009, the eightieth anniversary of the laying of the foundation stone for the Palais des Nations (now headquarters to the United Nations Office at Geneva) was celebrated with a special *heritage* ceremony targeting donors who might fund the restoration of buildings on the point of material collapse. Then there is the status of the United Nations. Its sixtieth anniversary invited a spate of historical endeavors, from speeches to conferences, to the collection of oral histories, to the constitution of a UN Intellectual History Project, based in New York, and an International Scientific Committee for the History of UNESCO, with its home in Paris.[30] All these efforts raise the question of how we should imagine the UN itself: as a lived history and living memory of twentieth-century internationalism, or a *lieu de mémoire* that does the ideological work of sustaining imagined national communities, empires, and civilizations?[31] Whatever we decide, in a new century of overwhelming international challenges, most of them less new than urgent, it might be too early to declare that the political ambitions and social expectations characteristic of the origins and apogee of twentieth-century internationalism have all but disappeared.

Notes

Introduction

1. *The United Nations and World Citizenship: Towards World Understanding* (Paris: UNESCO, 1949), and UNESCO, "Seminar on Teaching About the United Nations and Its Specialized Agencies," UNESCO/Sem.II/55, accessed 15 May 2012 unesdoc.unesco .org/images/0015/001556/155633eb.pdf. The countries were (using the names at the time) Afghanistan, Australia, Burma, Canada, Chile, China, Denmark, Egypt, Finland, France, Greece, Iceland, Italy, Lebanon, New Zealand, Norway, Pakistan, Philippine Republic, Poland, Siam, Switzerland, Syria, Turkey, United Kingdom, Union of South Africa, United States, and Uruguay.

2. UNESCO, "Seminar on Teaching About the United Nations and Its Specialized Agencies," 2–6.

3. Hans Morgenthau, *Politics Among Nations* (1948; repr., New York: Knopf, 1951), 413.

4. Ibid., 415.

5. Morgenthau's chapter drew on the theories of the Romanian-born David Mitrany, who was based at the London School of Economics. He also claimed that the argument rested upon "an analogy with national societies," Ibid., 395. See also the prefaces to the second and third editions published in 1954 and 1960.

6. *United Nations and World Citizenship*, 20.

7. See Micheline R. Ishay, *Internationalism and Its Betrayal* (Minneapolis: University of Minnesota Press, 1995), for a fuller discussion of the internationalism embedded in eighteenth century political theories of democracy and citizenship.

8. See Duncan Bell, "*Victorian Visions of Global Order*: An Introduction," in *Victorian Visions of Global Order: Empire and International Relations in Nineteenth Century British Political Thought*, ed. Bell (Cambridge: Cambridge University Press, 2007), 1–20, 4.

9. Immanuel Kant, "Idea for a Universal History with a Cosmopolitan Intent," (1784) in *Perpetual peace and other essays on politics, history, and morals,* translated by Ted Humphrey (Indianapolis, Cambridge: Hackett Publishing Company, 1983), 29–40, 34, 38. The italics are in the original.

10. Barbara Caine and Glenda Sluga, *Gendering European History* (London:

Leicester University Press, 2000), 72–74; Guiseppe Mazzini, *A Cosmopolitanism of Nations: Giuseppe Mazzini's Writings on Democracy, Nation Building, and International Relations*, ed. Stefano Recchia and Nadia Urbinati (Princeton, N.J.: Princeton University Press, 2009). Some of the mingled history of nineteenth-century nationalism and internationalism is taken up in Perry Anderson's "Internationalism: A Breviary," *New Left Review* 14 (March–April 2002): 5–25. Anderson assumes that internationalism is the intellectual property of a Marxist tradition. See also the discussion of historiography in the Afterword to this book, and Sunil Amrith and Glenda Sluga, "New Histories of the UN," *Journal of World History* 19, no. 3 (2008): 251–74.

11. Jean-Michel Guieu, *Le rameau et le glaive: Les militants français pour la Société des Nations* (Paris: Presses de Sciences Po, 2008), 21.

12. Some scholars argue that *internationalism* was first used in English in 1877 in a novel by a Miss M. M. Grant; see Clark Foreman, *The New Internationalism* (London: Allen & Unwin, 1934).

13. August Bebel, *Für und wider die Commune: Disputation zwischen den Herren Bebel und Sparig in der "Tonhalle" zu Leipzig* (Leipzig, 1876), quoted in Sebastian Conrad, "Globalization Effects: Mobility and Nation in Imperial Germany, 1880–1914," *Journal of Global History* 3 (2008): 45.

14. Dorothy Ross, *The Origins of American Social Science* (New York: Cambridge University Press, 1991), 68.

15. Warren F. Kuehl, *Biographical Dictionary of Internationalists* (Westport, Conn.: Greenwood, 1983), 6. Kuehl states that "Adams's own internationalism, founded upon a deeply religious worldview and nourished by a paternalistic Anglo-Saxon mystique, was altogether typical of his background and era."

16. See Carl Bouchard, *Le citoyen et l'ordre mondial (1914–1919): Le rêve d'une paix durable au lendemain de la Grande Guerre* (Paris: Editions A. Pedone, 2008).

17. Bob Reinalda, *Routledge History of International Organizations: From 1815 to the Present Day* (London: Routledge, 2009), 10, 37.

18. *United Nations and World Citizenship*, 22.

19. Akira Iriye, *Global Community: The Role of International Organizations in the Making of the Contemporary World* (Berkeley: University of California Press, 2004), 126, 129.

20. Each of these concepts are discussed more fully in chapter 4.

21. For more on this new history of the changing conception of state sovereignty in relation to international humanitarian intervention, see Brendan Simms and D. J. B. Trim, eds., *Humanitarian Intervention: A History* (Cambridge: Cambridge University Press, 2011), especially the concluding essay by Trim.

22. Liisa Malkki, "Citizens of Humanity: Internationalism and the Imagined Community of Nations," *Diaspora* 3, no. 1 (1994): 62.

23. See Akira Iriye, "The Internationalization of History," *American Historical Review* 94, no. 1 (1989): 1–10. And for an important global history of this trend, see Dominic Sachsenmaier, *Global Perspectives on Global History: Theories and Approaches in a Connected World* (Cambridge: Cambridge University Press, 2011).

24. See Glenda Sluga, "The Transnational History of International Institutions," *Journal of Global History* 6 (2011): 219–22.

25. Sunil Amrith, "Asian Internationalism: Bandung's Echo in a Colonial Metropolis," *Inter-Asia Cultural Studies* 6, no. 4 (2005): 557–69; idem, *Migration and Diaspora in Modern Asia* (Cambridge: Cambridge University Press, 2011); Emma Rothschild, "The Archives of Universal History," *Journal of World History* 19, no. 3 (2008): 375–401.

26. See Sugata Bose, *A Hundred Horizons: The Indian Ocean in the Age of Global Empire* (Cambridge, Mass.: Harvard University Press, 2006).

27. See Glenda Sluga, "Gender," in *Palgrave Advances in International History*, ed. Patrick Finney (Basingstoke: Palgrave Macmillan, 2005), 304; and Anthony Smith, "The Shifting Landscapes of 'Nationalism,'" *Studies in Ethnicity and Nationalism* 8, no. 2 (2008): 317–30.

28. For discussion of the four ages of nationalism, see Glenda Sluga, "A Short History of the Study of Nationalism," *European Studies Forum* 39, no. 1 (Spring 2009): 37–44.

29. Iriye, *Global Community*, 191, and Akira Iriye, *Cultural Internationalism and World Order* (Baltimore: Johns Hopkins University Press, 2000).

Chapter 1. The International Turn

1. J. A. Hobson, "The Ethics of Internationalism," *International Journal of Ethics* 17, no. 1 (1906): 16–28, in idem, *Writings on Imperialism and Internationalism*, ed. Peter Cain (London: Routledge/Thoemmes Press, 1992), 19. I refer throughout to J. A. Hobson as John Hobson.

2. Princeton University, Princeton, N.J., 1914, Robert Lansing Papers, Series 3, Writings and Speeches 1905-1928, box 8, folder 10, "Internationality." In 1919, Lansing accompanied Woodrow Wilson to the Paris peacetalks that gave birth to the League of Nations.

3. See Eric Hobsbawm, *Nations and Nationalism Since 1780: Programme, Myth, Reality* (Cambridge: Cambridge University Press, 1991),

4. These wars included the Ottoman massacre of Armenians, the American forced seizure of territory in the Pacific and Caribbean, the Boer War (1899–1902), the Russo–Japanese War (1904), and the Herero Revolt (1904–6) in which German troops in West Africa massacred local populations. For an accounting of the colonial violence of this period, see W. E. B. Du Bois, *Color and Democracy: Colonies and Peace* (New York: Harcourt, Brace, 1945).

5. On "the contamination of ideas" and an emergent public sphere or civil society, see Bouchard, *Le citoyen et l'ordre mondial*, 222. For more on the significance of internationalism in this period, see Iriye, *Cultural Internationalism*; the excellent essays in Martin H. Geyer and Johannes Paulmann, eds., *The Mechanics of Internationalism: Culture, Society, and Politics from the 1840s to the First World War* (Oxford: Oxford University Press, 2001); Daniel Laqua, ed., *Internationalism Reconfigured: Transnational Ideas and Movements Between the World Wars* (London: I. B. Tauris, 2011); Theodore Ruyssen, *La Société internationale* (Paris: Presses Universitaires de France, 1950); Elisabeth

Crawford, *Nationalism and Internationalism in Science, 1880–1939* (Cambridge: Cambridge University Press, 1992); G. P. Speeckaert, *Le Premier Siècle de la coopération internationale 1815–1914* (Brussels: Union des Associations Internationales, 1980); Frank Trentmann, "After the Nation-State: Citizenship, Empire and Global Coordination in the New Internationalism, 1914–1930," in *Beyond Sovereignty: Britain, Empire and Transnationalism 1860–1950*, ed. Frank Trentmann, Philippa Levine, and Kevin Grant (Basingstoke: Palgrave Macmillan, 2007), 34–53.

6. Christian Lange, *Histoire de l'internationalisme I: Jusqu'à la Paix de Westphalie (1648)* Publications de l'Institut Nobel Norvégien, Tome IV (Oslo: Aschehoug, 1919); and Nobel Peace Prize lecture, 1921, accessed 5/15/12 http://www.nobelprize.org/nobel_prizes/peace/laureates/1921/lange-lecture.html.

7. The idea of the "talk" that speaks to us historically is taken from Henry Kissinger, *A World Restored* (New York: Grosset and Dunlap, 1964), 3.

8. On the economic context of these change, see Ronald Findlay and Kevin H. O'Rourke, *Power and Plenty: Trade, War, and the World Economy in the Second Millennium* (Princeton, N.J.: Princeton University Press, 2007), chap. 8.

9. Iriye, *Global Community*, 17–19; this statistic concerns only nongovernmental organizations. See also Reinalda, *Routledge History of International Organizations* and Madeleine Herren, *Internationale Organisationen seit 1865: Eine Globalgeschichte der internationalen Ordnung* (Darmstadt: Wissenschaftliche Buchgesellschaft, 2009).

10. See the issues of *Annuaire de la vie internationale* (1905–1909) published by the Brussels Office Central de Institutions Internationales, and *Le Mouvement sociologique international*, as well as studies such as Paul S. Reinsch, *Public International Unions: Their Work and Organization: A Study in International Administrative Law* (Boston: Ginn and Company, 1911); Ruyssen, *La Société internationale*; Union pour la vérité, *Sur l'internationalisme: Libres entretiens*, deuxième série, 1905–6 (New York: Garland, 1971).

11. Quoted in Iriye, *Global Community*, 17.

12. See Iriye, *Cultural Internationalism*, 36–49.

13. The revival of historical interest in this "golden age" of international organizations tends to echo the motifs of these early twentieth-century observations; see Iriye, *Global Community*; Reinalda, *Routledge History of International Organizations*; and the very useful short essay by Jeremi Suri, "Non-governmental Organizations and Non-state Actors," in Finney, *Palgrave Advances in International History*, 223–47, 235.

14. Herren sees the number of dissertations that take up internationalism in this period as underlining the academic importance of the subject; Madeleine Herren, "Governmental Internationalism," in Geyer and Paulmann, *Mechanics of Internationalism*, 141n74.

15. Jean Claveirole, "L'Internationalisme et l'organisation internationale administrative: l'organisation internationale dans l'histoire, l'internationalisme libre et l'internationalisme officiel, les grandes unions administratives des États et les bureaux internationaux" (thèse pour le doctorat, Université de Lyon, 1910), xiii, xvi.

16. See Caine and Sluga, *Gendering European History*, chap. 3.

17. Hobson, "Ethics of Internationalism," 19.

18. J. A. Hobson, *Richard Cobden, the International Man* (New York: Henry Holt, 1919).

19. Claveirole uses Fried's documentation to support his own argument about the new era of international organizations; "L'Internationalisme et l'organisation internationale administrative," xiv.

20. Madeleine Herren, "Between Territoriality, Performativity, and Transcultural Entanglement (1920–39): A Typology of Transboundary Lives," in *Lives Beyond Borders: Toward a Social History of Cosmopolitans and Globalization, 1880–1960*, ed. Madeleine Herren, Ines Prodöhl, and Isabella Löhr (forthcoming).

21. A hundred years later, they tend to be known as intergovernmental organizations, or IGOs.

22. Herren, "Governmental Internationalism," 142.

23. Ibid.

24. The tradition of Inter-Parliamentary Unionism was linked to the post–World War II "World Association of Parliamentarians for World Government," still around in 1951 when a Welshman, Clement Davies, was its president.

25. Ibid., 129 and passim.

26. Ibid., 133ff.

27. Ibid., 137.

28. See Sandi E. Cooper, *Patriotic Pacifism: Waging War on War in Europe, 1815–1914* (New York: Oxford University Press, 1991); Bouchard, *Le citoyen et l'ordre mondial*; and Michael Clinton, "Jeunes Amis de la Paix: The Origins of the Association de la Paix par le Droit, 1885–1896" (paper, Peace History Society conference, Bellingham, Wash., April 2000), Academia.edu.

29. Theodore Ruyssen, *Rapport sur les congrès nationaux de la paix et leurs relations avec les congrès internationaux de la paix* (Toulouse, 1903). Ruyssen also believed that the universal ambitions of humanity were in effect historically French, by virtue of the Declaration of the Rights of Man and Citizen of 1789.

30. Tim Harper, "Empire, Diaspora and the Languages of Globalism, 1850–1914," in *Globalization in World History*, ed. A. G. Hopkins (New York: Norton, 2002), 148.

31. See Clinton, "Jeunes Amis de la Paix." For a thorough study of the French history of the connections between pacifism and law in this period, see Bouchard, *Le citoyen et l'ordre mondial* and Guieu, *Le rameau et le glaive*. For more on the longer history of humanitarianism and international law, see the essays in Simms and Trim, *Humanitarian Intervention*.

32. These conventional accounts are particularly prominent in popular and official histories of the League of Nations and the UN.

33. See Martti Koskenniemi, *The Gentle Civilizer of Nations: The Rise and Fall of International Law 1870–1960* (Cambridge: Cambridge University Press, 2002), 13; John

Westlake, *Treatise on Private International Law: Or the Conflict of Laws* (1858; repr., Whitefish, Mont.: Kessinger, 2009).

34. On the ambiguous legacy of international law and its liberal and humanitarian motivations, see Andrew Fitzmaurice, "Liberalism and Empire in Nineteenth Century International Law," *American Historical Review* 117 (February 2012): 122–40.

35. Kuehl, *Biographical Dictionary of Internationalists*, 448–49.

36. See Koskenniemi, *Gentle Civilizer of Nations*, 216, for a full discussion. On the intimate relationship between cosmopolitan thinking and empire, see Anthony Pagden, "Stoicism, Cosmopolitanism, and the Legacy of European Imperialism," *Constellations* 7, no. 1 (2000): 3–21.

37. Koskenniemi, *Gentle Civilizer of Nations*, 134ff.

38. Arthur Eyffinger, *The 1899 Hague Peace Conference* (The Hague: Kluwer Law International, 1999), 327.

39. Koskenniemi, *Gentle Civilizer of Nations*, 217.

40. Eyffinger, *1899 Hague Peace Conference*, 343.

41. For another example of the impact of the publishing industry on the peace movement, see Robert I. Rotberg, *A Leadership for Peace: How Edwin Ginn Tried to Change the World* (Stanford, Calif.: Stanford University Press, 2006).

42. Herren, "Governmental Internationalism," 140.

43. Bertha von Suttner, *Memoirs of Bertha von Suttner: The Records of an Eventful Life (Authorized Translation)* (Boston: Ginn, 1910); and Brigitte Hamann, *Bertha von Suttner: A Life for Peace* (Syracuse, N.Y.: Syracuse University Press, 1996).

44. Eyffinger, *1899 Hague Peace Conference*, 352.

45. Andrew White, quoted in ibid., 66.

46. Ibid., 342.

47. James Brown Scott, *The Hague Peace Conference of 1899 and 1907* (Baltimore: Garland, 1909); Calvin DeArmond Davis, *The United States and the Second Hague Peace Conference* (Durham, N.C.: Duke University Press, 1976).

48. W. T. Stead, "Letter to the Czar," quoted in Eyffinger, *1899 Hague Peace Conference*, 318. When Stead died in 1912, it was on the *Titanic* on his way to a peace conference at Carnegie Hall. See also Sandi E. Cooper, "Peace and Internationalism: European Ideological Movements Behind the Two Hague Conferences" (Ph.D. diss., New York University, 1967); W. T. Stead, *The United States of Europe on the Eve of the Parliament of Peace* (London: G. N. Morang, 1899); Frederic Whyte, *The Life of W. T. Stead, Vol. II* (London: Houghton Mifflin, 1925).

49. In 1911, Asser shared the Nobel Peace Prize with Fried.

50. Herren, "Governmental Internationalism," 142.

51. Eyffinger, *1899 Hague Peace Conference*, 318.

52. Ibid., 423.

53. The ICW originated in the United States and aimed to represent women workers through national branches.

54. Kuehl, *Biographical Dictionary of Internationalists*, 738. Van Kirk published *The Rainbow: A World Flag for Universal Peace* (1914).

55. See Lynn Hunt, *Inventing Human Rights: A History* (New York: Norton, 2007); Gary J. Bass, *Freedom's Battle: The Origins of Humanitarian Intervention* (New York: Knopf, 2009).

56. Cooper, *Patriotic Pacifism*, 60. Cooper's is the definitive history of pacifist movements in this period and their reconciliation of national patriotism and internationalism; it also provides useful listings of all the pacifist organizations. On women and the peace movement, there is the important American study by Harriet Hyman Alonso, *Peace as a Women's Issue: A History of the U.S. Movement for World Peace and Women's Rights* (Syracuse, N.Y.: Syracuse University Press, 1993).

57. Wilbur Crafts, *A Primer of Internationalism with Special Reference to University Debates* (Washington, D.C.: International Reform Bureau, 1908). See also Daniel Gorman's discussion in "Ecumenical Internationalism: Willoughby Dickinson, the League of Nations and the World Alliance for Promoting International Friendship Through the Churches," *Journal of Contemporary History* 45, no. 1 (2010): 51–73.

58. Crafts, *Primer of Internationalism*, 6.

59. Ibid., 92.

60. Ibid., 9.

61. William Henry Fremantle, *Patriotism and Cosmopolitanism: A Sermon for the Peace Conference Preached in the English Church at The Hague, Sunday, May 28th 1899, by the Very Rev. the Hon. W.H. Fremantle, D.D., Dean of Ripon* (Ripon: Thirlway and Son, 1899).

62. See Leila Rupp, *Worlds of Women: The Making of an International Women's Movement* (Princeton, N.J.: Princeton University Press, 1997).

63. *Conference on the Defence of Nationalities and Subject Races* (London: P.S. King, 1910), Appendix. See also Gregory Claeys, *Imperial Sceptics: British Critics of Empire, 1850–1920* (Cambridge: Cambridge University Press, 2010).

64. *Conference on the Defence of Nationalities and Subject Races.* By this time, the committee had added to its members the Anti-Imperialist League (USA), L'Alliance pour des Droits des Nations, and La Societé des amis du peuple Russe et des peuples annexés.

65. "Letter from M. Léon Bourgeois to Lord Weardale, President of the Congress," in *Papers on Inter-Racial Problems Communicated to the First Universal Races Congress Held at the University of London July 26–29, 1911*, ed. Gustave Spiller (London: King and Son, 1911), 462.

66. W. E. B. Du Bois, *The Souls of Black-Folk* (Charleston, S.C.: Forgotten Books, 1965), 11. For more on the international significance of the idea of the color-line, and of the Universal Races Congress, see Marilyn Lake and Henry Reynolds, *Drawing the Global Colour Line* (Cambridge: Cambridge University Press, 2008). Du Bois had already visited London in 1900 for the first pan-African conference. For more on the

pan-African genealogy of this internationalism, see Vijay *Prashad, The Darker Nations: A People's History of the Third World* (New York: New Press, 2007), 23.

67. "The Races in Conference," editorial, *The Crisis* 1, no. 2 (December 1910): 17.

68. "The Races Congress," *The Crisis* 2, no. 5 (September 1911): 199–200. See also W. E. B. Du Bois, *The Autobiography of W.E.B. Du Bois* (New York: International Publishers, 1968), 254–76.

69. Spiller, *Papers on Inter-Racial Problems.*

70. A Mrs. Elmer Black claimed that all national movements had had their moment last century and no new nations remained to be created; instead interdependence between existing nations had to be declared. Another theme was the respect that the white race owed to other races. Annie Besant complained about treatment of Hindus by the English. Olive Schreiner brought up the question of black and white equality in South Africa. Spiller, *Papers on Inter-Racial Problems,* passim.

71. Franz Boas, "Instability of Human Types," 99; Charles S. Myers, "On the Permanence of Racial Mental Differences," both in Spiller, *Papers on Inter-Racial Problems.*

72. The *Journal of Race Development* featured articles titled "French Scheme of Empire in Africa," "Turkey and the United States," "Japanese in America," and the "Anglo-Saxon in India and the Philippines." See Robert Vitalis, "Birth of a Discipline," in *Imperialism and Internationalism in the Discipline of International Relations,* ed. Brian Schmidt and David Long (Albany: State University of New York Press, 2005), 159–82.

73. Hall and Blakeslee were colleagues at Clark University in Massachusetts and both supporters from a distance of the race congress.

74. See G. Sluga, *The Nation, Psychology and International Politics* (Basingstoke: Palgrave, 2006), chap. 1.

75. J. A. Hobson, "Character and Society," in *Character and Life: A Symposium by Alfred Russell Wallace, J. A. Hobson, Walter Crane, Harold Begbie, Emil Reich,* ed. P. L. Parker (London: Williams and Northgate, 1912), 6.

76. Marilyn Fischer, "Mead and the International Mind," *Transactions of the Charles S. Peirce Society* 44, no. 3 (2008): 508–31.

77. Nicholas Murray Butler, *The International Mind: An Argument for the Judicial Settlement of International Disputes* (New York: Scribner, 1912), 102.

78. Kuehl, *Biographical Dictionary of Internationalists,* 131. For a sympathetic account of Butler's influence after the war, see Joseph W. Winn, "Nicholas Murray Butler, The Carnegie Endowment for International Peace, and the Search for Reconciliation in Europe, 1919–1933," *Peace and Change* 31, no. 4 (2006): 555–84.

79. "Want Japanese Here to Stay for Good," *New York Times,* March 10, 1912.

80. Tsunejiro Miyaoka, "Growth of Internationalism in Japan," pub. no. 6, report to the trustees of the endowment (Washington, D.C.: Carnegie Endowment for International Peace, 1915), 2.

81. Ibid., 1.

82. See Sinclair Lewis, *Main Street,* "Though a Gopher Prairie regards itself as part

of the Great World, . . . it will not acquire the scientific spirit, the international mind, which would make it great." Quoted in Fischer, "Mead and the International Mind," 510.

83. H. G. Wells, *An Englishman Looks at the World* (London: Cassell, 1914), 19–20.

84. Fischer, "Mead and the International Mind," 510.

85. It is no coincidence that Miyaoka went on to a study of the growth of liberalism in Japan in order to integrate the Japanese more fully into the narrative of the new internationalism.

86. Jane Addams, "The Revolt Against War," in *Women at The Hague: The International Congress of Women and Its Results,* ed. Mercedes M. Randall (New York: Garland, 1972), 55–81.

87. Ibid., 60, 62.

88. Edward Krehbiel, *Nationalism, War and Society: A Study of Nationalism and Its Concomitant, War, in Their Relation to Civilization; and of the Fundamentals and the Progress of the Opposition to War* (New York: Macmillan, 1916), 219. Krehbiel like Hobson believed that international facts were out of sync with subjectivities.

89. Gustave Hervé, *L'Internationalisme* (Paris: Giard & Brière, 1910). See also Bouchard for a thorough study of the significance of this idea among French wartime supporters of a League of Nations; Bouchard, *Le citoyen et l'ordre mondial.*

90. Joseph Preston Baratta, *The Politics of World Federation: From World Federalism to Global Governance* (New York: Praeger, 2004), chap. 3.

91. Kuehl, *Biographical Dictionary of Internationalists,* 197.

92. Ibid., 114.

93. David Lloyd George, *The Truth About the Peace Treaties* (London: Victor Gollancz, 1938), 622; H. Duncan Hall, *Mandates, Dependencies and Trusteeship* (London: Stevens and Sons, 1948), 14.

94. Harper, "Empire, Diaspora and the Languages of Globalism," 141–66,152; Keng wrote, in Chinese, English, and Malay, *The Great War from a Confucian Point of View* (Singapore: Straits Albion Press, 1917).

95. Maxime LeRoy, *L'Ère Wilson: La Société des Nations* (Paris: Giard & Brière, 1917).

96. Among political advocates of a Société were Cardinal Amette, archbishop of Paris, members of the French Academy, all former prime ministers, Barthou, Briand, Viviani, Ribot, Painlevé, many former ministers, such as Millerand, Doumer, Siegfried, and Albert Thomas, and republicans of varying shades of opinion.

97. Léon Bourgeois, preface to *Vers la Société des Nations: Leçons professées au Collège libre des Sciences Sociales pendant l'année 1918 par MM. Ferdinand Buisson, Jean Brunhes, Aulard, J. Charles-Brun, Maxime Leroy, J. Ernest-Charles, Jean Hennessy* (Paris: Giard & Brière, 1919), ix.

98. Meetings at the hotels des Sociétés Savantes Aulard, February 1918, in ibid., 180. For more discussion, see Sluga, *Nation, Psychology and International Politics,* 114–15.

99. LeRoy, *L'Ère Wilson,* 92.

100. Guieu, *Le rameau et le glaive,* 95.

101. Ruhl Bartlett, *The League to Enforce Peace* (Chapel Hill: University of North Carolina Press, 1944), 127–30.

102. Guieu, *Le rameau et le glaive*, 95.

103. Warren F. Kuehl, *Seeking World Order: The United States and International Organization to 1920* (Nashville, Tenn.: Vanderbilt University Press, 1969), 218.

104. See Sluga, *Nation, Psychology and International Politics*, 112, 113.

105. Addams, "Revolt Against War," 60.

106. See Gertrude Busey and Margeret Tims, *Pioneers for Peace: The Women's International League for Peace and Freedom 1915–1965* (London: WILPF British Section, 1980) and Rupp, *Worlds of Women.*

107. "Editorial," *Foreign Affairs* 1, no. 1 (July 1919): 2.

108. Helena Swanwick, "Democracy and the League of Nations," *Foreign Affairs* (August 1919): 14.

109. See Bouchard, *Le citoyen et l'ordre mondial.*

110. Andrew Williams, *Failed Imagination? The Anglo-American New World Order from Wilson to Bush* (Manchester: Manchester University Press, 2007), 30. Bouchard argues that the national theme was prominent because the war had been about defining nations, so the peace had to be about nations too; *Le citoyen et l'ordre mondial*, 222.

111. See Sluga, *Nation, Psychology and International Politics*, chap. 3.

112. J. A. Hobson, *Towards International Government* ([London: Allen & Unwin, 1915); See also *Confessions of an Economic Heretic* (London: Allen & Unwin, 1938).

113. Emma Rothschild, "What Is Security?" *Daedalus* 124, no. 3 (1995): 78.

114. International Association for the Struggle Against Unemployment, quoted in ibid., 78; J. A. Hobson, "A League of Nations," pamphlet, October 1915, Union of Democratic Control, 5.

115. H. W. V. Temperley, ed., *History of the Peace Conference of Paris* (London: Oxford University Press, 1924), 6:429.

116. Ministère des Affaires étrangères (MAE), Paris, Série A. Paix, tome 6 Fragments, Including Margburg to Briand, November 18, 1916, F/7/13146.

117. United States National Archives and Records Administration (USNARA), College Park, Maryland, M1107, *The Inquiry*, General Correspondence, box 1, 1917, "Letters Between Lippmann and Laski." For a survey of the range of ideas about a new international order, see Bouchard, *Le citoyen et l'ordre mondial*, 25ff. and his appendix.

118. Quoted in Temperley, *History of the Peace Conference*, 6:397.

119. Havelock Ellis, introduction to Ellen Key, *Love and Marriage* (New York: Putnam, 1911).

120. This was not a completely novel perspective. Woolf was also suggesting that national communities were as utopian as international communities because they could never be adequately representative. The point was to choose the most constructive kind of community.

121. Ellen Key, *War, Peace and the Future: A Consideration of Nationalism and Internationalism, and of the Relation of Women to War* (London: Knickerbocker, 1916).

122. Ibid., 17, 18.

123. Morton Prince, "A World Consciousness and Future Peace" (address, Concordia Association of Japan, Tokyo, June 13, 1916), *Journal of Abnormal Psychology* 11 (1917): 287.

124. William McDougall, *The Group Mind: A Sketch of the Principles of Collective Psychology with Some Attempt to Apply Them to the Interpretation of National Life and Character* (London: Putnam, 1920); and *The American Nation: Its Problems and Psychology* (London: Allen & Unwin, 1925), preface, xi.

125. Walter B. Pillsbury, *The Psychology of Nationality and Internationalism* (New York: Appleton, 1919), 150.

126. Pillsbury, *Psychology of Nationality and Internationalism*, 309.

127. Fischer, "Mead and the International Mind," 515.

128. Henry Winkler, *The League of Nations Movement in Great Britain, 1914–1919* (New Brunswick, N.J.: Rutgers University Press, 1952), 132; see Leonard Woolf, *International Government: Two Reports by L. S. Woolf Prepared for the Fabian Research Department, Together with a Project by a Fabian Committee for a Supernational Authority That Will Prevent War* (London: Allen & Unwin, 1916).

129. J. H. Rose, *Nationality in Modern History* (New York: Macmillan, 1916), 153, see 207. Rose also refers to his ideal for the new Europe, when like will be sorted out with like, and nationalism will merge into wider and nobler sentiment of human brotherhood.

130. A. Zimmern, "True and False Nationalism," June 28, 1915, in Zimmern, *Nationality and Government, with Other Wartime Essays* (London: Chatto and Windus, 1918), 61.

131. "Letters Between Lippmann and Laski."

132. Lange, Nobel Peace Prize lecture, 1921.

133. Hobson, *Richard Cobden*, 275.

134. Rabindranath Tagore, *Personality: Lectures Delivered in America* (London: Macmillan, 1917), 47.

135. Robert Lansing Papers, Series 2, Personal Papers, box 3, folder 17: "Robert Lansing to Edward N. Smith, Watertown, NY," March 23, 1919.

136. Robert Lansing Papers, box 3, folder 1: "Memorandum on the Spiritual Weakness of a World Union," November 1918.

137. "World-Brotherhood," *Expository Times*, 1919. Their congress, organized in London in the wake of the Paris Peace Treaty, was "undenominational," "international and interracial, both in its basis and its membership."

138. Ibid., 61.

139. Krehbiel, *Nationalism, War and Society*, 219.

140. Bouchard argues this is to be expected given that the war was fought on behalf of the protection of nations; *Le citoyen et l'ordre mondial*, 222.

141. William McDougall, *Ethics and Some Modern World Problems* (New York: Methuen, 1924), xiii.

142. Tomas Masaryk, "Masaryk o pom ru národnoti a mezinárodnosti" [Masaryk on the Relationship of National Identity and Internationalism], *Československá samostatnost* (Czechoslovak Independence) 4, no. 28 (December 11, 1918): 343, 354, 357.

143. James Baldwin, "France and the War," *Sociological Review* 8, no. 2 (1915): 65–80, 73.

144. Hobson, *Richard Cobden*, 76.

Chapter 2. Imagine Geneva, Between the Wars

1. The title of Chapter 2 is borrowed from Nicholas Brown, "Enacting the International: R.G. Watt and the League of Nations Union," in *Transnational Ties: Australian Lives in the World*, ed. Desley Deacon, Penny Russell, and Angela Woollacott (Canberra: ANU ePress, 2008), 75–94. League of Nations Archives, Geneva, Women's Questions, section 23: R64212/8302/8302, Mrs. Ogilvie Gordon, "The New Patriotism," address to the National Council of Women of Great Britain and Ireland, June 25, 1919, 7.

2. Yale Sterling Library, Edward Mandell House Papers, MS466, Series II, Diaries, box 302, folder 1–2, vol. 7, p. 29: "House to Wilson," January 31, 1919.

3. Treaty of Versailles, pt. 13, Labour, sec. 1.

4. Ibid.

5. Hobson, *Confessions of an Economic Heretic*, 111–13; Hobson argued not only that no element of "supersovereignty" had been introduced but also that a "perverted nationalism" had taken over. See also J. M. Keynes, *The Economic Consequences of the Peace* (Cambridge: Cambridge University Press, 1971) for a different and powerful early attack on the peace and the league.

6. Quoted in Fischer, "Mead and the International Mind," 520.

7. For a survey of this tradition, see Susan Pedersen, "Back to the League of Nations: Review Essay," *American Historical Review*, 112:4 (2007): 1091–1117; for more on the failures of the league to enforce arbitration and disarmament, see Andrew Webster, "The Transnational Dream: Politicians, Diplomats and Soldiers in the Pursuit of International Disarmament, 1920–1938," *Contemporary European History* 14, no. 4 (November 2005): 493–518; "From Versailles to Geneva: The Many Forms of Interwar Disarmament," *Journal of Strategic Studies* 29, no. 2 (April 2006): 225–46; and "Making Disarmament Work: The Implementation of the International Disarmament Provisions in the League of Nations Covenant, 1920–25," *Diplomacy & Statecraft* 16, no. 3 (September 2005): 551–69.

8. Harold Nicolson, *Peacemaking, 1919* (London: Constable, 1945).

9. D. H. Miller, Plenary Session May 31, 1919, in *My Diary at the Conference of Paris* (New York: Appeal, 1924), 73; and *The Drafting of the Covenant* (New York: Putnam, 1928), 7:182.

10. Schücking was professor at the conservative Marburg law faculty. He had been part of the Carnegie Inquiry into the Balkan wars and had links to The Hague international law community see chapter 1; Temperley, *History of the Peace Conference*, 2:457.

11. See ibid., 6:457.

12. Ibid., 6:455.

13. For more on the influence of Bourgeois and other French enthusiasts of the league, see Guieu, *Le rameau et le glaive*, chaps. 4 and 5.

14. Temperley, *History of the Peace Conference*, 6:428.

15. Other member states included, at various times, Albania, Argentina, Australia, Austria, Belgium, Bolivia, the British Empire, Bulgaria, Canada, Chile, the Republic of China, Colombia, Cuba, Czechoslovakia, Denmark, the Dominican Republic, Ecuador, El Salvador, Estonia, Ethiopia, Finland, France, Greece, Guatemala, Haiti, Honduras, Hungary, India, Iraq, Ireland, Italy, Latvia, Liberia, Lithuania, Luxembourg, Mexico, the Netherlands, New Zealand, Nicaragua, Norway, Panama, Paraguay, Persia/Iran, Peru, Poland, Portugal, Romania, Siam, Spain, Sweden, Switzerland, Turkey, the Union of Soviet Socialist Republics, the Union of South Africa, the United Kingdom, and Uruguay.

16. See Jasmien Van Daele, "The International Labour Organization (ILO) in Past and Present Research," *International Review of Social History* 53 (2008): 485–511.

17. Temperley, *History of the Peace Conference*, 2:34; and Iwao Frederick Ayusawa, *International Labor Legislation* (New York: Columbia University Press, 1920), vol. 91, nos. 1–2.

18. Treaty of Versailles, pt. 13, Labour, sec. 1.

19. Temperley, *History of the Peace Conference*, 2:466.

20. Edward Mandell House Papers, Series II. Diaries, 302/1-2, vol. 7, p. 34: February 4, 1919.

21. See Naoko Shimazu, *Japan, Race and Equality: The Racial Equality Proposal of 1919* (London: Routledge, 2002), 119; and Lake and Reynolds, *Drawing the Global Colour Line*.

22. Shimazu, *Japan, Race and Equality*, 182.

23. See, e.g., Beatrice McKenzie, "The Power of International Positioning: The National Woman's Party, International Law and Diplomacy, 1928–34," *Gender and History* 23, no. 1 (2011): 130–46.

24. Sluga, *Nation, Psychology and International Politics*, 19ff.

25. See William Roger Louis, *Imperialism at Bay: The United States and the Decolonization of the British Empire, 1941–1945* (New York: Oxford University Press, 1978). The British Foreign Office commented, "The Americans baulked at permitting the use of the imperialist-sounding term [mandate] in the records." National Archives, London, FO 608/219, "Proposed United States Protectorate over Liberia," FO comment on memo, February 1919; in Sluga, *Nation, Psychology and International Politics*, 19.

26. Miller, *Drafting of the Covenant*, vol. 3, document 110.

27. See Paul Gordon Lauren, *Power and Prejudice: The Politics and Diplomacy of Racial Discrimination* (Boulder, Colo.: Westview, 1988), 77. The delegates of the Pan-African conference assembled at the Grand Hotel "with the declared purpose of securing the protection of the natives of Africa and the people of African descent in other countries" on behalf of the representatives of countries "inhabited by 85,000,000 Negroes and persons of African descent." "Frank Lyon Polk to the American Commissioners,

Washington Jan 17, 1919. Very Confidential," in *The Papers of Woodrow Wilson*, ed. A. S. Link (Princeton, N.J.: Princeton University Press, 1966–94), 54:126.

28. USNARA, Records of the American Commission to Negotiate Peace, record group 256, 540.16/4 Paris, February 18, 5, P. M. POLK; Mr. King, Secretary of State for Liberia, and Mr. Dunbar, Liberian Senator.

29. Records of the American Commission to Negotiate Peace, record group 256, 540.16/8 Resolutions, votées par le Congrès Pan-Africa, 20, 21 fev. 1919. Grand Hotel, Paris. "Pour la protection des indigènes d'Afrique et des peuples d'origine Africane."

30. Sluga, *Nation, Psychology and International Politics*, 11.

31. A. Toynbee, *The World after the Peace Conference: Being an Epilogue to the "History of the Peace Conference of Paris" and a Prologue to the "Survey of International Affairs, 1920–1923"* (London: Oxford University Press, 1926), 82. See also A. Toynbee, "The Main Features in the Landscape," in *The Treaty of Versailles and After*, ed. Lord Riddell et al. (London: Allen & Unwin, 1935), 42–55.

32. W. R. Keylor, "Versailles and International Diplomacy," in *The Treaty of Versailles: A Reassessment After 75 Years*, ed. M. F. Broemeke, G. D. Feldman, and E. Glaser (Cambridge: Cambridge University Press, 1998), 495.

33. National Archives, London, FO 608/154 511/1/2, "Proceedings at Third Plenary Session of Peace Conference Feb 14 League of Nations," 12.

34. J. C. Smuts, *The League of Nations: A Practical Suggestion* (New York: Hodder and Stoughton, 1918), 40.

35. See the Greece and Turkey Convention Concerning the Exchange of Greek and Turkish Populations and Protocol, signed at Lausanne, January 30, 1923 [1925], LNTSer 14, 32 LNTS 75; Treaty of Lausanne, 1923, *League of Nations Treaty Series* Accessed 15 May 2012 at http://treaties.un.org/pages/LONOnline.aspx.

36. See Carole Fink, *Defending the Rights of Others: The Great Powers, the Jews, and International Minority Protection, 1878–1938* (New York: Cambridge University Press, 2004).

37. Temperley, *History of the Peace Conference*, 6:437, 458.

38. Glenda Sluga, "Inventing Ethnic Spaces: 'Free Territory,' Sovereignty and the 1947 Peace Treaty," *Acta Histriae* 4 (1998): 173–86.

39. See Kumari Jayawardena, *Feminism and Nationalism in the Third World* (London: Zed Books, 1986).

40. See Erez Manela, *The Wilsonian Moment: Self-Determination and the International Origins of Anticolonial Nationalism* (New York: Oxford University Press, 2007), 71, 96.

41. National Archives, London, FO 608/170 802/1/1, "From Port au Prince, Haiti, April 27 1919 June 1919."

42. Temperley, *History of the Peace Conference*, 6:461.

43. Ibid., vol. 2, appendix 2, pt. 5, "Extracts from President Wilson's Speeches Subsequent to the Armistice," Woodrow Wilson, Rome, January 3, 1919.

44. Temperley, *History of the Peace Conference*, 6:461.

45. Nicolson, "Letter to Vita Sackville-West," Monday, May 19, 1919, in *Peacemaking 1919*, 344.

46. Egon Ranshofen-Wertheimer, *The International Secretariat—A Great Experiment in International Administration* (Washington, D.C.: Carnegie Endowment for International Peace, 1945), chap. 12.

47. Ibid., 192, 196.

48. Covenant of the League of Nations, art. 7.

49. National Archives, London, FO 608/37 92/1/4, "Proceedings at Committee Meeting of 20th February on Greek Territorial Questions." Swiss membership was problematic because the league's covenant was seen to undermine Switzerland's historic "neutrality" (as defined in 1815). A compromise was reached in 1920 that allowed Switzerland to become a member and to retain its domestic obligations over and above its legal obligations to the league. See also Ranshofen-Wertheimer, *International Secretariat*.

50. Helena Swanwick, *I Have Been Young* (London: Gollancz, 1935), 32.

51. "American Woman Who Was Attached to Secretariat Tells How Questions Are Handled," *New York Times*, August 14, 1921.

52. Thomas W. Burkman, "Nationalist Actors in the Internationalist Theatres: Nitobe Inazo and Ishii Kikujiro and the League of Nations," in *Nationalism and Internationalism in Imperial Japan: Autonomy, Asian Brotherhood, or World Citizenship?* ed. Dick Stegewerns (New York: Routledge, 2006), 90.

53. Brown, "Enacting the International," 84. Ray Stannard Baker, Wilson's press secretary in Paris in 1919, had his conversion to internationalism (from nativism) during the war. As the league took form, he began to write novels pseudonymously (as David Grayson) that were concerned with the restoration of community on a global scale, see Kuehl, *Biographical Dictionary of Internationalists*, 56.

54. For an engrossing and historically astute fictional account of this enthusiasm, see Frank Moorhouse, *Grand Days* (Sydney: Vintage, 2000).

55. Burkman, "Nationalist Actors," 103.

56. Burkman explains that Nitobe was taught social Darwinism by the progressive economist Richard Theodore Ely at Hopkins. Nitobe also believed the British philosopher Herbert Spencer was right to think that "modern Japan, like Europe and the United States, was evolving inexorably from a stage of violent militarism to a stage of peaceful industrialism, where the man of arms would become an anachronism." Ibid., 103.

57. Ranshofen-Wertheimer, *International Secretariat*, 337.

58. Herren, Prodöhl, and Löhr, *Lives Beyond Borders*, especially Herren, "Between Territoriality."

59. Ranshofen-Wertheimer, *International Secretariat*, 338.

60. See Kathryn Lavelle, "Exit, Voice, and Loyalty in International Organizations: U.S. Involvement in the League of Nations," *Review of International Organizations* 2, no. 4 (2007): 372.

61. Ibid., 335–36.

62. Ibid.

63. Butler was secretary-general of its first conference, deputy director of the office, and associate of Albert Thomas until the latter's death in 1932. See Sandrine Kott, ed., *Une autre approche de la globalisation: socio-histoire des organisations internationales (1900–1940),* special issue of *Critique internationale* 52, no. 3 (2011).

64. Ranshofen-Wertheimer, *International Secretariat,* 244.

65. Ibid., 356.

66. Salvador de Madariaga y Rojo, *Englishmen, Frenchmen, Spaniards: An Essay in Comparative Psychology* (London: Oxford University Press, 1929), 243, 465. (Alfred Zimmern wrote the prefatory note.)

67. Ibid., 242–43.

68. See Sydney Dawson Bailey, *The Secretariat of the United Nations* (New York: Carnegie Endowment for International Peace 1962), 19.

69. Ranshofen-Wertheimer, *International Secretariat,* xiii.

70. Madariaga y Rojo, *Englishmen, Frenchmen, Spaniards,* 35. Madariaga also published his memoirs: *Morning Without Noon* (London: Saxon House, 1974).

71. Ranshofen-Wertheimer, *International Secretariat,* xiv.

72. Until 1930 he lived in Germany, after which he moved to London, and then to Geneva to work for the league. He migrated one last time to the United States in 1940. Following World War II, he found a home at the new United Nations organization.

73. Ibid., 243.

74. See League of Nations Archives, Geneva, Registry Files, 1934–1937, sec. 5 B and sec. 5 C (Intellectual Cooperation); International Institute for Intellectual Cooperation, *An International Series of Open Letters* (Paris: IIIC, 1933); *The League of Nations and Intellectual Cooperation* (Geneva: League of Nations, 1927).

75. See Derek Heater, *Peace Through Education: The Contribution of the Council for Education in World Citizenship* (Brighton: Falmer, 1984).

76. Suri, "Non-governmental Organizations," 237. In 1914 there were 330.

77. Ibid., 236.

78. Kuehl, *Biographical Dictionary of Internationalists,* 81.

79. Harper, "Empire, Diaspora and the Languages of Globalism," 164.

80. For more on the history of the IPR, see Paul Hooper, *Elusive Destiny: The Internationalist Movement in Modern Hawaii* (Honolulu: University Press of Hawaii, 1980), and Tomoko Akami, *Internationalizing the Pacific: The United States, Japan and the Institute of Pacific Relations in War and Peace, 1919–1945* (London: Routledge, 2002).

81. Kuehl, *Biographical Dictionary of Internationalists,* 155–56.

82. Ibid., 795–97.

83. Ibid., 359.

84. Winn, "Nicholas Murray Butler," 562.

85. Kuehl, *Biographical Dictionary of Internationalists,* 405–6.

86. Ibid., 596.

87. Ibid.

88. Michael Lang, "Globalization and Global History in Toynbee," *Journal of World History* 22, no. 4 (2011): 747–83.

89. Kuehl, *Biographical Dictionary of Internationalists*, 72–73.

90. Ibid., 283.

91. Stuart Macintyre, *A History for a Nation*, quoted in Brown, "Enacting the International," 88.

92. Quoted in Ben Keppel, *The Work of Democracy: Ralph Bunche, Kenneth B. Clark, Lorraine Hansberry, and the Cultural Politics of Race* (Cambridge, Mass.: Harvard University Press, 1995), 37.

93. Ralph Bunche, "That Man May Dwell in Peace," in *Ralph J. Bunche: Selected Speeches and Writings*, ed. Charles P. Henry (Ann Arbor: University of Michigan Press, 1996), 18.

94. Ibid., 19, italics in original.

95. Benjamin Rivlin, ed., *Ralph Bunche: The Man and His Times* (New York: Holmes and Meyer, 1990), 223, and appendix.

96. Bouchard, *Le citoyen et l'ordre mondial*, 6.

97. Bellegarde was linked to Howard University, where Bunche taught; see Clifford L. Muse Jr., "Howard University and U.S. Foreign Affairs During the Franklin D. Roosevelt Administration, 1933–1945," *Journal of African American History* 87 (Autumn 2002): 403–15.

98. Saul Dubow, "Smuts, the United Nations and the Rhetoric of Race and Rights," *Journal of Contemporary History* 43, no. 1 (January 2008): 45–74.

99. Quoted in Léon Dénius Pamphile, *Haitians and African Americans: A Heritage of Tragedy and Hope* (Gainesville: University Press of Florida, 2001), 125.

100. Du Bois, *Autobiography*, 254–76.

101. Quoted in "Mary Hicks, "The Coverage of World War I by the Radical Black Press, 1917–1919," *Iowa Historical Review*, 1 no.1 (2007): 57–82, 74.

102. Jane K. Cowan, "Who's Afraid of Violent Language? Honour, Sovereignty and Claims-Making in the League of Nations," *Anthropological Theory* 3, no. 3 (2003): 271–91.

103. See John Munro, "Empire and Intersectionality: Notes on the Production of Knowledge About U.S. Imperialism," *Globality Studies* 12 (2008): 6. Munro quotes Robert Lee Nichols, "Realizing the Social Contract: The Case of Colonialism and Indigenous Peoples," *Contemporary Political Theory* 4, no. 1 (February 2005): 43. Deskaheh's endeavors at the league are further recounted in Anthony Hall, *The American Empire and the Fourth World* (Montreal: McGill-Queen's University Press, 2003), 489–95; and Ronald Niezen, *The Origins of Indigenism: Human Rights and the Politics of Identity* (Berkeley: University of California Press, 2003), 31–36.

104. Fiona Paisley, "Mock Justice: World Conservation and Australian Aborigines in Interwar Switzerland," *Transforming Cultures e-journal* 3, no. 1 (2008): 196–226, 196, http://epress.lib.uts.edu.au/journals/TfC

105. Tilman Dedering, "Petitioning Geneva: Transnational Aspects of Protest and Resistance in South West Africa/Namibia After the First World War," *Journal of Southern African Studies* 35, no. 4 (2009): 785–801.

106. Ralph J. Bunche, "French Administration in Togoland and Dahomey" (Ph.D. diss., Harvard University, 1934).

107. Susan Pedersen, "Metaphors of the Schoolroom," *History Workshop Journal* 66 (2008): 188–207, 196.

108. Ibid. Pedersen's work on the mandates has renovated the study of the league.

109. Quoted in "The Deliberations of the Council of Four, Lloyd George, May 17, 1919," in Miller, *Drafting of the Covenant*, 2:91. See also Sir James Headlam-Morley, *A Memoir of the Paris Peace Conference, 1919*, ed. Agnes Headlam-Morley et al. (London: Methuen, 1972).

110. Kuehl, *Biographical Dictionary of Internationalists*, 66–68.

111. Ibid., 10.

112. For a more cynical view, see Stephen Bonsal, *Unfinished Business* (New York: Doubleday, Doran, 1944), from his diary for March 27, 1919.

113. Ranshofen-Wertheimer, *International Secretariat*, 365.

114. Ibid.

115. Pedersen, "Metaphors of the Schoolroom."

116. Swanwick, *I Have Been Young*, quoted in Sluga, "Gender," 315–16.

117. To be sure, Westminster was the locus of a League of Nations Conference of Women's Organizations. Eighty delegates represented forty-three women's organizations, with the explicit aim of ensuring "an adequate share for women in the work of the Assembly, the Commissions, and the Secretariat of the League"; League of Nations Archives, Geneva, Women's Questions, sec. 23: R1356 23/1042/1042, "Women and the League of Nations Conference of Women's Organisations."

118. For more on the Health Organization's work, see *League of Nations Health Organization* (Geneva: Information Section, 1931); and for the growing literature on the international politics of health in this period, see Sunil Amrith, *Decolonizing International Health: India and Southeast Asia, 1930–65* (Basingstoke: Palgrave Macmillan, 2006); Amrith and Sluga, "New Histories of the UN."

119. For more on this history, see Carol Miller, "Geneva—the Key to Equality: Interwar Feminists and the League of Nations," *Women's History Review* 3 (1994): 219–45.

120. League of Nations Archives, Geneva, R1356 23/1042/1042: "Women and the League of Nations Conference of Women's Organizations," letter from E. Shepherd to Drummond. Her coauthor was to be Clarence W. Alvord, a celebrated American historian from Missouri.

121. See Caine and Sluga, *Gendering European History*, chap. 6.

122. Swanwick, *I Have Been Young*, 385, 246.

123. McKenzie, "Power of International Positioning," 142: "These powerful women—powerful by professional class and national citizenship—carved out a space

between the domestic and the international to vie for additional rights. They drew on international law and diplomacy to pass legislation that allowed U.S. women to transmit citizenship to their children born overseas."

124. The figures are taken from Guieu, *Le rameau et le glaive*, 96, 97.

125. Ibid., 98–119.

126. On Fosdick, see Lavelle, "Exit, Voice, and Loyalty," 376.

127. Kuehl, *Biographical Dictionary of Internationalists*, 78–80.

128. Ibid., 405–6.

129. Ibid., 396–97.

130. See Guieu, *Le rameau et le glaive*, 56.

131. Ibid., 63.

132. See Bouchard, *Le citoyen et l'ordre mondial*, 228.

133. Guieu, *Le rameau et le glaive*, 59.

134. The International Union had held three "General Assembly" meetings in 1919, one in Paris, then London, then Brussels. Guieu, *Le rameau et le glaive*, 64, 68.

135. Brown, "Enacting the International," 83ff.

136. Ibid., 78.

137. Ibid. 83.

138. Ibid. 87.

139. H. Duncan Hall, *The News Bulletin of the Institute for Pacific Relations*, June–July 1927, 7–9. Hall had worked in the league's Opium Trade Committee.

140. Willoughby Dickinson, "Speech at League of Nations Union Meeting," Tottenham, January 15, 1930, quoted in Gorman, "Ecumenical Internationalism," 68. The International Federation of League of Nations Societies was also known as a union in the French literature.

141. Ibid., 80.

142. In another example, Janet Mitchell was education secretary for YWCA 1924–26, and an Australian delegate to the first Institute of Pacific Relations conference in Honolulu in 1925. See Fiona Paisley, *Glamour in the Pacific: Cultural Internationalism and Race Politics in the Women's Pan-Pacific* (Honolulu: University of Hawaii Press, 2009), 34.

143. Swanwick, *I Have Been Young*, 440.

144. Sudhin Ghose, "Three Conversations: Tagore Talks with Einstein, with Rolland and with Wells," *Asia* 31 (1931): 139–43, 196-97, 196, 142.

145. Ibid, 142.

146. *The Case of Rosika Schwimmer: Alien Pacifists Not Wanted!* (New York: American Civil Liberties Union, June 1929).

147. She finally won her appeal in 1946, two years before her death. See Sluga, *Nation, Psychology and International Politics*; and Edith Wynner, "Lippmann and the Schwimmer Case," in response to *The Mysteries of Mr. Lippmann*, by Anthony Lewis, *New York Review of Books*, March 19, 1981.

148. Kuehl, *Biographical Dictionary of Internationalists*, 524–25.

149. Kenneth Thompson, "Quincy Wright," in *American Political Scientists: A Dictionary*, ed. G. Utter and C. Lockhart (New York: Greenwood, 1993), 345.

150. Madeleine Herren, "'Outwardly . . . an Innocuous Conference Authority': National Socialism and the Logistics of International Information Management," *German History* 20, no. 1 (2002): 67–92.

151. Daniel Varè, *Laughing Diplomat*, quoted in Ranshofen-Wertheimer, *International Secretariat*, 251.

152. Ranshofen-Wertheimer, *International Secretariat*, 251.

153. For more on the history of pan-Asianism in this context, see Prashad, *Darker Nations*, 27; and Cemil Aydin, *The Politics of Anti-Westernism in Asia: Visions of World Order in Pan-Islamic and Pan-Asian Thought* (New York: Columbia University Press, 2007).

154. Quoted in Burkman, "Nationalist Actors," 97.

155. Nitobe's replacement in 1927 as under secretary-general and director of the Political Section of the Secretariat was Sugimura Yotaro, one of many such Japanese international figures; see Francis P. Walters, *A History of the League of Nations* (London: Oxford University Press, 1952), 705.

156. Lavelle, "Exit, Voice, and Loyalty," 377.

Chapter 3. The Apogee of Internationalism

1. Mass Observation, *Peace and the Public: A Study by Mass Observation* (London: Longmans, Green, 1947), 39. The rest of the report was devoted to assessing "how far ordinary people are prepared to go in sacrificing national sovereignty in the interests of world peace." They found that two out of three people liked the idea of world government, one in two thought it practical in the future, one in six thought it "possibly practical during the twentieth century." Ibid., 47.

2. James Speer II, "Hans Morgenthau and the World State," *World Politics* 20, no. 2 (1968): 214.

3. MAE, Nations unies [NUIO], S-50-3-8-6: "Report on the Relation of Women to the UN Organization to the Sec. Gen. of the UN Organization from the Women's Advisory Committee of the United Nations Information Office," 2.

4. Manu Bhagavan, "Princely States and the Making of Modern India," *Indian Economic and Social History Review* 46, no. 3 (2009): 428; see also the excellent survey of these wartime movements in Marika Sherwood, "The United Nations: Caribbean and African-American Attempts to Influence the Founding Conference in San Francisco in 1945," *Journal of Caribbean History* 29, no. 1 (1996): 25–58.

5. Quoted in Manu Bhagavan, "A New Hope: India, the United Nations and the Making of the Universal Declaration of Human Rights," *Modern Asian Studies* 44, no. 2 (2010): 318.

6. This is Eric Hobsbawm's argument; see *Nations and Nationalism Since 1780*, chap. 5.

7. The specific clauses of the Atlantic Charter that resonated were "the right of all peoples to choose the form of government under which they will live" and "securing,

for all, improved labor standards, economic advancement and social security." Atlantic Charter, August 14, 1941, available at http://avalon.law.yale.edu/wwii/atlantic.asp.

8. Quoted in Bhagavan, "New Hope," 318.

9. See Mamoru Shigemitsu, *Japan and Her Destiny: My Struggle for Peace*, ed. F. S. G. Piggott, trans. O. White (London: Hutchinson, 1958), written while he was in jail, in the wake of the Tokyo military tribunals.

10. Du Bois, *Color and Democracy*, preface.

11. China was represented at these talks, but with a weak voice.

12. Du Bois, *Color and Democracy*, 85.

13. See also Arnold Toynbee, "*World* Sovereignty and *World* Culture," *Pacific Affairs* 4 (September 1931): 753-78.

14. See Glenda Sluga, *The Problem of Trieste and the Italo-Yugoslav Border* (Albany: State University of New York Press, 2001), 14, 36.

15. Cited in Alfred Cobban, *National Self-Determination* (London: Oxford University Press, 1944), 176. The geographer Arthur Moodie more simply calculated that in Europe linear borders were inappropriate; *The Italo-Yugoslav Boundary: A Study in Political Geography* (London: George Philip and Son, 1945), 158, 187.

16. David Mitrany, "The Functional Approach to World Organization," *International Affairs* (Royal Institute of International Affairs 1944–) 24, no. 3 (1948): 350–63. See also Rothschild, "What Is Security?" 57; and David Long, *Towards a New Liberal Internationalism: The International Theory of J. A. Hobson* (Cambridge: Cambridge University Press, 1996), 186.

17. Quoted in Sluga, *Problem of Trieste*, 138.

18. Ibid., 139.

19. Quoted in Glenda Sluga, "UNESCO and the One World of Julian Huxley," *Journal of World History* 21, no. 3 (2010): 405.

20. Guieu, *Le rameau et le glaive*, 67, 83.

21. MAE, Paris, NUOI, S-1, Dumbarton Oaks, "Commission pour l'étude des principes d'une organisation internationale," Séance Dossiers Générale; and Glenda Sluga, "René Cassin: *Les droits de l'homme* and the History of Human Rights," in *Human Rights in the Twentieth Century*, ed. Stefan Ludwig-Hoffman (Cambridge: Cambridge University Press, 2009), 107-24.

22. For more on Cassin's life in this period, see Antoine Prost and Jay Winter, *René Cassin* (Paris: Fayard, 2011), chaps. 6–7; and the chapter on Cassin in Jay Winter, *Dreams of Peace and Freedom: Utopian Moments in the Twentieth Century* (New Haven, Conn.: Yale University Press, 2006).

23. See Paul Gordon Lauren, *The Evolution of International Human Rights: Visions Seen*, 2nd ed. (Philadelphia: University of Pennsylvania Press, 2003), 148.

24. H. G. Wells, *'42 to '44: A Contemporary Memoir upon Human Behaviour During the Crisis of the World Revolution* (London: Secker and Warburg, 1944), 30.

25. David Levering Lewis, *W. E. B. Du Bois: The Fight for Equality and the American Century, 1919–1963* (New York: Henry Holt, 2009), 518.

26. See Liang Pan, *The United Nations in Japan's Foreign and Security Policymaking, 1945–1992: National Security, Party Politics, and International Status* (Cambridge, Mass.: Harvard University Press, 2005).

27. Bhagavan argues that in the rather unlikely setting of "total war" the world experienced its "first, true 'global moment,' when people everywhere actually participated with heretofore unseen parity." See "New Hope," 320.

28. Wendell Willkie, *One World* (New York: Simon & Schuster, 1943), 2.

29. See Mark Mazower, *No Enchanted Palace: The End of Empire and the Ideological Origins of the United Nations* (Princeton, N.J.: Princeton University Press, 2009) for detailed analysis of the imperialist perspectives of a specific generation of British supporters of the league and the UN.

30. Bhagavan, "Princely States," 429. Within the context of Indian nationalism, the idea of one world took hold as a kind of "world government, plenary in character, even though informally so, which would save humanity." Ibid., 435.

31. Ibid., 436.

32. The first Congress of Pan-Europe met in Vienna in 1926. Coudenhove-Kalergi, born in Tokyo in 1894, the son of an Austrian nobleman father and Japanese mother, educated in Vienna, stood for the cosmopolitan image of the hybrid international man; Kuehl, *Biographical Dictionary of Internationalists*, 172–74. French versions of the United States of Europe were as prominent in the interwar period; Guieu, *Le rameau et le glaive*, chap. 10.

33. Clarence Streit, *Union Now: A Proposal for a Federal Union of the Democracies of the North Atlantic* (New York: Harper, 1939).

34. Kuehl, *Biographical Dictionary of Internationalists*, 155–56.

35. Wayne Hudson, *Australia and the New World Order: Evatt at San Francisco, 1945* (Canberra: Australian National University, 1993).

36. Brian Urquhart, *Ralph Bunche: An American Odyssey* (New York: Norton, 1998), chaps. 8 and 9.

37. Heater, *Peace Through Education*, 147.

38. Ibid. Jo-Ann Pemberton provides a useful genealogy of the twentieth-century usage and variety of meanings of world citizenship and one world-ism in *Global Metaphors* (London: Pluto Press, 2001), see esp. 121ff. She describes the use of the notion of a "world mind," "discussed as though it were a viscous fluid penetrating and fusing together individual minds," 111.

39. Cf. the United World Federalists, a nonpartisan, nonprofit organization founded in 1947 as the result of a merger of five existing world government groups: Americans United for World Government; World Federalists, U.S.A.; Student Federalists; Georgia World Citizens Committee; and the Massachusetts Committee for World Federation. The organization became World Federalists, USA in the 1960s, before changing its name again in the 1970s to the World Federalists Association; see Baratta, *Politics of World Federation*.

40. Kuehl, *Biographical Dictionary of Internationalists*, 524–25.

41. Ibid., 184.

42. After the UN's creation, Culbertson worked through the Citizens Committee for UN Reform, trying to put his ideals into practice.

43. Suri, "Non-governmental Organizations," 238.

44. Guieu, *Le rameau et le glaive*, 272.

45. See E. Meyer, *Report on San Francisco* (Washington, D.C.: Washington Post, 1945), 12; H. V. Evatt, *The United Nations* (Cambridge, Mass.: Harvard University Press, 1948), 14ff.; Sherwood, "United Nations."

46. Hedda Hopper, "The Press: San Francisco Spectacle," *Time*, May 7, 1945, available at http://www.time.com/time/magazine/article/0,9171,797505,00.html.

47. Ibid, and "Danish Writer in Hollywood to Supply Data for UN," *Box Office*, November 5, 1949, 16.

48. Ibid.

49. Virginia Gildersleeve, *Many a Good Crusade* (New York: Macmillan, 1954), 344. Lukas Hanyes and Michael Ignatieff, "Mobilizing Public Support for the United Nations" (working paper, Center for Public Leadership, John F. Kennedy School of Government, Spring 2003), 69.

50. Marika Sherwood, "'There Is No New Deal for the Blackman in San Francisco': African Attempts to Influence the Founding Conference of the United Nations, April–July, 1945," *International Journal of African Historical Studies* 29, no. 1 (1996): 71–94.

51. For more on Smuts, see Sluga, *Nation, Psychology and International Politics*; Dubow, "Smuts, the United Nations and the Rhetoric of Race and Rights"; and Mazower, *No Enchanted Palace*.

52. Gildersleeve, *Many a Good Crusade*, 331; and B. Lutz, "Reminiscences of the San Francisco Conference That Founded United Nations, Bertha Lutz Brazilian Plenipotentiary Delegate" (typescript, n.d.), Women's Library, London, Papers of Margery Irene Corbett Ashby, 6B/106/7/MCA/C2.

53. Glenda Sluga, "National Sovereignty and Female Equality: Gender, Peacemaking, and the New World Orders of 1919 and 1945," in *Frieden–Gewalt–Geschlecht: Friedens-und Konfliktforschung als Geschlechterforschung*, ed. J. Davy, K. Hagemann, and U. Katzel (Essen: Klartext, 2005), 166–83; and Karen Offen, "Women's Rights or Human Rights? International Feminism Between the Wars," in *Women's Rights and Human Rights: International Historical Perspectives*, ed. P. Grimshaw, K. Holmes, and M. Lake (Basingstoke: Palgrave, 2001), 243.

54. Sluga, "National Sovereignty and Female Equality." See also Glenda Sluga, "'Spectacular Feminism': The International History of Women, World Citizenship, and Human Rights," in *Women's Activism: Global Perspectives from the 1890s to the Present*, ed. Francisca De Haan, June Purvis, Margaret Allen, and Krassimira Daskalova (London: Routledge, 2012).

55. Lutz added, "Nevertheless, they collaborated very fully on all points of special interest to women"; Lutz, "Reminiscences of the San Francisco Conference."

56. Churchill College, Cambridge University, Papers of Florence Horsbrugh, Baroness Horsbrugh, United Nations Conference, San Francisco, "The Women's World

Section," *San Francisco Chronicle*, April 28, 1945; Zilfa Estcourt, "British Women in War," *San Francisco Chronicle*, April 28, 1945, n.p.

57. *Free World*, June 1945, n.p., cutting in ibid.

58. For more on Lutz's life, see Rachel Soihet, *O feminismo tatico de Bertha Lutz* (Florianopolis: Editora Mulheres, 2006).

59. "Jessie Street," in *Stirring Australian Speeches: The Definitive Collection from Botany to Bali*, ed. Michael Cathcart and Kate Darian-Smith (Melbourne: Melbourne University Press, 2004), 208–11.

60. See Sherwood, "'There Is No New Deal.'"

61. UNCIO Commission II General Assembly 2683/5/6, folder 24, Verbatim Minutes of the Third Meeting of Commission II, Opera House, June 20, 1945, 8.30 p.m.

62. For more on the fate of the mandates, see Michael Callahan, *A Sacred Trust: The League of Nations and Africa, 1929–1946* (Brighton: Sussex Academic Press, 2004).

63. See Duncan Hall, "The British Commonwealth and Trusteeship," Talk at Chatham House 1945, *International Affairs* 22, no. 2 (1946): 203.

64. Dubow, "Smuts, the United Nations and the Rhetoric of Race and Rights."

65. UN Charter, chap. 11, art. 73.

66. UN Charter, chap. 12, "The International Trusteeship System," arts. 82–83.

67. UN Charter, chap. 13, "The Trusteeship Council," arts. 87–88.

68. Ralph Bunche, *A World View of Race* (Washington D.C.: Associates in Negro Folk Education, 1936), 374.

69. Urquhart, *Ralph Bunche*, 102–4. UCLA, Papers of Ralph Bunche, box 128, folder 85: Letter to Kay Fremin of *Ebony* magazine, 1947.

70. Lawrence S. Finkelstein, "Bunche and the Colonial World: From Trusteeship to Decolonization," in Rivlin, *Ralph Bunche*, 116–17.

71. Charles P. Henry, *Ralph Bunche: Model Negro or American Other?* (New York: New York University Press, 1999), 137; Urquhart, *Ralph Bunche*, 121–23; and W. J. Hudson, *Australia and the Colonial Question at the United Nations* (Sydney: Sydney University Press, 1970).

72. UCLA, Papers of Ralph Bunche, box 100, folder 14: 16th Plenary Session of the West Indian Conference, March 12, 1946.

73. UN Charter, chap. 1, art. 1.3.

74. UN Charter, chaps. 1–5.

75. On Evatt, the best accounts remain Hudson, *Australia and the Colonial Question* and idem, *Australia and the New World Order*. See also Emma Ede, "An Internationalist Vision" (honors thesis, Department of History, University of Sydney, 2008).

76. Others set up in the 1940s included the International Civil Aviation Organization (Montreal). For more on the United Nations "system," see Reinalda, *Routledge History of International Organizations*, pt. 8.

77. League of Nations, *The Development of International Cooperation in Economic and Social Affairs: Report of the Special Committee* [The Bruce Report] (Geneva, August 1939). See Martin D. Dubin, "Toward the Bruce Report: The Economic and Social

Programs of the League of Nations in the Avenol Era," in *The League of Nations in Retrospect: Proceedings of the Symposium Organized by the United Nations Library and the Graduate Institute of International Studies*, ed. Graduate Institute of International Studies (Geneva: de Gruyter, 1983), 42–72; and Lavelle, "Exit, Voice, and Loyalty," 381.

78. Bailey, *Secretariat of the United Nations*, 19.

79. Sluga, *Problem of Trieste*, chap. 6.

80. Mercedes M. Randall, ed., *Beyond Nationalism: The Social Thought of Emily Greene Balch* (New York: Twayne, 1972), xxxi. Randall also provides a useful bibliography to the many writings Balch produced in this period, at the age of eighty.

81. Emma Rothschild notes the origins of the UN flag in the context of the 1947 Commission of Investigation Concerning Greek Frontier Incidents. "Archives of Universal History," 393. Notably, the league did not have an official flag.

82. See Levering Lewis, *W. E. B. Du Bois*, 513ff.

83. Sherwood, "United Nations," 42.

84. See "Status of Women," *UN Weekly Bulletin* 1, no. 7 (September 16, 1946): 11.

85. "Lady Pethick-Lawrence Talks on Equal Rights," *Equal Rights*, March–April 1946, 11. See also Sluga, "National Sovereignty and Female Equality."

86. Lord Gladwyn, *The Memoirs of Lord Gladwyn* (London: Weidenfeld and Nicolson, 1972), 182.

87. Gildersleeve, *Many a Good Crusade*, 348.

88. Other sites discussed in the United States included Chicago, Philadelphia, Boston, Queens, Rhode Island, South Dakota, and North Carolina.

89. CARAN, Paris, Fonds Cassin, AP382, cote 158, Lettre "vendredi matin 16 mai 1946" [letter to his wife, Simone], author's translation.

90. Churchill College, Papers of First Lord Gladwyn, GLAD 1/4/1 1943–45 Documents, typed extracts from letter to Mr. Jebb from Brian Urquhart, n.d.

91. One noted example is the film *North by Northwest* (1959).

92. Quoted in Keppel, *Work of Democracy*, 66.

93. University of Adelaide, Barr Smith Library, Crocker Papers, MSS 327 C938p/ series 8, "The United Nations at First Hand," draft of a book on the UN, 1949–50.

94. See Samuel Moyn, *The Last Utopia: Human Rights in History* (Cambridge, Mass.: Harvard University Press, 2010); Roland Burke, *Decolonization and the Evolution of International Human Rights* (Philadelphia: University of Pennsylvania Press, 2010); Lauren, *Evolution of International Human Rights*.

95. UN Department of Public Information, Press Division, press release PM/273 27, January 1947, "Address by Henri Laugier, Assistant Sec-Gen in charge of Social Affairs Before the Commission on Human Rights." Laugier, a former professor of physiology, was also president of the Ligue des Droits de l'Homme.

96. MAE, Paris, NUOI, S-1, Dumbarton Oaks, "Commission pour l'étude des principes d'une organisation internationale, 20 janvier 1945."

97. See Johannes Morsink, *The Universal Declaration of Human Rights: Origins, Drafting, and Intent* (Philadelphia: University of Pennsylvania Press, 2000), 33.

98. Library of Congress, Charles Malik Collection, "Commission on Human Rights, First Session, Verbatim Record, 31 January 1947," box 76, file 1: First Session, Commission on Human Rights—Minutes 1947. Chang earned his doctoral degree at Columbia University, specializing in Chinese studies.

99. Ibid.

100. Romulo served as the president of the Fourth Session of the United Nations General Assembly in 1949–50 and chairman of the United Nations Security Council. He later ended up a defender of the Marcos regime, just as Cassin became an apologist for de Gaulle's creeping authoritarianism in the 1950s—until de Gaulle verbally attacked Israel.

101. Charles Malik Papers, Library of Congress, Manuscript Division, Box 76, Human Rights Commission, Drafting Committee, Meeting 7, February 1, 1947, verbatim records, Ronald LeBeau, E/61.

102. "UN: Applied Euthenics," Time, May 20, 1946.

103. Mehta became a member of the Constituent Assembly of India, parliamentary secretary to the minister of education and health. She was also president of the All-India Women's Conference (AIWC). Her early education encompassed time in London, the United States, and Japan, in the throes of first-wave feminism and the social science movements around education and social welfare that almost uniquely invited in women. See Bhagavan's discussion of her role in "New Hope."

104. When Mehta articulated the need for a charter of rights for women that established "the freedom of woman and her equality with man, equality of identity," she looked to already-formulated Indian models including a 1931 resolution of the Indian National Congress; Nehru Memorial Museum and Library, New Delhi, Papers of Hansa Mehta,, "Presidential Address Before the 18th Session of the All India Women's Conference at Hyderabad (Sind) by Mrs. Hansa Mehta," Roshni, February 1946, 21.

105. Bhagavan, "New Hope."

106. "Letter from Embassy of India Chancery, Washington DC, 2nd Jan 1947 to Mrs. Hansa Mehta," quoted in ibid., 16.

107. Bhagavan, "Princely States," 429: "Mehta, involved with both the UDHR and the Indian Constituent Assembly, entangled the idea of globalism with the idea of the postcolonial and sought to redefine the relationships between individuals, groups, states and meta-state frames. This raised a variety of questions regarding sovereignty, notions of belonging and of rights, limits of citizenship and so on."

108. See Laura Reanda, "Human Rights and Women's Rights: The United Nations Approach," Human Rights Quarterly 3, no. 2 (1981): 11–31.

109. CARAN, Paris, Fonds Cassin, AP382, cote 128, dossier 3: "Declaration," Statement on Equality for Women, May 27, 1948.

110. Reanda, "Human Rights and Women's Rights," 18.

111. Morsink, Universal Declaration of Human Rights, 93, 118. See articles 23 and 25 of the declaration, which refer to "himself and his family."

112. Ibid.

113. University of Adelaide, Barr Smith Library, Crocker Papers, MSS 327 C938p/ series 5, Perham to Crocker, March 19, 1947.

114. See the preamble to the constitution of the United Nations Educational, Scientific and Cultural Organization, adopted in London on November 16, 1945.

115. Ibid.; John Partington, "H.G. Wells and the World State: A Liberal Cosmopolitan in a Totalitarian Age," *International Relations* 17, no. 2 (2003): 233–46.

116. UNESCO General Conference First Session, First Plenary Meeting, November 20, 1946.

117. Walter H. C. Laves and Charles A. Thomson, *UNESCO: Purpose, Progress, Prospects* (Bloomington: Indiana University Press, 1957), 222.

118. Julian Huxley, *Memories*, vol. 2 (London: Allen & Unwin, 1973), chap. 1; John C. Greene, "The Interaction of Science and World View in Sir Julian Huxley's Evolutionary Biology," *Journal of the History of Biology* 23, no. 1 (Spring 1990): 40. For more on the circumstances surrounding his appointment, see James Sewell, *UNESCO and World Politics* (Princeton, N.J.: Princeton University Press, 1975), 105–7.

119. Laura Vitray, "UNESCO: Adventure in Understanding," *Free World*, November 1946, 24.

120. Sewell, *UNESCO and World Politics*, 84, 105–7.

121. Ernest O. Hauser, "Doctor Huxley's Wonderful Zoo," *Saturday Evening Post*, October 2, 1948, 76.

122. Elazar Barkan, and Diane B. Paul, cited in C. K. Waters and A. Van Helden, "Introduction," in *Julian Huxley: Biologist and Statesman of Science*, ed. C. K. Waters and A. Van Helden (Houston: Rice University Press, 1992), 20.

123. Sewell, *UNESCO and World Politics*, 109.

124. Ellen Wilkinson, "Conference for the Establishment of the United Nations Educational, Scientific and Cultural Organisation, Held at the Institute of Civil Engineers, London, from the 1st to the 16th November, 1945," ECO/CONF./29, available at UNESDOC; for more on Wilkinson, see the biography by Betty D. Vernon, *Ellen Wilkinson* (London: Croom Helm, 1982), although not much is made of her UNESCO role.

125. Huxley, Report of the Executive Secretary of the Preparatory Commission, General Conference of Unesco First Session (20 November to 10 December 1946), Unesco, Paris, 1947, 20; Gerard Mangone, *The Idea and Practice of World Government* (New York: Columbia University Press, 1951).

126. UN Archives, New York, S-0544-004 UN Education Science and Culture Section, Ivan Borisoc to Henri Laugier, Ass. Secretary General, Dept of Social Affairs, Comments on the Second Session of the General Conference of UNESCO, December 3, 1947.

127. There was little transparency or procedure in the early recruitment process. Although over thirty thousand people applied for positions, most of the recruitment occurred on a haphazard basis, through connections and networks, proximity achieved through residence or through experience in the processes leading up to the UN's

creation. See Walter Crocker, "Some Notes on the United Nations Secretariat," *International Organization* 4, no. 4 (1950): 609. Bailey, *Secretariat of the United Nations*, 19.

128. "This Is Our Power: Speeches Delivered by Julian Huxley and Mr. Jaime Torres Bodet During the Third Session of the General Conference of the UNESCO, Beirut, December 10, 1948" (Paris: UNESCO, 1948), 10.

129. Heater, *Peace Through Education*, 140.

130. Huxley, *Memories*, 2:15.

131. Basil Karp, "The Development of the Philosophy of UNESCO" (Ph.D. diss., University of Chicago, 1951), 41.

132. *UN Bulletin*, January 1, 1949.

133. For more on this point, see Liang Pan, "Behind the Cultural Enterprise of an Economic Superpower," in *Kokusai seiji keizaigaku kenkyu* (Journal of International Political Economy), no. 19, March (2007): 1–20.

134. See Peter Mandler, "One World, Many Cultures: Margaret Mead and the Limits to Cold War Anthropology," *History Workshop Journal* 68, no. 1 (2009): 149–72.

135. "Tensions Affecting International Understanding Project" (Paris: UNESCO, 1947), UNESDOC.

136. Oxford University, Papers of Gilbert Murray, dossier 3, "Letter to Cassin, 23 June 1947"; "Letter to Cassin, 23 Jan 1953."

137. Rice University, Julian Sorell Huxley Papers, "Verbatim Report of Talk by Dr. Huxley at the Sorbonne University, Paris, on Thursday, 26 February, 1948, at 9.00 pm. Paris," 12.

138. Thomas Besterman, *UNESCO: Peace in the Minds of Men* (New York: Methuen, 1951). Besterman was head of the Department of Information at UNESCO and a supporter of Huxley.

139. For a brief discussion of the internationalization of development, see Frederick Cooper and Randall Packard, "Introduction," in *International Development and the Social Sciences: Essays on the History and Politics of Knowledge* (Berkeley: University of California Press, 1998), 9; Frederick Cooper, "Modernizing Colonialism and the Limits of Empire," in *Lessons of Empire: Imperial Histories and American Power*, ed. Craig Calhoun, Frederick Cooper, and Kevin W. Moore (New York: New Press, 2006), 63–72; Roger Louis, *Imperialism at Bay*, 104.

140. Rice University, Julian Sorell Huxley Papers, MS 50, box 99, folder 2: Julian Huxley, "West African Possibilities," *Yale Review*, Winter 1945, 263; Julian Huxley (with P. Deane), *Future of the Colonies* (London: Pilot Press, 1944). Huxley had close links to the British Colonial Office through his consulting work, his cousin Elspeth, and his relationship with Arthur Creech-Jones, who was eventually the postwar Labor Government's secretary of state for the colonies.

141. John Bowers, "Fundamental Education," *UNESCO Courier* 1, no. 1 (1948): 5. Phillip Jones has traced the influence of fundamental education through Bowers; see *International Policies for Third World Education: UNESCO, Literacy and Development* (London: Routledge, 1988); and UNESCO, "Nyasaland Protectorate Mass Education

Pilot Project," Edc./61—31 March 1948, "Fundamental Education: Pilot Project in Nyas-aland (Malawi) 1948," UNESDOC.

142. UNESCO, Paris, Social Questions, Economic and Social Council, Commission on Human Rights, Correspondence, "To: Director-General, Deputy Director-General, Assistant Director-General, From: A. Cortesao 'Provisional Questionnaire on Trust Territories,'" August 11, 1947.

143. While there are numerous assessments of this project in histories of British imperialism and Tanganyika, there is no scholarly study of UNESCO's role; Cyril Ehrlich, "Some Antecedents of Development Planning in Tanganyika," *Journal of Development Studies* 2, no. 3 (1966): 254–67.

144. Commission on Human Rights, Correspondence, "To: Director-General, Deputy Director-General, Assistant Director-General, From: A. Cortesao 'Provisional Questionnaire on Trust Territories,'" August 11, 1947.

145. Ehrlich, "Some Antecedents of Development Planning in Tanganyika."

146. Bowers, "Fundamental Education," 5.

147. Chloé Maurel, "L'UNESCO de 1945 à 1974" (Univ. Paris I. Sous la direction de Pascal Ory, 2005). Maurel dates UNESCO's interest in Africa and the influence of the British Colonial Office to a later phase of UNESCO's policy making, the 1950s and 1960s.

148. Huxley, *Memories*, 2:23. Gabriel was on a succession of temporary contracts at grade 11; his European equivalents were grade 14. See also Sluga, "UNESCO and the One World of Julian Huxley."

149. Quoted in "Rural Schooling Poses Problem for Haitians," *UNESCO Courier*, April 1948, 5; see also "Highlights of Haitian Project," *UNESCO Courier*, March 1948, 4 and Edmund Wilson, *Red, Black, Blond and Olive: Studies in Four Civilizations: Zuñi, Haiti, Soviet Russia, Israel* (New York: Oxford University Press, 1956), 95–96.

150. For a useful assessment of the fate of the project, see Chantalle Francesca Verna, "Haiti's 'Second Independence' and the Promise of Pan-American Cooperation, 1934–1956" (Ph.D. diss., Michigan State University, Department of History, 2005), chap. 4; Joseph Watras, "Was Fundamental Education Another form of Colonialism?," *Review of Education* 53 (2007): 55–72; and Craig N. Murphy, *The United Nations Development Programme: A Better Way?* (Cambridge: Cambridge University Press, 2006), 86.

151. Laves and Thomson, *UNESCO,* 52.

152. For more on the significance of developmentalism in Africa in this period among scientific "progressives" and their links to Huxley, see Peder Anker, "The Politics of Ecology in South Africa on the Radical Left," *Journal of the History of Biology* 37 (2004): 303–31.

153. There is a growing literature on the UN's role in the postwar reconstruction of Europe, which includes the tragic problem of refugees; see, e.g., Jessica Reinisch, "Internationalism in Relief: The Birth (and Death) of UNRRA," in *Post-War Reconstruction in Europe: International Perspectives, 1945–1949*, ed. Mark Mazower, Jessica Reinisch, and David Feldman (Oxford: Oxford University Press, 2011), 258–89; idem, "'We Shall

Rebuild Anew a Powerful Nation': UNRRA, Internationalism and National Reconstruction in Poland," *Journal of Contemporary History* 43, no. 3 (2008): 451–76; Jessica Reinisch and Elizabeth White, eds., *The Disentanglement of Populations: Migration, Expulsion and Displacement in Post-war Europe, 1943–1949* (New York: Palgrave Macmillan, 2011); Pam Ballinger, "Opting for Identity: The Politics of International Refugee Relief in Venezia Giulia, 1948–1952," *Acta Histriae* 14, no. 1 (2006): 115–36.

154. Murphy, *United Nations Development Program*, 53.

155. Oxford University, United Nations Archive, Henry Fowler CD, Jamaican Ambassador to UNESCO, "UNESCO, Past, Present and Future," March 30, 1999, http://una.oxfordcity.org/index.php?option=com_content&ta.

156. See Herschelle S. Challenor, "The Contribution of Ralph Bunche to Trusteeship and Decolonization," in Rivlin, *Ralph Bunche,* 132‒56, and Robert A. Hill and Edmond J. Keller, *Trustee for the Human Community: Ralph J. Bunche and the Decolonization of Africa* (Athens: Ohio University Press, 2010).

157. Arbetarrörelsens Arkiv, Stockholm, Myrdal Papers, AMb, 3.1.3:4, "Myrdal to Laugier, Amb. July 6 1949."

158. Laves and Thomson, *UNESCO,* 53.

159. Arbetarrörelsens Arkiv, Stockholm, Myrdal Papers, AMb, 3.1.3:4, "Memorandum to Monsieur Henri Laugier, Assistant Secretary-General in Charge of the Department of Social Affairs from Mme Alva Myrdal, Top-Ranking Director, Department of Social Affairs, 5 April 1949."

160. Arbetarrörelsens Arkiv, Stockholm, Myrdal Papers, AMb, 3.1.3:4, "Alva Myrdal Diary Sent to Mr. Henri Laugier from Mrs. Alva Myrdal, 1 March 1950."

161. Alva Myrdal, "Population Trends in Densely Populated Areas," *Proceedings of the American Philosophical Society* 95, no. 1 (February 13, 1951): 1–7, 6.

162. UNESCO, "Resolutions for the 1950 Programme at the Fourth Session of UNESCO's General Conference," UNESDOC.

163. Elazar Barkan, *The Retreat of Scientific Racism: Changing Concepts of Race in Britain and the U.S. Between the World Wars* (Cambridge: Cambridge University Press, 1992), 341.

164. Ivan Hannaford, *Race: The History of an Idea in the West* (Washington, D.C.: Woodrow Wilson Center Press, 1996), 386.

165. Ibid., 397.

166. London School of Economics, Redcliffe-Maud Papers, 8/56: "Letter to John Maud from Pierson Dixon, Internal 5th June, 1950 Confidential," 3.

167. Laves and Thomson, *UNESCO,* 330.

168. Ibid., 221.

169. UNESCO, UNESCO/ED/124, Paris, 24 January 1953: "*Teaching About Human Rights*: A Report on the UNESCO Seminar on Active Methods of Education for Living in a World Community, 1952," UNESDOC.

170. For more on this McCarthyist period, see Shirley Hazzard, *Defeat of an Ideal: A Study of the Self-Destruction of the United Nations* (New York: Little, Brown, 1973);

Keppel, *Work of Democracy*, 70. Bunche was eventually exonerated, but the episode ended in tragedy for a trusteeship colleague who, faced with the public charge of being a communist, killed himself.

171. UNESCO, *An Appraisal of the United Nations Educational, Scientific and Cultural Organisation, UNESCO, July 1953* [Prepared by Mr. Irving Salomon of California, chairman of the U.S. delegation, with approval of other two delegates], UNESDOC.

172. Ibid.

173. Cf. Stuart Chase, *The Proper Study of Mankind: An Inquiry into the Science of Human Relations* (London: Phoenix House, 1950).

174. Guieu, *Le rameau et le glaive*, 272–76.

175. A critical world history of the UN associations is still to be written.

176. See Marco Duranti, *Human Rights and Conservative Politics in Postwar Europe* (New York: Oxford University Press, forthcoming).

177. CARAN, Paris, Fonds Cassin, AP382, cote 128, dossier 3: "Cassin, Declaration universelle de droits de l'homme," text typed, no author. In the late 1950s, Cassin, as vice president of the Conseil d'État, authorized the enactment of "emergency powers" for the French president for use in the management of anticolonial opposition in North Africa.

178. See Christine Fauré, *Ce que déclarer des droits veut dire* (Paris: Les Belles Lettres, 2011).

179. CARAN, Paris, Fonds Cassin, AP382, cote 147: "Europe 1944–74, I, Angleterre 1944–72," newspaper cutting, *News Chronicle*, n.d.

180. CARAN, Paris, Fonds Cassin, AP382, cote 134: UNESCO, dossier 4, "Letter from Alva Myrdal to Cassin, 19 août 1953."

181. UNESCO Archives, Paris, X07.83, *Missions of Myrdal*. Myrdal was disillusioned by what scholars have since identified as the "high modernism" of international development programs and the marginalization of local knowledge; see Suri, "Nongovernment Organizations," 240.

182. E. Franklin Frazier, "World Community and a Universal Moral Order," in *Approaches to Group Understanding*, ed. Lymon Bryson, Louis Finkelstein, and R. M. MacIver (New York: Harper, 1947), 443–52.

183. Ibid., 447.

184. Brian Urquhart, *A Life in Peace and War* (New York: Harper & Row, 1987), 92, 96.

185. Ibid., 96.

Chapter 4. What Is the International?

1. Henry Kissinger, in James Reston, "Now for the Last Quarter," *New York Times*, 19 January 1975, 19.

2. Stanley Hoffmann, "International Organization and the International System," *International Organization* 3 (1970): 389. Hoffmann is a professor of government at Harvard University.

3. Iriye, *Global Community*, 126, 129. Iriye charts a shift in the 1970s from

intergovernmental institutions as sites of significant "global" transnational agendas to a burgeoning international "civil society."

4. Kissinger, in Reston, "Now for the Last Quarter."

5. Daniel P. Moynihan, *A Dangerous Place* (London: Secker & Warburg, 1979), 82.

6. See Findlay and O'Rourke, *Power and Plenty,* chap. 9.

7. U Thant, *View from the UN* (New York: David and Charles, 1968), 441.

8. Philippe de Seynes, "Prospects for a Future Whole World," *International Organization* 26, no. 1 (1972): 1.

9. Bailey, *Secretariat of the United Nations,* 23; and Frederick C. Turner, "The Implications of Demographic Change for Nationalism and Internationalism," *Journal of Politics* 27 (1965): 89; On this view, "internationalism" constituted "a system of loyalty" and facility to communicate between the inhabitants of national states in ways that was equal to "their facility of communication with their own nationals."

10. See, e.g., Joseph S. Nye, "Neo-realism and Neoliberalism," *World Politics* 40, no. 2 (1988): 235–51, and Hedley Bull, *The Anarchical Society* (London: Macmillan, 1977). I discuss this point more fully later in this chapter.

11. See James A. Field, "Transnationalism and the New Tribe," *International Organization* 25 (1971): 353–72; and David Armstrong, Lorna Lloyd, and John Redmond, *From Versailles to Maastricht: International Organisation in the Twentieth Century* (London: St. Martin's, 1996), 250: "international regime" was a distinct analytical category that implied "sets of rules which aim to regulate some specific activity of international interest."

12. Iriye, *Global Community,* 181.

13. Consultative status has its foundation in article 17 of chapter 10 of the United Nations Charter, introduced as a result of the lobbying of NGOs at San Francisco.

14. Reinalda, *Routledge History of International Organizations,* 319.

15. In 2011, there were 3,382 NGOs in consultative status with the Economic and Social Council (ECOSOC) and some 400 NGOs accredited to the Commission on Sustainable Development (CSD).

16. Leland Goodrich, "San Francisco in Retrospect," *International Journal* 25, no. 2 (1970): 239. Goodrich had been director of the World Peace Foundation from 1942 to 1946 as well as professor of international organization and administration at Columbia University.

17. The others were India (independent from 1947, but with a seat because of membership of the league even as part of British Raj), China, the Philippines (newly independent in 1945), Ethiopia and Liberia, and seven countries from the Middle East.

18. Thant's appointment came after Hammarskjold's death in a plane crash on a UN mission in the Congo.

19. U Thant, *View from the UN,* 36.

20. In 1955, a meeting of the U.S. National Security Council noted that the president "referred to the widespread growth of nationalism which had become obvious in the world since the end of the war." Eisenhower was most alarmed that the communists had

managed "to identify themselves and their purposes with this emergent nationalism' and the United States had failed to recognize the importance of utilizing 'this new spirit of nationalism in its own interest"; quoted in J. Parker, "Cold War II: The Eisenhower Administration, the Bandung Conference, and the Reperiodization of the Postwar Era," *Diplomatic History* 30 (2006): 877.

21. See Burke, *Decolonization and the Evolution of International Human Rights,* chap. 2.

22. Anghie argues that the UN General Assembly was acting as a de facto site of international lawmaking, or at least attempts to remake international laws, in the interests of postcolonial states. Antony Anghie, *Imperialism, Sovereignty, and the Making of International Law* (New York: Cambridge University Press, 2004), 226; Hedley Bull made a similar point, disparagingly, in *Anarchical Society,* chap. 6.

23. See the argument in Anghie, *Imperialism, Sovereignty,* chap. 4.

24. Armstrong, Lloyd, and Redmond, *Versailles to Maastricht,* 103.

25. See the discussions of the sense of significance attached to the creation of UNCTAD at the time in Thomas G. Weiss et al., *UN Voices: The Struggle for Development and Social Justice* (Bloomington: Indiana University Press, 2005), chaps. 5–6; Hugh Tinker, *Race, Conflict and the International Order* (London: Macmillan, 1977), 117; Stephen Ryan, *The United Nations and International Politics* (New York: St. Martin's, 2000), chap. 3.

26. Weiss et al., *UN Voices,* 188–92.

27. For more on this complicated history of population politics, see Matthew Connolly's observations in "Seeing Beyond the State: The Population Control Movement and the Problem of Sovereignty," *Past and Present* 193, no. 1 (2006): 197–233, and *Fatal Misconception: The Struggle to Control World Population* (Cambridge, Mass.: Harvard University Press, 2008).

28. Rice University, Julian Sorell Huxley Papers, box 117, Report on the 11th Session of the General Conference of UNESCO, Paris, December 14–15, 1960.

29. See Hilkka Pietilä, *The Unfinished Story of Women and the United Nations* (New York: UN Non-Governmental Liaison Service, 2007), 23.

30. See Bhagavan, "A New Hope," 318.

31. On Bandung, see *Prashad, Darker Nations* and the useful discussion in Burke, *Decolonization and the Evolution of International Human Rights.*

32. Amrith, "Asian Internationalism," 558. Amrith neatly sums up the relationship of this internationalism to the work of the UN: "The post-war architecture of international organisations contained seeds of both visions of the international order. The language of the United Nations charter, on the one hand, enshrined the language of rights, citizenship and moral community. On the other hand, the institution of the UN's agencies as apolitical purveyors of 'technical assistance for economic development' strengthened the primacy of the developmental state."

33. By this time too, the UN had a gradually increasing number of African staff; Thant Myint-U and Amy Scott, *The UN Secretariat: A Brief History (1945-2006),* (New York: International Peace Academy, 2007), 48.

34. Suri, "Non-governmental Organizations," 240–41; David Mackenzie, *A World Beyond Borders: An Introduction to the History of International Organizations* (Toronto: University of Toronto Press, 2011), chap. 5; Peter Willetts, ed., *"The Conscience of the World": The Influence of Non-Governmental Organisations in the UN System* (London: Hurst, 1996).

35. Andrew Preston, "Universal Nationalism: Christian America's Response to the Years of Upheaval," in *The Shock of the Global: The 1970s in Perspective* (Cambridge, Mass.: Belknap of Harvard University Press, 2010).

36. See Iriye, *Global Community*, 131.

37. J. R. *McNeill*, "The Environment, Environmentalism, and International Society in the Long 1970s," in *The Shock of the Global*.

38. De Seynes, "Prospects for a Future Whole World," 1.

39. "Wonders of the Atomic Age," *Montreal Standard* 2 February, 1946, 4–5.

40. Goodrich, "San Francisco in Retrospect," 239.

41. Nye, "Neo-realism and Neoliberalism," 236.

42. The Organization of Petroleum Exporting Countries was an intergovernmental organization created in 1960 out of an agreement among Iran, Iraq, Kuwait, Saudi Arabia, and Venezuela.

43. Armstrong, Lloyd, and Redmond, *Versailles to Maastricht*, 95. Some analyses of the oil crisis explain the OPEC decisions as economically inevitable. See also from the period Gillian White, "A New *International* Economic Order," *Virginia Journal of International Law* 16, no. 2 (1976): 323–45; Burns H. Weston, "The Charter of Economic Rights and Duties of States and the Deprivation of Foreign-Owned Wealth," *American Journal of International Law* 75, no. 3 (1981): 437–75; Robin C. A. White, "A New International Economic Order," *International and Comparative Law Quarterly* 24 (1975): 542–52.

44. See R. Keohane and J. Nye, "International Interdependence and Integration," in *International Politics: Handbook of Political Science*, vol. 8, ed. F. Greenstein and N. Polsby (Reading, Mass.: Addison-Wesley, 1975), chap. 5.

45. Ivor Richards, "The United Nations and the New International Economic Order," *Millennium—Journal of International Studies* 4 (1975): 68.

46. Richard Jolly, "Society for International Development, the North-South Round-table and the Power of Ideas," *Development* 50 (2007): 55. See also Weiss et al., *UN Voices*, 227.

47. Ronald I. Meltzer, "Restructuring the United Nations System: Institutional Reform Efforts in the Context of North-South Relations," *International Organization* 32 (1978): 998.

48. Ibid., 1008.

49. Ibid., 1017. Ironically, the mooted structural changes were less popular among the developing bloc than among the industrialized nations—at least partly because they augured a shift from "voting" as the site of decision making at the UN to governance by professionals, in effect the shift from the "tyranny of the majority" to the rule of experts.

50. Quoted in Armstrong, Lloyd, and Redmond, *Versailles to Maastricht*, 95.

51. De Seynes, "Prospects for a Future Whole World," 133.

52. Hoffmann in a letter written in 1975, quoted in Jonathan Haslam, *No Virtue Like Necessity* (Princeton, N.J.: Princeton University Press, 2002), 227.

53. Richards, "United Nations and the New International Economic Order," 68.

54. Tucker, quoted in Haslam, *No Virtue Like Necessity,* 227. Some theorists argued that if NIEO had succeeded it would have constituted a "new internationalism" committed to "an ever-increasing interdependence" that was as likely to lead to conflict.

55. Armstrong, Lloyd, and Redmond, *Versailles to Maastricht*, 88.

56. Quoted in Tinker, *Race, Conflict.* 110.

57. John Reginald P. Dumas, "Moynihanism at the UN," *Third World Quarterly* 2 (1980): 518. See also United Nations, "Summary Records of the Third Committee, 43rd meeting (32nd session), A/C.3/32/SR. 43," para. 26. For more on Moynihan's position, see also Daniel Patrick Moynihan, "The Politics of Human Rights," *Commentary* 64, no. 2 (1977): 22; Moynihan, "The United States in Opposition," *Commentary* 59, no. 3 (1975): 31-44.

58. Quoted in Moynihan, *Dangerous Place*, 114.

59. J. N. Bhagwati and John Gerard Ruggie, introduction to *Power, Passions, and Purpose: Prospects for North-South Negotiations* (Cambridge, Mass.: MIT Press, 1984), 1.

60. Du Bois died in 1963, aged ninety-five.

61. See Chapter 3.

62. "Personal Note," April 2, 1952, quoted in Urquhart, *Ralph Bunche*, 242.

63. Ibid., 240.

64. *United Nations and World Citizenship*, 20.

65. Carol Anderson, "International Conscience, the Cold War, and Apartheid: The NAACP'S Alliance with the Reverend Michael Scott for South West Africa's Liberation, 1946–1951," *Journal of World History* 19 (September 2008): 297–325.

66. Quoted in Giuliano Ferrari Bravo, "National and International Trusteeship: Some Notes on UN Intervention in the System of Chapters XII and XIII of the Charter," *L'Africa romana* 34, no. 4 (1979): 416.

67. Ibid., 399.

68. Ibid., 401.

69. These included the International Convention on the Elimination of All Forms of Racial Discrimination (1969) and the Committee on Elimination of Racial Discrimination.

70. Pietilä, *Unfinished Story of Women*, 27.

71. For the effective role of the politics of international embarrassment on civil rights in this era, see Carol Anderson, *Eyes Off the Prize: The United Nations and the African American Struggle for Human Rights, 1944–1955* (New York: Cambridge University Press, 2003) and John Maynard, "Transcultural/Transnational Interaction and Influences on Aboriginal Australia," *Connected Worlds—History in Transnational Perspective* (Canberra: ANU ePress, 2005), 195–208.

72. Tinker, *Race, Conflict*, 130, 135.

73. Tinker, *Race, Conflict*, 77–132.

74. Harold R. Isaac, "Color in World Affairs," *Foreign Affairs* 47 (1969): 235.

75. Turner, "Implications of Demographic Change," 89.

76. Edward Shils, "Colour and the Afro-Asian Intellectual," in *Colour and Race,* ed. John Hope Franklin (Boston: Beacon, 1968), 5.

77. Talcott Parsons, "The Problem of Polarization on the Axis of Color," in Franklin, *Colour and Race*, 349–69.

78. Tinker, *Race, Conflict,* 129. He acknowledged R. Preiswerk, "Race and Colour in International Relations," in *The Year Book of World Affairs, 1970* (London: Stevens and Sons, 1970), 54–87; Isaac, "Color in World Affairs"; and Franklin, *Colour and Race.*

79. Tinker, *Race, Conflict,* 100, 132.

80. Preiswerk, "Race and Colour," 60.

81. Ibid., 87.

82. Bernard Lewis, quoted in Moynihan, *Dangerous Place,* 173.

83. The United States withdrew from the ILO completely in 1977, returning in 1981.

84. Tinker, *Race, Conflict,* 126.

85. Australia, Parliament, Senate, Standing Committee on Foreign Affairs and Defence, "The Role and Involvement of Australia and the United Nations in the Affairs of Sovereign Australian Territories: Official Hansard Report" (Canberra, 1979), 849–50.

86. In the years since Australian federation (in 1901), Australian governments were influential founding members of first the league and then the UN. After the end of World War II, a Labour government had cultivated the high international idealism of the UN, even as it retained the state's founding "White Australia" platform of policies directed specifically (although not only) against the indigenous Aboriginal population and "Asian" immigrants. As that race platform came under increasing international and national pressure in the 1960s, it was eventually dismantled. In the 1970s, another Labour government began a radical program to rekindle Australia's reputation as an enthusiast of the UN, and of its anticolonial and antiracist agenda.

87. Gerald Ford, Address to the 29th Session of the General Assembly of the United Nations, September 18, 1974, http://www.presidency.ucsb.edu/ws/index .php?pid=4718, accessed 15 May 2012.

88. Quoted in Moynihan, *Dangerous Place,* 114.

89. Ibid.

90. See also Cynthia Enloe, "The Military Uses of Ethnicity," *Millennium—Journal of International Studies* 4, no. 3 (1975): 220.

91. Moynihan, *Dangerous Place,* 65; and idem, "Introduction," in Nathan Glazer and Daniel Moynihan, *Ethnicity: Theory and Experience* (Cambridge, Mass.: Harvard University Press, 1975), 3.

92. Ralph Bunche, "On Race: Alienation and the Modern Man" (Fifth East-West Philosophers Conference, Honolulu, 1969), in Rivlin, *Ralph Bunche,* appendix F.

93. Quoted in Benjamin Rivlin, "The Legacy of Ralph Bunche," in Rivlin, *Ralph Bunche*, 21.

94. In the mid-1980s, the United States and Britain abandoned UNESCO to its Senegalese secretary-general Amadou M'Bow, returning only after the end of the Cold War.

95. Patrick Wilcken, *Claude Lévi-Strauss: The Poet in the Laboratory* (New York: Penguin, 2010), 198, 318–19.

96. It was hard not to be cynical about even the possibility of race-based confraternities when, according to Tinker, "concern for the right of repressed peoples to fight for their liberty has not included the black tribes of South Sudan who struggled for ten years against the army sent to subdue them by the Nilotic northerners, nor has it included the Kurds, fighting for their own state against the forces of Iraq." *Race, Conflict*, 126.

97. Prashad, *Darker Nations*, xviii, 274; Hoffmann, "International Organization," 392.

98. Bull, *Anarchical Society*, 318.

99. Ibid., xiv.

100. Adam Watson, "Recollection of my discussions with Hedley Bull about the place in the history of International Relations of the idea of the Anarchical Society" Paris, July 2002, available at http://www.leeds.ac.uk/polis/englishschool/watson-bull02 .doc, accessed 15 May 2012.

101. Bull, *Anarchical Society*, 257.

102. Hedley Bull, "The *State's Positive Role* in World Affairs," *Daedalus* 108, no. 4 (1979): 121. For a discussion see Pemberton, *Global Metaphors*, 155.

103. Bull, "*State's Positive Role*," 120.

104. Ibid.

105. See Connolly, "Seeing Beyond the State."

106. Hoffmann, "International Organization," 393, 400. See Haslam's chapter on this period in *No Virtue Like Necessity*, as well as E. Haas, *Beyond the Nation-State: Functionalism and International Organization* (Palo Alto, Calif.: Stanford University Press, 1964); Keohane and Nye, "International Interdependence and Integration."

107. Haslam, *No Virtue Like Necessity*, 242.

108. Nye, "Neo-realism and Neoliberalism," 237.

109. Armstrong, Lloyd, and Redmond, *Versailles to Maastricht*, 117.

110. UN General Assembly, "United Nations Moon Treaty" (1979), *UN Chronicle* 17, no. 2 (March 1980).

111. James Rosenau, quoted in Y. H. Ferguson and R. W. Mansbach, eds., *Remapping Global Politics: History's Revenge and Future Shock* (Cambridge: Cambridge University Press, 2004), 2; Yasemin Soysal, *Limits of Citizenship: Migrants and Postnational Membership in Europe* (Chicago: University of Chicago Press, 1994); and David Jacobson, *Rights Across Borders: Immigration and the Decline of Citizenship* (Baltimore: Johns Hopkins University Press, 1996).

112. James Rosenau, *Turbulence in World Politics* (Princeton, N.J.: Princeton University Press, 1990). The concept was based on the kind of evidence that Iriye has

uncovered in regard to the expansion of NGOs in China in the 1990s: Iriye, *Global Community*, 190–91.

113. Matthew Jamison, "Humanitarian Intervention Since 1990 and 'Liberal Interventionism,'" in Simms and Trim, *Humanitarian Intervention*, 365–80, 366.

114. Gunter Grass, quoted in Rothschild, "What Is Security?" 65.

115. See Anthony Smith, "The Shifting Landscapes of 'Nationalism,'" for a survey of the new preference for "an open cosmopolitan society after the terrors of the ages of nation-states and nationalism," 324.

116. Nicholas J. Wheeler, "Pluralist or Solidarist Conceptions of International Society: Bull and Vincent on Humanitarian Intervention," *Millennium—Journal of International Studies* 21, no. 3 (1992): 463–87; Nicholas Wheeler, *Saving Strangers: Humanitarian Intervention in International Society* (New York: Oxford University Press, 2002); John Williams, "Pluralism, Solidarism and the Emergence of World Society in English School Theory," *International Relations* 19, no. 1 (2005): 19–38.

117. See Daniele Archibugi, "The Reform of the UN and Cosmopolitan Democracy," *Journal of Peace Research* 30, no. 3 (1993): 301–15; Liisa Malkki, "Things to Come: Internationalism and Global Solidarities in the Late 1990s," *Public Culture* 10, no. 2 (1998): 431–42.

118. Glenda Sluga, "Writing History into Politics: Balkan Boundaries," in *Europe: Rethinking Boundaries*, ed. L. Holmes and P. Murray (London: Ashgate, 1998), 105–20.

119. Haslam, *No Virtue Like Necessity*, 243.

120. Ibid., 245; see also Ian Robinson, "Progressive Unilateralism? U.S. Unilateralism, Progressive Internationalism, and Alternatives to Neoliberalism" (Washington, D.C.: Foreign Policy in Focus, November 1, 2000).

121. See Jamison, "Humanitarian Intervention," 376.

122. I am grateful to Patricia Clavin for introducing me to the literature on human security and its significance.

123. In 1998 Amartya Sen, the Nobel Prize–winning Indian economist, was tasked with writing the widely cited report *Human Security Now: Protecting and Empowering People. Report. Commission on Human Security* (New York: United Nations, 2003).

124. See Pietilä, *Unfinished Story of Women*, 76–77.

125. Jamison, "Humanitarian Intervention," 371.

126. See "Human Security Unit: Overview and Objectives," available at ochaonline.un.org.

127. *Human Security Now.*

128. J. A. Hobson, *Wealth and Life: A Study in Values* (London: Macmillan, 1929), 400.

129. See Chapter 3.

130. Heidi Hudson, "'Doing' Security as Though Humans Matter: A Feminist Perspective on Gender and the Politics of Human Security," *Security Dialogue* 36, no. 2 (2005): 155–74.

131. See S. Neil Macfarlane and Yuen Foong Khong, *Human Security and the UN: A Critical History* (Bloomington: Indiana University Press, 2006).

132. Stephen Spender, *World Within World* (London: Faber, 1977), 292; see also Inis L. Claude, Jr., *Swords into Ploughshares: The Problem and Progress of International Organization* (New York: Random House, 1956), 407

133. See Mackenzie, *World Beyond Borders,* chap. 7; and Jamison, "Humanitarian Intervention."

134. Edward Said, "Preface to *Orientalism,*" *Al-Ahram Weekly Online* 650 (August 7–13, 2003), http://weekly.ahram.org.eg/2003/650/op11.htm, accessed 15 May 2012.

135. Said continues, "In all this, however, we must admit that no one can possibly know the extraordinarily complex unity of our globalised world, despite the reality that the world does have a real interdependence of parts that leaves no genuine opportunity for isolation." Ibid., para. 22.

136. Koskenniemi, *Gentle Civilizer of Nations,* 524. It was a perspective that reached back to Cassin's disillusionment with the human rights debates of the 1950s.

137. Rothschild, "Archives of Universal History," 391. Rothschild bemoans the relative lack of interest in the archives of international or transnational history.

138. Ibid., 392.

139. Quoted in ibid., 394.

140. See Jeremy Waldron, "What Is Cosmopolitan?" *Journal of Political Philosophy* 8, no. 2 (2000): 227, 228. Cf. David Simpson, "The Limits of Cosmopolitanism and the Case for Translation," *European Romantic Review* 16, no. 2 (2005): 141–52 who argues that most studies of cosmopolitanism begin with a disclaimer about being able to specify what exactly it is.

141. See, e.g., Kwame Appiah's autobiographical *Cosmopolitanism: Ethics in a World of Strangers* (New York: Norton, 2006).

142. Suri, "Non-governmental Organizations," 242.

143. These last sentences adapt Hobsbawm's conclusion to *Nations and Nationalism.* For more discussion, see the postscript. Of course one could argue Hobsbawm was wrong about the nation, the more it is studied, the more real it becomes. See Ulf Hannerz, "The Withering Away of the Nation? An Afterword," *Ethnos* 58 (1993): 377–90.

Afterword

1. Theodore Ruyssen, *Les sources doctrinales de l'internationalisme,* vol. 1 (Paris: Presses Universitaires de France, 1954). Ruyssen even claimed that Christianity was the first international community.

2. The best example of the cultural internationalism is, of course, Akira Iriye's work; and of the emphasis on race and empire, Mazower's *No Enchanted Palace.*

3. See Smith, "Shifting Landscapes."

4. B. Anderson, *Imagined Communities: Reflections on the Origin and Spread of Nationalism,* 3rd ed. (London: Verso, 2006), 4.

5. Ibid., 24.

6. Ibid., 6.

7. Given his own emphasis on the imperial setting of the earliest outbreaks of

nationalism in South America, and on the significant political role played by a limited number of imperial languages (English, French, and Spanish), Anderson's argument runs into some difficulties.

8. Anderson, *Imagined Communities* also refers to three kinds of nationalism: creole, linguistic, and official.

9. See Glenda Sluga, "Identity, Gender, and the European History of Nations and Nationalisms," *Nations and Nationalisms*, 4 (1998): 87–111.

10. Anderson, *Imagined Communities*, 4.

11. Ibid., 113. This separation out of nationalism and internationalism contrasts sharply with his later work, *Under Three Flags: Anarchism and the Anti-Colonial Imagination* (London: Verso, 2006).

12. Hobsbawm, *Nations and Nationalism*.

13. Ibid., 38.

14. Ibid., 207.

15. Ibid., 179.

16. See also Geyer and Paulmann, "Introduction," in *Mechanics of Internationalism*.

17. Hobson, "Ethics of Internationalism," 16, emphasis added.

18. Iriye also makes the point that it is not only national communities that are imagined; Iriye, *Cultural Internationalism*, 15. Here I want to emphasize the entangled imagining of national and international communities.

19. Claveirole, "L'Internationalisme et l'organisation internationale administrative," xi.

20. Historians also find it difficult to include in their narratives transnational actors, or the complex history of the intersecting personal and political ambitions of women as well as men. That story is emerging in works such as : C. A. Bayly and Eugenio F. Biagini, eds., *Giuseppe Mazzini and the Globalisation of Democratic Nationalism, 1830–1920: Proceedings of the British Academy* (Oxford: Oxford University Press, 2008), 419; Ros Pesman, "The Marriage of Giorgina Saffi and Aurelio Saffi: Mazzinian Nationalism and the Italian Home," in *Intimacy Across Borders: The Italian Nation in a Mobile World*, ed. Loretta Baldassar and Donna Gabaccia (New York: Fordham University Press, 2010), 58.

21. See Chapter 1.

22. Hoffmann, "International Organization," 392.

23. Moyn, *Last Utopia*.

24. These have included an interest in transcending the territorial sovereignty of nations through the enunciation of specific rights of mobility and of asylum; the demand for the right of individuals to be represented in the new international organization, rather than merely states; the idea of an international organization that could act to implement human rights; an interest in adding animal rights to a universal declaration of rights; using the new organization to reinvent economic relations, to contribute to social planning on a worldwide scale, and to democratize through modernization and industrialization; the idea of an international territory; the idea that women should have an equal role to play in international political life; the redrawing of the color line;

absolute disarmament. All of these were features of the debate in the 1940s regarding a new "world"-identified internationalism and its scope.

25. E. Renan, *Qu'est-ce qu'une nation? Et autres essais politiques*, ed. J. Roman (Paris: Agora Pocket, 1992).

26. This discussion draws on the report by William J. Millard, "International Public Opinion of the United Nations: A Comparative Analysis," *International Journal of Public Opinion Research* 5, no. 1 (1993): 92–99.

27. Ibid., 93.

28. Claveirole, "L'Internationalisme et l'organisation internationale administrative," ix.

29. Pierre Nora, "Between Memory and History: Les Lieux de Mémoire," trans. Marc Roudebush, *Representations* 26 (1989): 12.

30. I am a member of the committee. For more details on these historical developments, see Glenda Sluga, "The Transnational History of International Institutions," *Journal of Global History* 6 (2011): 219–22, 219.

31. On the political uses of that past, see Glenda Sluga, "Was the Twentieth Century the Great Age of Internationalism?" (Hancock Lecture 2009), in *Australian Academy of Humanities Proceedings 2009* (Canberra, 2010), 157–74.

Acknowledgments

I have accrued an extensive geography of national and international debts in the writing of this book to, first and foremost, the Australian Research Council, the wonderful national funding body that boldly supports international excellence in the humanities as a national benefit. Without it Australia would be an intellectually poorer and less interesting place. So would the Department of History and the School of Philosophical and Historical Inquiry at the University of Sydney, a disciplinary congregation that outshines its national peers and regularly finds itself in the top ranks of international tables. Thank you to internationalized colleagues, especially Barbara Caine, Marco Duranti, Andrew Fitzmaurice, Stephen Garton, Moira Gatens, Chris Hilliard, Julia Horne, Julia Kindt, Jennifer Milam, Dirk Moses, Ros Pesman, Shane White, the International Society research cluster, especially Dany Celermajer, and the best reading group in the world (you know who you are). In Melbourne, I owe Roland Burke, Kate Darian-Smith, and Marilyn Lake, at least.

Like many international historians, I exist in a virtual society of intellectual networks and ideas. I am indebted to Akira Iriye, the Harvard historian who has almost single-handedly legitimated the historical study of internationalism. Where would any international historian be these days without Iriye—as mentor and friend? Or without Jens Boel, whose archival and intellectual role at UNESCO in the support of the history of international organizations is the benchmark for archivists the world over. The International Scientific Committee for the History of UNESCO was his idea, and it provided me with many years of stimulating settings and collegiality. Among those colleagues count the model intellectual and font of wisdom on all things international, Emma Rothschild, and the genial and gifted, and much missed, Ilya Gaiduk.

The primary research for this book was undertaken with the kind help of librarians and archivists at the following institutions: the League of Nations Archive and UN Archives in Geneva and New York; UNESCO; Butler

Library, Columbia University; New York Public Library; the Schomburg Center for Research in Black Culture; the Bodleian Library, Oxford; the Library of Congress, Washington D.C.; Seeley G. Mudd Manuscript Library, Princeton University; Young Research Library, UCLA; Sterling Memorial Library, Yale University; Nehru Memorial Museum and Library, New Delhi; Churchill College, Cambridge; Archives Nationales and Ministère des Affaires Étrangères, Paris; National Archives, National Women's Library, and LSE Library, London; Fondren Library, Woodson Research Center, Rice University; Barr Library, Adelaide University; Flinders University; and the Arbetarrörelsens Arkiv och Bibliotek, Stockholm.

Some of the thinking in this book was worked through in previously published essays, including "UNESCO and the (One) World of Julian Huxley," *Journal of World History* 21, no. 3 (2010): 393–418; "The Transformation of International Institutions: Global Shock as Cultural Shock," in *The Shock of the Global: The International History of the 1970s*, ed. N. Ferguson et al. (Cambridge, Mass.: Harvard University Press, 2010); and "Was the Twentieth Century the Great Age of Internationalism?" (Hancock Lecture, 2009), in *The Australian Academy of Humanities Proceedings 2009* (Canberra, 2010), 157–74.

The ideas in this book have also been rehearsed in numerous fora—at the UNESCO conference at King's College, Cambridge, in 2008; at the Australian Academy of Humanities as the Hancock Lecture for 2009; at the Cambridge Economic history seminar (thank you Tim Harper, William Reilly, and Emma Rothschild); with Sydney History department graduate students in the European History seminar; the Oxford European Studies seminar (thank you Jane Caplan, Patricia Clavin, and Anne Deighton); the EUI (thanks Sebastian Conrad); at the Bologna-Sydney workshop on the History of Twentieth Century Internationalism (funded by the Australian Academy of Humanities, with the always-stimulating collaboration of Patrizia Dogliani); and with my colleagues at Sydney named above, and many others. Thank you David Armitage for the emails, Peter Mandler for the ear, and Gilles Pecout for the empathy.

A special nod to Alex, Andrew, Armen, and Eppie, who indulged my writing of this book while they were writing their own international histories; to my students in HSTY2691 who lived the argument as it took shape; to all my research assistants for putting up with my disorder, especially Roderic Campbell, Juliet Fleisch, Olivian Cha, and Louise McLeod. Usha Nair, of the

All India Women's Alliance, was extremely generous with her time and help. And in its last days, Marigold Black saved me.

Thank you finally Liang Pan and Sunil Amrith for much-needed regional expertise, and kindness; Madeleine Herren and Sandrine Kott for their deep knowledge of the history of internationalism, and camaraderie; Peter Jackson and Patricia Clavin for reading through the whole manuscript with wisdom. Peter Agree, the most agreeable editor I know, for his support and patience. If Alexander Zahar hadn't taken that job at the UN, and then left it, this project may never have been born. As always, and in everything, this book is for that irrepressibly international as much as transnational girl, Anna-Sophia.

CPSIA information can be obtained
at www.ICGtesting.com
Printed in the USA
LVOW12s1926290416

485956LV00001B/192/P